Green Acres School's

Going Places
With Children

in Washington, D.C.

13th Edition

Edited by

Derry G. Koralek

First edition 1958, Second edition 1961, Third edition 1963, Fourth edition 1965, Fifth edition 1968, Sixth edition 1971, Seventh edition 1974, Eighth edition 1976, Ninth edition 1979, Tenth edition 1982, Eleventh edition 1984, Twelfth edition, 1988, Thirteenth edition, 1992.

Text Copyright 1992 by Green Acres School, All rights reserved

Library of Congress Catalog number 84-081568; ISBN-0-9608998-3-9

Production by Irvin Shapell, Woodbine House

Cover design by Jennifer Barrett

Illustrations by the students of Green Acres School

Typesetting by Edington-Rand Inc.

Metro map courtesy of Washington Metropolitan Area Transit Authority

Mall map courtesy of the National Park Service

Published by Green Acres School
11701 Danville Drive
Rockville, Maryland 20852

Library of Congress Cataloging-in Publication Data

Going places with children in Washington, DC
    Green Acres School's going places with children in Washington, DC/ edited by Derry Koralek; (cover by Jennifer Barrett, illustrations by students of Green Acres School). — 13th ed.
p. cm.
    Rev. ed. of: Green Acres School's going places with children in Washington, DC. 12th ed. c1988.
    Includes index.
    ISBN -0-9608998-3-9: $9.95
    1. Washington (DC) — Description — 1992 — Guide-books.
2. Washington Region — Description and travel — Guide-books.
3. Family recreation — Washington (DC). 4. Family Recreation — Washington Region. I. Koralek, Derry G. II. Green Acres School III. Going places with children in Washington. IV. Title.
F192.3.G63   1992   88-36773
917.53'044 — dc19   CIP

About Green Acres School

Green Acres was founded in 1934 as a nursery school and now provides a full curriculum for **nursery** to **eighth grade**. For over 50 years, Green Acres has welcomed girls and boys of diverse backgrounds who grow and work in small groups, achieving academic excellence while developing their individual personalities and abilities.

Located in the Washington suburb of Rockville, Maryland, Green Acres is an independent school with historic roots in progressive traditions. It is organized as a non-profit corporation with a Board of Trustees composed of parents and teachers.

As a progressive school, all programs and curriculum are planned in accordance with the developmental stages, needs, and interests of the children. Small classes allow teachers to work with children individually and in small groups. An emphasis is placed on children being intrinsically involved in their own learning: touching, exploring, experimenting, talking, reading, discussing, and practicing. It is often through play that children extend their ability to think symbolically and "problem solve." This process is highly respected as children engage in challenges each day.

The 15-acre campus invites children to become familiar with the seasonal patterns of animal and plant life. Environmental concerns are raised spontaneously by our youngest children and become part of the science curriculum in the older classes. Children spend time outside every day.

Surrounded by woods, a naturalized amphitheater, and many play areas, its modern buildings house classrooms, a library, science lab, art and music studios, and a gymnasium/performing arts center. Art, music, and drama are often integrated with classroom projects. A fleet of school buses permits teachers to plan numerous field trips to further extend classroom learning.

Green Acres is a cooperative community with a nurturing dynamic faculty, an involved parent body, and children who pursue their learning with zest. May we all continue "Going Places."

About This Book

Green Acres School's 1958 publication of *Going Places with Children in Washington* was a mimeographed booklet put together by parent volunteers. This unique guidebook was an instant success and 13 editions have now been produced by parent volunteers. All proceeds from the sale of the book go to the Green Acres School, and over 300,000 copies of the book have been sold.

Families visiting Washington, DC often find *Going Places* more valuable than the conventional guidebook because our school parents have actually explored and evaluated the places listed. We welcome your suggestions, compliments, and criticisms. Send them to Green Acres School, 11701 Danville Drive, Rockville, Maryland 20852.

Please send me ___ copies of **Going Places with Children** at $11.20 ($9.95 + MD tax [.50] and postage).

Name: _____

Address: _____

_____

_____

Total enclosed: $ _____

Checks payable to Green Acres School

Send to **Green Acres School**
Going Places
11701 Danville Drive
Rockville, Maryland 20852
(301) 881-4100

Acknowledgements

To complete a book of this magnitude takes the contributions and cooperation of numerous dedicated individuals. First, this book could not have been completed without the ongoing guidance and support provided by Joan Adler, Green Acres' Development Officer. The chapter editors listed below, volunteered numerous hours to update and revise each chapter, and contributed many ideas on how to create a "family-friendly" guidebook.

Chapter Editors

1. Starting Out — Amy Fox and Susan Greif
2. Main Sights and Museums in Washington, DC — Susan Friend
3. Main Sights and Museums in Maryland and Virginia — Pamela McDermott
4. Baltimore and Beyond — Joan Adler
5. Nature — Derry G. Koralek
6. Parks and Recreation — Derry G. Koralek
7. Arts and Entertainment — Jocelyn Schaffer and John Starrels
8. Behind the Scenes — Susan Greif
9. Shopping — Candyce Stapen
10. Restaurants — Barbara and Paul Silberman
11. Annual Events for Children and Families — Derry Koralek and Chapter Editors

We also would like to acknowledge the contributions of a number of other members of the Green Acres' community. Before this book went to press, every fact (admission fees, hours of operation, phone number, etc.) was checked for accuracy and completeness by our team of fact checkers: Lois Colberg, Kelly Dorfman, Diana Eastridge, Dorrit Green, Judy Higgins, Carol Jason, Harriet Kelman, Elizabeth Rosenstein, Margot Russel, Jocelyn Schaffer, and Cheryl Shirley. Thanks also go to Mace Rosenstein, for proofreading the final document under very tight time pressures, to Travis Gosselin for carrying a year's worth of *Going Places'* correspondence back and forth between school and home, to Ginny Spevak for creating the index, and to Mary Grogan and Peter Greif for their computer expertise.

Under the direction of Green Acres' art teacher, Karen Mc-Laughlin Gallant, with assistance from her colleague Marilyn Banner, Green Acres' students contributed the illustrations included in the book. The names of these student artists appear below.

Student Artists

Alexandra Alper
Ruthie Basham
Anders Bjorgung
Jonathan Burt
Andrew Clark
David Cohen
Stella Emsellem
Trevor Gartenhaus
Adam Goldstein
Leah Goldstein
Travis Gosselin
Bobby Gravitz
Cliff Kaplan
J. J. Kee
Christine Kim
Laura Marlin
Aaron Paul

Seth Pukatch
Kimberly Roseman
Brittany Ross
Adam Sacks
Carley Schaffer
Charlotte Semmes
Anna Shapell
Joel Silberman
Leah Silver
Daniel Smith
Joel Stillman
Rachel Stinson
Paul Ulane
Kina Wihl
Alexis Wolfe
Nora Yoo

Contents

1 Starting Out

The key to successful family trips — whether brief excursions or extended sightseeing — is planning ahead. Before embarking on an outing in the Washington, DC area, leaf through the pages of this idea-packed book for literally hundreds of suggestions. This section tells how to keep up to date on what's happening, lists transportation possibilities, describes some of the special services available, and includes a sample three-day tour for visitors. Hours, rates, and offerings change frequently, so the best advice we can give you is: PHONE AHEAD.

Special Information Centers And Services

Baltimore Area Visitors' Center

300 West Pratt Street, Baltimore, MD 21201 (1-800-282-6632, for touch tone information).

Call for information about the many exciting places to visit in Baltimore. You can order a general tourism packet which includes maps and information on attractions and entertainment. Baltimore is less than a one hour drive or train ride from Washington, DC. See Chapter 4, Baltimore and Beyond, for suggested sites to visit.

Braille Maps of the Capitol and Mall

Your Senator's office can help you order a braille map of the Capitol and Mall areas. Call or write to your Senator to request a map. A map will be printed and mailed to you.

Columbia Lighthouse for the Blind, Services Office

1421 P Street, NW, Washington, DC 20071 (202-462-2900).

This organization provides free maps for the visually impaired. Call or write to receive either large print or braille maps. You will receive both a large map and a pocket-sized strip map.

Information, Protection, and Advocacy Center For Handicapped Individuals

300 I Street, NE, Suite 202, Washington, DC 20002. (202-547-8081).

This agency, which has wheelchair access, offers free information, follow-up, and referral services to handicapped persons of all ages in the metropolitan area. It is open from 8:30 A.M. to 5:30 P.M. The closest Metrorail stop is Union Station.

International Visitors' Information Center

1623 Belmont Street, NW, Washington, DC 20009 (202-939-5566)

This center provides pamphlets and brochures on the Washington sights in English and several other languages — German, French, Spanish, Japanese, Russian, Chinese, and Italian. You can write or call in advance or come to the center to pick up information.

Maryland Department of Economic and Community Development, Office of Tourist Development

46 Calvert Street, Annapolis, MD 21401 (301-269-3517).

Write or call this office to receive a map and a package of information to help you plan your visit to sites in Maryland.

Senate and House Visitors' Galleries

- □ United States House of Representatives, House Office Building, Washington, DC 20515
- □ United States Senate, Senate Office Building, Washington, DC 20510.
- □ Switchboard 202-224-3121.

Out-of-town school groups (or individuals) should write or call their senators or representatives before coming to Washington to arrange for passes to the visitors' galleries of the House and Senate. If you are planning to visit Washington, DC in the busy spring season, be sure to do this six months prior to your visit. Elected officials will often arrange to meet with their young constituents and even have their picture taken with the group on the steps of the Capitol.

Virginia Division of Tourism

202 North Ninth Street, Suite 500, Richmond, VA 23219 (804-786-4484).

This office will send an assortment of pamphlets about the many historic and recreational sites in Virginia.

Washington Visitor Information Center

1455 Pennsylvania Avenue, NW, Washington, DC 20004 (202-789-7038).

The Center is open Monday through Saturday, from 9 A.M. to 5 P.M.; closed Sunday and Federal holidays. This is a good first stop if you are new to the area or visiting from out of town. The Center has free maps of DC, brochures on the major attractions and special exhibits, and a quarterly calendar of events. They will also provide information on area hotels and motels. You can call or write for information before you visit or walk in once you get to Washington.

Public Transportation

Metrorail and Metrobus

Washington Area Transit Authority, 600 5th Street, NW, Washington, DC 20001 (202-637-7000).

Parking in many downtown areas is expensive and difficult to find. Avoid frustration by using Metro, Washington's subway and bus system. Metro is an excellent (although not inexpensive) alternative for getting to and around downtown Washington, DC. Children will enjoy the Metrorail train rides and the spacious vaulted underground stations.

Metrorail system guides are available from the Washington Area Transit Authority (address and phone listed above) or at the Metro Center station. Metrobus routes dovetail with Metrorail, and together they provide a comprehensive transportation system for both city and suburbs. Metro parking lots, adjacent to many suburban stations, are convenient places to leave your car while riding the Metro. You must have a bus transfer, available at any Metro station, as proof that you were using the Metro system in order to pay a discounted parking fee. Many Metro parking lots fill early on weekday mornings, but space is often available on weekends at no cost.

The five Metrorail lines are designated by color: Red, Blue, Yellow, Orange, and Green. Transferring between the lines is possible at several points. Metrorail operates from 5:30 A.M. to midnight on weekdays, 8 A.M. to midnight on Saturday, and 10 A.M. to midnight on Sundays. (The operating hours do change from time to time, so check on this before you start out.) Entrance to Metrorail is by farecard, which can be purchased at any Metrorail station. The amount charged depends on the distance traveled and the time of day. Each passenger (including children over five) must have a farecard; those under 5 ride free when with a paying passenger. The farecard vending machines will not take bills over $5. The highest fares are charged during rush hours — 5:30–9:30 A.M. and 3–6:30 P.M. There are substantial fare savings during nonrush hours.

A family (up to four persons) can purchase a ticket good for unlimited Saturday or Sunday travel on the entire Metro system for $8. These tickets must be purchased for a specific date and are available at the Metro Center station. Free transfers are available for riders going from rail to bus. Look for transfer machines near the escalators.

Metro has elevators and train space for wheelchairs, features to assist the blind, and devices to assist the deaf. Information regarding reduced fares for handicapped persons may be obtained at the Handicapped Services Unit, 202-637-1245. Metro TTY-teletypewriter for deaf and hearing-impaired is 202-638-378. For route information on any part of the Metro system call 202-637-7000, and be prepared to be put on hold for several minutes.

Exact fare (85¢ in DC) is required on Metrobus. Operators do not make change. There are no transfers from bus to rail.

Ride-On Buses, Montgomery County, MD

The blue and white Ride-On buses are part of the transportation network in Montgomery County, Maryland. They stop only at the blue and white Ride-On signs every 30 minutes. Exact change is required here, too ($1 at peak times). Special multi-ride tickets can be purchased at Metro Center and other locations. Call the Montgomery County Transit Information Center at 301-217-RIDE for details. TTY/TDD for the hearing impaired is 301-217-2222.

DASH, Alexandria, VA

DASH operates along 4 routes within the City of Alexandria, connecting several Metrorail stations with locations throughout the City, including the Old Town shopping and restaurant area. Base fare is 65¢ with a 30¢ surcharge to the Pentagon Metrorail station. DASH operates from approximately 5:30 A.M.–midnight, Monday–Saturday, with reduced Sunday operations. Phone 703-370-DASH for more information.

Northern Virginia Transportation Commission

In addition to DASH, there are several other mass transit options in Northern Virginia. Some are designed to serve commuters, others may be of interest to visitors to Washington, DC. This organization publishes a guide to the transit network in Northern Virginia. Call 703-524-3322 for your free copy.

MARC Trains

(1-800-325-RAIL, recorded message with instructions for touch tone phones).

This commuter rail service links DC with Baltimore and points in Maryland and West Virginia. The Camden Line from Baltimore includes stops at College Park and Riverdale, while the Penn Line stops at BWI Airport, Bowie State, and New Carrollton, to name a few. Along the West Virginia line which eventually stops in Duffields, WV, the MARC makes stops in Silver Spring, Kensington, Gaithersburg, Germantown, Boyds, and Harpers Ferry. All three services have their Washington, DC terminal at Union Station. These trains operate on weekdays only, about every half hour during the commuter rush and approximately every hour otherwise. Weekly and monthly tickets are available.

Sightseeing

Old Town Trolley Tours of Washington, Incorporated

5225 Kilmer Place, Hyattsville, MD 20781 (301-985-3021 or 301-985-3020, recording).

- Trips daily from 9 A.M.–4 P.M. every thirty minutes. The complete route takes 2 hours.
- Adults, $14; children 5–12, $5; children under 5, free.
- Metrorail Blue and Orange lines (Federal Triangle) and Red line (Union Station).
- Wheelchair access, but wheelchairs must be collapsible.

The Old Town Trolley Tours offer a wide-ranging tour of 13 major sites in Washington, including Georgetown, Embassy Row, the Washington Cathedral, Capitol Hill, Dupont Circle, and the Mall. Passengers can get off and reboard at their leisure. The ride in an old fashioned trolley car makes the sightseeing all the more enjoyable. Check to see if the trolleys stop near your hotel.

Potomac Riverboat Company Cruises

205 The Strand, Alexandria, VA 22314 (703-684-0850 or 703-548-9000, recording). The dock is located behind the Torpedo Factory Arts Center, North Union and Cameron Streets in Old Town Alexandria.

- Open April–October. Closed Monday. Morning, afternoon and evening tours are available. Departure times vary with the day and season.
- Adults, $6; senior citizens, $5; children 2–12, $4. Tickets may be purchased at the dock.
- Wheelchair access, but wheelchairs must be collapsible.
- Strollers permitted.

The Admiral Tilp offers a 40-minute narrated cruise along the waterfront of historic Alexandria. A beverage stand is on board; you may bring your own lunch or snacks.

Spirit Cruises

Pier 4, 6th and Water Streets, SW, Washington, DC 20024 (202-554-8000).

- Tours on the Spirit of Washington coordinate with the meal being served. The Spirit of Mount Vernon cruises depart at 9 A.M. and 2 P.M. Both cruises are closed on Monday.
- Costs vary with the day of the week and the meal being served. Call for information on current prices.
- Call for information on wheelchair access.
- Strollers permitted.

Both the Spirit of Washington and The Spirit of Mount Vernon operate from Pier 4 in Washington, DC. The Washington offers 2-hour lunch cruises, 3-hour dinner cruises, and 2½-hour evening and moonlight cruises. Sites along the route include the

Capitol and historic monuments, Fort McNair, National Airport, and the Potomac skyline. The Mount Vernon tours are 4½ hours long stopping, naturally, at George Washington's estate.

Tourmobile® Sightseeing Incorporated

1000 Ohio Drive, SW, Washington, DC 20024 (202-554-7020 or 202-554-7950, recording for tour information).

Tourmobile® is a concessionaire of the National Park Service offering a convenient way to get from one main attraction to another. The open-air vehicles, accompanied by guides, stop at 18 major sites along the Mall. For an additional fee you may add Arlington National Cemetery, Mount Vernon, and the Frederick Douglass Historic Site to your tour. You are allowed unlimited stops along the route, and reboarding is free throughout the day. This is an efficient and energy-saving way to see numerous

attractions. Several Tourmobile® stops are located near Metrorail stations.

- Hours of operation, June 15–Labor Day; 9 A.M.–6:30 P.M.; remainder of the year, 9:30 A.M.–4:30 P.M. Closed Christmas. Board every 15 to 30 minutes, depending on the season, at any stop. The complete tour, without the swing to Arlington, takes about 90 minutes.
- Adults, $10.50; children 3–11, $5. June 15 through Labor Day, for a slightly higher fee, you may also purchase a ticket at Tourmobile® ticket booths or from the drivers, after 4 P.M. (or after 2 P.M. the rest of the year) that can be used for the remainder of that afternoon and again the next day.
- Call 202-554-7022 for information on discount rates for groups of 20 or more. Charter tours are also available.

General Information

Calendars

In addition to the calendar of events included in Chapter 11 of this book, the following calendars will help you plan your visits to Washington-area sights.

- *Calendar of the Smithsonian* is a schedule of Smithsonian Institution happenings which appears near the end of the month in the *Washington Post*.
- *Kiosk* is a free monthly calendar of events scheduled to take place in the National Capital Parks System. Call 202-619-7222 for a copy.
- *Nutshell News* is a free, monthly publication of the Maryland National Capital Parks and Planning Commission. Pick up your copy at nature centers and libraries, write to Brookside Nature Center, 1400 Glenallen Avenue, Wheaton, MD 20902, or call 301-946-9071.

- *Tabloid* is a free publication of the DC Department of Recreation and Parks, 3149 16th Street, NW, Washington, DC 20010. Call 202-673-7660 to ask for a copy or look for it at recreation centers and libraries. There are two issues a year — spring/summer and fall/winter.

Newspapers and Magazines

- *Alexandria Gazette Packett,* 717 N. St. Asaph Street, Alexandria, VA (703-549-0004) is published on Thursday.
- Arlington Courier, P.O. Box 7560, Arlington, VA 22207 (703-538-5044) is published on Wednesday.
- *Jewish Week,* 12300 Twinbrook Parkway, Suite 250, Rockville, MD 20852 (301-230-2222) includes "What's Happening" in the Thursday edition.
- *Journal Newspapers, Inc.,* 6883 Commercial Drive, Springfield, VA 22159 (703-750-2000) are published daily in Arlington, Alexandria, Fairfax, Montgomery, and Prince George's Counties; weekly in Prince William County. "Community Calendar" appears in the Friday editions.
- *Montgomery County Sentinel,* P.O. Box 1272, Rockville, MD 20849 (301-948-4630) and Prince Georges County Sentinel, P.O. Box 1247, Seabrook, MD 20703 (301-306-9500) are published every Thursday.
- *Parent and Child Magazine,* published bimonthly, includes a comprehensive calendar of events for children and educational programs for parents. It is available free in retail establishments, children's book stores, libraries, child care centers, schools, and doctors' offices; or by subscription. Send requests to 7048 Wilson Lane, Bethesda, MD 20817 (301-229-2216).
- *Washingtonian Magazine,* 1828 L Street, NW, Suite 200, Washington, DC 20036 (202-296-3600) includes a monthly schedule of events titled, "Where and When."
- *Washington Afro-American,* 20002 11th Street, NW, Washington, DC 20001 (202-332-0080) is published on Thursday.
- *Washington Post,* 1150 15th Street, NW, Washington, DC 20071 (202-334-6000) includes Maryland, Virginia, and

Washington *Weekly* sections in the Thursday edition, which feature a calendar of events. The *Weekend* section in Friday's paper provides information on a wide variety of recreational and cultural events. The *Show* section in the Sunday paper highlights arts and entertainment events.

- *Washington Times*, 3600 New York Avenue, NE, Washington, DC 20002 (202-636-6000) publishes a *Weekend* section on Thursday.

Telephone Recorded Messages

The area code for Washington, DC is (202). Maryland is (301) in the Washington suburbs and western Maryland and (410) in Baltimore and the eastern half of the state. Northern Virginia is (703). When you place a call from one area to another in the Washington metropolitan area you must use the area code even though the call is a local one.

- **Dial-an-Event**, 202-737-8866, provides information on events scheduled to take place throughout metropolitan Washington.
- **Dial-a-Museum**, 202-357-2020, includes information on the Smithsonian Institution Museums, including the National Zoo.
- **Sky-Watcher's Report**, 202-357-2000, comes from the Albert Einstein Planetarium.
- **Dial-a-Park**, 202-619-PARK, provides information on National Capital Parks events, including schedules for the Arboretum, monuments, and memorials.
- **Dial-a-Hike**, 202-547-2326, from the Sierra Club, describes upcoming day and evening hikes and educational programs for outdoor enthusiasts.
- **Local weather and 2-day forecast**, 301-936-1212.
- **Audubon Voice of the Naturalist**, 301-652-1088, provides an update on the birds arriving in and departing from Washington.

Doing Washington in Three Days

It's a challenge, but if you vary the type of sites and keep the pace comfortable it's possible for the whole family to see the major attractions AND have fun. It is probably best to abandon your car, except at night. Comfortable walking shoes and strollers are critical. Touring can be a tiring endeavor, especially during Washington's hot and humid summers. Keep a supply of snacks and drinks with you if possible.

This tour includes most of the main attractions and should be altered to fit your family's interests (or those of visiting friends and relatives). It is written with the spring or summer traveler in mind. Sound advice for any time of year is ALWAYS CHECK OPERATING HOURS AND ADMISSION FEES BEFORE YOU BEGIN.

First Day

Start out early at the Washington Monument. A trip to the top is a beautiful introduction to the scope of the activities to come. Walk up the Mall to the National Museum of American History (gowns of the First Ladies, locomotives, ceramics, glass, coins) or the National Museum of Natural History (dinosaurs, minerals, insect zoo). After a quick carousel ride, walk through the Arts and Industry building for a trip back in time to the Philadelphia Centennial of 1876.

Buy a Tourmobile® ticket in the late afternoon for the slightly higher fee. Check that this ticket can be used tomorrow. Now board the Tourmobile® for the 90-minute tour of the major sights.

You can get off the Tourmobile® at the White House when you are ready for dinner and walk down Pennsylvania Avenue to The Shops at National Place. Those with more stamina can go back to the Lincoln, Jefferson, or Washington Monuments for beautiful nighttime views.

Second Day

Take the tour of the Bureau of Engraving and Printing, which opens early. On a nice day, a paddle boat ride on the Tidal basin is a real joy. Then take the Tourmobile® up to Capitol Hill, where you can lunch in the Supreme Court cafeteria before touring the Capitol. Young children might enjoy going to the Capital Children's Museum.

Walk down the Capitol steps to the Botanic Gardens for a change of pace and go on to the Air and Space Museum. As an alternative you can use your Tourmobile® ticket to return to any of the sights such as the Kennedy Center for the Performing Arts.

Third Day

Line up first thing in the morning for the Federal Bureau of Investigation tour, then walk to the National Archives and study the Declaration of Independence, the Constitution, and the Bill of Rights. Spend the afternoon at the National Zoo, shopping for souvenirs, or visiting the new National Museum of Women in the Arts.

2 Main Sights and Museums in Washington, DC

Taking trips to new places can awaken interests, stimulate curiosity, and be just plain fun. In Washington, however, it is easy to feel overwhelmed. To help you decide where to begin, look in this chapter at the "On the Mall," "Capitol Hill," or "Around Town" sections. Each begins with a brief overview and is followed by alphabetic listings of attractions in that section of town. If you prefer an already-arranged tour, look in the preceding chapter, Starting Out, where a three-day tour is profiled for you.

On The Mall

The Mall is the heart of Washington, home to many of the monuments, museums and main attractions that draw visitors to the nation's capital. Although several visits are required to view all the Mall buildings, it is possible to see the highlights quickly (see "Doing Washington in Three Days" in Chapter 1, Starting Out, for suggestions). Almost two miles long, a quick stroll from one end to the other is unrealistic at best and tortuous on a hot August day. A good stroller is a must for young children, as are comfortable shoes for everyone else.

The Tourmobile® is one solution for visitors who want to see as much as possible in a short time. There are several Tourmobile® stops on the Mall, although the lines can build up at popular stops during the heavy tourist times. For more information on Tourmobile® see Chapter 1, Starting Out.

If time is short, a good way to squeeze in all the main attractions is to save the monuments for the evening when they're dramatically lit. Evening temperatures are more comfortable in the hot summer months. The Lincoln and Jefferson Memorials are open all the time, and the Washington Monument is open until midnight from April through Labor Day.

A visit to the Smithsonian Information Center, located in The Castle, will provide you with an orientation to all 13 Smithsonian museums. See the listing below for this information center.

The museums on the Mall offer many special attractions for children. In addition to the dinosaurs, diamonds, and a great blue whale inside the Natural History Museum, there's the unusual insect zoo (with live insects) and a "Discovery Room," where children can handle and intimately explore museum objects. Across the Mall is an old-fashioned carousel, offering rides all year round, weather permitting, for a small fee. The Museum of American History contains the First Ladies Hall, early cars, trains, and machines. At Air and Space there are fighter planes, rockets, a planetarium, and several award-winning films.

The unusual architecture of both the Hirshhorn and the East Wing of the National Gallery makes these contemporary art museums fascinating stops. The many large canvases and bright colors captivate even the youngest visitors. Special exhibits, the "people mover," and the glass-enclosed waterfall will interest children at the East Wing, and the Hirshhorn sculpture garden is always a pleasant place for a rest. One caution: strollers are not allowed in the Hirshhorn (they must be checked, but the museum provides backpacks for babies).

Eating in the Mall area used to be limited to the cafeterias at most of the museums, which offer fairly ordinary food and can be very crowded. Fortunately, a number of restaurants, cafes and eateries have emerged both on Pennsylvania and off Independence Avenues. Of particular interest are the "food courts" at the Old Post Office and at The Shops at National Place. See Chapter 10, Restaurants, for details. Ice cream, hot dogs, and other snacks are available at several refreshment stands on the Mall. You can picnic on the benches or grass.

Admission to all museums and monuments on the Mall is free. Parking on Mall streets is free, but hard to get, and meter parking on side streets is likewise hard to find. Use Metrorail if possible. Otherwise try your luck or find a nearby parking garage.

Arts and Industries Building

900 Jefferson Drive, SW, Washington, DC 20560 (202-357-2700).

- Open daily, 10 A.M.–5:30 P.M. Closed Christmas.
- Metrorail Blue and Orange lines (Smithsonian, Mall exit).
- Tourmobile® stop.
- Wheelchair access ramp located at the north entrance.
- Strollers permitted.
- Walk-in tours of the 1876 Centennial exhibit are available on Saturdays only. Call 202-357-1481 for schedule information.

Just as it did in the 1880s, the Smithsonian's Arts and Industries Building houses items that were or might have been displayed at the 1876 Centennial Exposition in Philadelphia. The exhibit has three main areas: machinery, technology, and displays from the 37 states that were part of our nation more than 100 years ago. January 1991 marked the opening in the building's South Hall of the new Experimental Gallery: a changing exhibition space featuring innovative and creative exhibitions from the museums of the Smithsonian and from around the world.

Special activities include children's performances in the Smithsonian Discovery Theater, which is located in this building (see Chapter 7, Arts and Entertainment).

The United States Botanic Garden

First Street and Maryland Avenue, at the foot of Capitol Hill (202-225-8333). Mailing address: 245 First Street, SW, Washington, DC 20024.

- Open daily, 9 A.M.–5 P.M.; June–August, until 9 P.M. Open until 7:30 P.M. when there is a special show.
- Metrorail Orange and Blue lines (Federal Center).
- Wheelchair access.
- Strollers are permitted.
- No walk-in tours. You may call to arrange a guided tour weekdays at 10 A.M. or 2 P.M.

A waterfall, a jungle, prickly cacti, and an orchid collection are included in this lush conservatory. A nice break between museums, children delight in the pathways amid the colorful flowers as parents relax and enjoy their children as well as the garden. Advice on plant care is available on request, and there are a number of free classes and special programs on plants and gardens.

Special activities include several plant and flower shows scheduled throughout the year: spring flowers (before Palm Sunday), summer flowers (May), chrysanthemums (early November), and poinsettias and Christmas greens (December).

Freer Gallery of Art

Jefferson Drive at 12th Street, SW, Washington, DC 20560 (202-357-2700).

- Closed for renovation through 1992.
- Metrorail Blue and Orange lines (Smithsonian, Mall exit).
- Wheelchair access.
- Strollers permitted.
- Call for information on tours.

Chinese jades, bronzes, and paintings, Buddhist sculpture, Japanese screens, early Biblical manuscripts, miniatures from India and Persia — these are some of the exotic art objects in the distinguished Oriental collection at the Freer. Exhibits are continuously rotated since only a fraction of the catalogued art works can be displayed at one time. The Freer is also noted for its select collection of important works by American artists, especially James Whistler. Children will be particularly fascinated by Whistler's "Peacock Room," which offers an extraordinary visual experience for all ages.

Hirshhorn Museum and Sculpture Garden

Independence Avenue at 8th Street, SW, Washington, DC 20560 (202-357-2700).

- Open daily, 10 A.M.–5:30 P.M. Closed Christmas.
- Metrorail Yellow, Blue, and Orange lines (Smithsonian, Mall exit; L'Enfant Plaza, Maryland Avenue exit).
- Wheelchair access through swinging doors on plaza. Sculpture garden accessible from the Mall.
- Strollers must be left at checkroom to prevent damage to paintings; infant backpacks are available without charge.
- Walk-in tours: Monday–Saturday, 10:30 A.M., noon, 1:30 P.M.; Sunday, 12:30 and 2:30 P.M. Call in advance for groups, 202-357-3235.
- Sculpture tours for the blind and visually impaired and sign-language tours are available by appointment, 202-357-3235.

This monumental collection of 19th and 20th century paintings and sculpture displayed in an unusual circular building offers children an exciting introduction to art. The paintings are massive, vivid, and often very colorful — making a direct impact on viewers, young and old. Exhibits from the comprehensive permanent collection (nearly 14,500 paintings, sculptures, and works on paper) and changing loan shows provide opportunities to study major modern artists such as Rodin, Calder, Eakins, and Matisse. Diverse art movements including realism, pop, and abstract expressionism can be considered in depth.

The building itself immediately fascinates visitors. Paintings and larger works are displayed in a windowless outer circle. Sculptures fill an inner circle that offers comfortable chairs to relax in and view the central courtyard through its window-walls. Or you can relax in the outdoor sculpture garden, but warn children not to touch or climb on the art work.

An outreach program is available to schools in the metropolitan area. The program ranges from elementary level through high school and provides incentive and encouragement for upcoming museum tours.

Special activities include children's films shown on various Saturdays throughout the school year (see Chapter 7, Arts and Entertainment).

Jefferson Memorial

On the southern edge of the Tidal Basin. Mailing address: National Park Service Mall Operations, 900 Ohio Drive, SW, Washington, DC 20242 (202-426-6841).

- Open 24 hours daily. Park Service rangers on duty 8 A.M.–midnight.
- Metrorail Blue line (Smithsonian), but this is a long walk for children.
- Parking lot.
- Tourmobile® stop.
- Elevator for wheelchairs.
- Strollers permitted.

This pillared rotunda is a tribute to our third President, Thomas Jefferson, who was also the author of the Declaration of Independence. Like the Lincoln Memorial, it is impressively floodlit at night. Park Service rangers are available to answer questions and give brief interpretive speeches every half-hour by request.

Lincoln Memorial

On Memorial Circle, between Constitution and Independence Avenues, SW. Mailing address: National Park Service Mall Operations, 900 Ohio Drive, SW, Washington, DC 20242 (202-426-6841).

- Open 24 hours daily. Park Service rangers on duty 8 A.M.–midnight.
- Handicapped parking next to the memorial. Other parking is a short walk away.
- Tourmobile® stop.
- Special ramp and elevator for wheelchairs.
- Strollers permitted.

This classical Greek memorial to the Great Emancipator, Abraham Lincoln, is one of the most beautiful sights in Washington. Thirty-six marble columns, representing the 36 states of the Union at the time of Lincoln's death, surround the impressive seated statue of Lincoln. Two of his great speeches, the Second

Inaugural Address and the Gettysburg Address, are carved on the walls. At the foot of the memorial is the 2,000-foot Reflecting Pool, which mirrors the Washington Monument at its other end. Try to visit the Lincoln Memorial twice — once in the daytime and once at night. Call for information on tours of the cavern located under the statue.

National Air and Space Museum

6th Street and Independence Avenue, SW, Washington, DC 20560 (202-357-2700).

- Open daily, 10 A.M.–5:30 P.M. Extended summer hours set each year. Closed Christmas.
- Metrorail Yellow, Blue, and Orange lines (L'Enfant Plaza, Maryland Avenue exit).
- Tourmobile® stop.
- Wheelchair access through ramps on both sides of building.
- Strollers permitted.
- Highlight tours daily at 10:15 A.M. and 1 P.M.; no reservations. Tour groups should schedule in advance, 202-357-1400.
- Flight Line fast-food cafeteria and Wright Place restaurant on upper level.
- Films shown daily on the museum's five-story-tall movie screen and a presentation at the museum's Albert Einstein Planetarium (nominal fee for both).
- Baby service station next to Gallery 107 on the first floor.

This great aerospace center has 26 exhibit areas, a puppet theater, film theater, and planetarium. The central display on "Milestones of Flight" includes the Wright brothers' Kitty Hawk Flyer, the X-1 (first plane to break the sound barrier), Lindbergh's "Spirit of St. Louis," and the command module of the Apollo 11 moon-landing mission. In another section, children can walk through the Skylab orbital workshop and examine the astronauts' living and lab quarters. Each gallery explores a different theme: helicopters, satellites, World War I planes, World War II planes, rockets, and more. Many exhibits use motion pictures or a moving display to explain a particular subject.

This is a great place for children. To avoid crowds, go early on a weekday morning or late in the evening during extended summer hours. Purchase film tickets when you arrive, as the day's showings can be sold out quickly.

National Archives

Constitution Avenue between 7th and 9th Streets, NW, Washington, DC 20408 (202-501-5000, recording).

- Open daily, 10 A.M.–5:30 P.M. Extended summer hours set each year. Closed Christmas.
- Metrorail Yellow line (Archives).
- Wheelchair entrance on Pennsylvania Avenue at 8th Street.
- Strollers permitted.
- Guided tours weekdays. Call 202-501-5205 or write in advance.

This is the repository of America's records and documents. Permanently on display are the nation's three great charters of freedom: the Declaration of Independence, the Constitution, and the Bill of Rights. These documents are kept in sealed glass and bronze cases, which are lowered every night into a bomb- and fire-proof vault 20 feet below floor level. Other documents are displayed on a rotating basis in the Exhibition Hall.

For information about film series, lectures, intermittent special programs for children and adults, and exhibits, call the Office of Public Programs, 202-501-5200.

National Gallery of Art

East Building, 4th Street and Constitution Avenue, NW, Washington, DC 20565; West Building, 6th Street and Constitution Avenue (202-737-4215).

- Open Monday–Saturday, 10 A.M.–5 P.M.; Sunday, 11 A.M.–6 P.M. Extended summer hours set each year. Closed Christmas and New Year's Day.

- Metrorail Red line (Judiciary Square, 4th Street exit); Yellow line (Archives).
- Parking for handicapped visitors provided next to entrance to East Building, located on 4th Street between Madison Drive and Pennsylvania Avenue. Wheelchair access at entrance to the East Building and at Constitution Avenue entrance to the West Building. Wheelchairs are available.
- Tourmobile® stop.
- Strollers permitted. You may borrow them at the coat check areas of both the East and West Buildings.
- Introductory tours: East Building, weekdays, 11:30 A.M.; Saturday, 11 A.M.; Sunday, 2 and 4 P.M. West Building, weekdays, 1:30 and 3 P.M.; Saturday, 3 P.M.; Sunday, 1 and 3 P.M. Group tours should be arranged 3 weeks in advance. A variety of school tours are available.
- Cafeteria and table service cafes in both buildings.

One of the world's great art museums, the National Gallery contains major collections of European and American paintings and sculpture. Among its Renaissance and Dutch paintings are masterpieces by Raphael, Rembrandt, and Titian. As well as presenting its own special exhibitions, the gallery hosts major loan shows from around the world.

There are West and East Wings to this museum. The West Wing's main foyer is huge and awe-inspiring. Loud whispers are fun around its circular indoor fountain. For a tour of the main collection, children do well with Acoustiguide, the museum director's recorded tour of his favorite paintings. Special recorded tours are also available for most major special exhibits (for a small fee).

It's a quick trip on the lower-level "people mover" from West to East Buildings, and a pleasant break for young museum goers. At one end is the bottom of the outdoor waterfall, all well encased in glass. The Gallery's East Building is a feast for the eyes; children love the geometric shapes and unusual visual spaces. Look for isosceles triangles in the architecture; they're everywhere. Mostly 20th century art and special temporary exhibits are displayed here.

Most major special exhibits require a pass for admittance. These passes are distributed free of charge for each day beginning at 10 A.M. Some passes may be reserved in advance or purchased through Ticketron, 202-628-6661.

Free chamber music concerts are performed in the delightful East Garden Court Sunday at 7 P.M., September to June. You must have an advance free pass to attend. Call for information. At other times, the court and other open spaces in the West Building offer visitors a peaceful place to rest their feet and backs.

National Museum of African Art

950 Independence Avenue, SW, Washington, DC 20560 (202-357-4600).

- Open daily, 10 A.M.–5:30 P.M. Closed Christmas.
- Metrorail Blue and Orange lines (Smithsonian, Mall or Independence Avenue exits).
- Wheelchair access.
- Strollers permitted.

Located in the new Smithsonian Quadrangle next to the Arthur M. Sackler Gallery and the Smithsonian Arts and Industries Building, this new underground structure opened to the public in September 1987. It is the only museum in the United States devoted to the collection, study, and exhibition of the traditional arts of sub-Sahara Africa.

Its initial exhibitions are drawn from the museum's collection of 6,000 African art objects in wood, metal, clay, ivory and fiber. They highlight West African weaving traditions, Royal Benin art, and utilitarian art objects. The geometric patterns are appealing to many children.

Special activities include the African Art Club for children, films, workshops, lectures, and musical performances. Call for information.

National Museum of American History

14th Street and Constitution Avenue, NW, Washington, DC 20560 (202-357-2700).

- Open daily, 10 A.M.–5:30 P.M. Extended summer hours set each year. Closed Christmas.
- Metrorail Blue and Orange lines (Smithsonian, Mall exit; Federal Triangle, 12th Street exit).
- Tourmobile® stop.
- Wheelchair access at two main entrances.
- Strollers permitted.
- Walk-in tours: check at the Information Desk for starting times and locations of the Highlights, Ceremonial Court, and Field to Factory tours. Generally, the first tour starts at 10 A.M. and the last at 1:30 P.M. Special tours and demonstrations vary according to season and temporary exhibits. Call in advance for groups, 202-357-1481. Demonstration centers are offered in various exhibit halls, Monday–Saturday. Check at the Information Desk.
- Fast-food cafeteria on basement level; ice cream parlor on first floor.

Massive and modern outside, spacious and fascinating inside, this Smithsonian building is the home of the original Star Spangled Banner, gowns of our nation's First Ladies, and the Foucault pendulum. Other popular exhibits include musical instruments, early cars, trains, coins, printing, and Everyday Life in the American Past. The diversity of the collections makes this museum most likely to appeal to every family member. An excellent bookstore specializes in Americana. The museum shop has museum-related reproductions from all over the world and lots of small things for collection-minded children.

In the three Discovery Corners (open Monday–Saturday, noon–3 P.M.) children can experience hands-on activities and demonstrations. The Relief of Pain and the Electricity Discovery Corners are located on the first floor; the Spirit of 1776 Discovery Corner is located on the third floor.

Special activities include an annual display of Christmas trees, laden with handcrafted decorations.

National Museum of Natural History/ Museum of Man

10th Street and Constitution Avenue, NW, Washington, DC 20565 (202-357-2700).

- Open daily, 10 A.M.–5:30 P.M. Extended summer hours set each year. Closed Christmas.
- Metrorail Blue and Orange lines (Smithsonian, Mall exit; Federal Triangle, 12th Street exit).
- Wheelchair access at Constitution Avenue entrance only.
- Strollers permitted.
- Walk-in tours daily (no tours in July and August). Free self-guided tour pamphlets available at the Information Desk at the Mall entrance.
- Cafeteria on main floor. Smithsonian Associates dining room on the lower floor.
- Discovery Room offering hands-on examination of rocks and animal skins, and a new computer simulation of how bones become fossils among other items. Pick up free tickets at Information Desk. (The description below has more information).

It's hard to decide where to begin a visit to this incredible Smithsonian center for the study of man and his natural environment. The fossils (highlighted by reconstructions of dinosaur skeletons), mammals (animals in lifelike settings), sea life (a living coral reef and 92-foot blue whale model), and birds are all worthwhile choices. The exhibit of American Indian life is fun. All children are dazzled by the gems and minerals collection, which includes the world-famous Hope Diamond.

The Insect Zoo, with giant centipedes and tiny fruit flies, is not to be missed. It offers fascinating up-close views of working bee hives, ant hills, and other insect communities, some of whose inhabitants a museum guide will hold for you to touch. Well-marked exhibits and an enthusiastic staff make this display a highlight for children.

Plan to visit the Discovery Room, a special place where children can look at, smell, touch, or study various animal, vegetable, and mineral specimens and make their own discoveries about them. The Discovery Room is open for families and individuals weekdays, noon–2:30 P.M.; Saturday and Sunday, 10:30 A.M.–3:30 P.M. Free admission tickets, available at the Discovery Room entrance, are required. Children under 12 must be accompanied by an adult. Groups may visit the Discovery Room on weekdays from 10–11:30 A.M. Call 202-357-2747 to schedule a visit.

For budding scholars, the museum offers a Naturalist Center, where visitors 12 years and older can use the library-resource center and can examine over 30,000 specimens to identify objects (your own or others) or to answer questions about natural history. Staff members are available to help you. The Center is open Monday–Saturday, 10:30 a.m to 4 P.M., Sunday, noon to 5 P.M.

The museum shop on the first floor sells cards, books, crafts, posters, jewelry, and other museum-related objects. An additional small gems and minerals shop is on the second floor.

Arthur M. Sackler Gallery

1050 Independence Avenue, SW, Washington, DC 20560 (202-357-2700).

- Open daily, 10 A.M.–5:30 P.M. Closed Christmas.
- Metrorail Blue and Orange lines (Smithsonian, Mall exit).
- Wheelchair access.
- Strollers permitted.
- Call for tour information.

One of the newest additions to the Smithsonian Institution, this museum of Asian art opened to the public in September 1987. It is located underground, in a quadrangle formed by the Arts and Industries Building and the Freer Gallery, and will be connected to the Freer by underground exhibition areas when the Freer re-opens in 1993. This will emphasize the links between the two Asian art galleries. The Sackler Gallery houses one of the finest collections of Asian art, including ancient Chinese jades and bronzes and important Chinese paintings. It also offers an attractive schedule of loan exhibitions.

Of particular interest to children is the "Monsters, Myths, and Minerals" exhibit that displays Chinese animal imagery crafted in jade, silver, and other materials. Special steps help youngsters view the items on display.

Smithsonian Information Center, "The Castle"

1000 Jefferson Drive, SW, Washington, DC 20560 (202-357-2700 or 202-357-1729, TTD).

- Open daily, 9 A.M.–5:30 P.M. Closed Christmas.
- Metrorail Blue and Orange lines (Smithsonian, Mall exit).
- Wheelchair access.
- Strollers permitted.

For the visitor who wishes to be introduced to the 13 Smithsonian museums in Washington, the Castle is the place to start. This aptly named building is the Smithsonian Institution's first, designed by James Renwick, Jr. and completed in 1855. Today it houses the Smithsonian Information Center. Provided are two orientation theaters which continuously show a 20 minute video overview of the Institution, "touch screen" programs in seven languages on the Smithsonian museums and on other capital highlights, electronic wall maps, and scale models of famous Washington monuments. The "touch screen" programs and electronic maps are very appealing to children, although some are displayed too high for younger children to do on their own.

Vietnam Veterans Memorial

Constitution Avenue between Henry Bacon Drive and 23rd Street, NW. Mailing address: National Park Service Mall Operations, 900 Ohio Drive, SW, Washington, DC 20242 (202-426-6841).

- Open daily, 24 hours. Park Service rangers on duty 8 A.M.–midnight.
- Park during the day on Ohio Drive off Independence Avenue or on Constitution Avenue during non-rush hours and on weekends.
- Wheelchair access. Handicapped parking on Constitution Avenue between 20th and 22nd Streets.
- Strollers permitted.

This memorial to Vietnam veterans was dedicated November 13, 1982. It consists of two black granite walls set in the ground in a shallow V. In 1984 a life-size sculpture of three soldiers was added. The walls are inscribed with 58,175 names of the dead in chronological order of casualty. Books are available at the entrances to guide visitors to specific names.

Although set in the peaceful, contemplative surroundings of Constitution Gardens (near the Lincoln Memorial), the memorial is stark and imparts an overpowering sense of loss. People touch and make rubbings of the names and leave tokens of every description. Be prepared to answer hard questions from children about the Vietnam War.

Washington Monument

15th Street near Constitution Avenue, SW. Mailing address: National Park Service Mall Operations, 900 Ohio Drive, SW, Washington DC 20242 (202-426-6841).

- Open daily, Labor Day–March, 9 A.M.–5 P.M.; April–Labor Day, 8 A.M.–midnight.
- Limited parking.
- Tourmobile® stop.

- Wheelchair ramp and elevator.
- Strollers permitted while waiting in line, but must be parked before going up in the Monument.
- Call 202-426-6841 to arrange for tours to walk down the Monument.

An impressive obelisk rising 555 feet is our nation's memorial to its founder. An elevator takes visitors to the top for a magnificent view of the city. Energetic children like to count the 897 steps as they walk down. Go early in the morning on a good, clear day or on a summer evening when the temperature is cooler and the lines are shorter.

Special activities include military band concerts held at the Sylvan Theater on the grounds of the Washington Monument on Sunday, Tuesday, Thursday, and Friday evenings in the summer at 8 P.M.

On Capitol Hill

There's a lot more to see on Capitol Hill than the Capitol. Plan to stop by the office of your Representative or Senator. Not only will you get a glimpse of your legislator at work, but he or she can arrange passes for you to view the House or Senate in session, arrange for a VIP tour of the White House (see White House listing), and obtain passes to the FBI Building tour. (See Chapter 1, Starting Out, for information on arranging for passes in advance.)

Just across from the Capitol are the Supreme Court and Library of Congress, both impressive buildings. Another block away is the Folger Shakespeare Library amidst streets lined by charming 19th century town houses. A car or taxi ride away is the Capital Children's Museum, a "must" stop for families.

There are several cafeterias in the Capitol and its office buildings, but they have limited hours for the public and often are very crowded. Happily there is a wide variety of eateries down Pennsylvania Avenue, SE and along Massachusetts Avenue, NE (see Chapter 10, Restaurants). In addition there is a food court and several restaurants at Union Station.

Capital Children's Museum

800 3rd Street, NE, Washington, DC 20002 (202-543-8600).

- Open daily, 10 A.M.–5 P.M. Closed Easter, Thanksgiving, Christmas, and New Year's Day.
- Adults and children, $5; senior citizens, $2; children under 2, free. Memberships and special rates available.
- Metrorail Red line (Union Station).
- Limited on-street parking or in commercial lot.
- Wheelchair access.
- Strollers permitted.
- Group tours $3 per person; you must call in advance, 202-675-4162.
- Vending machine food and drink and tables and chairs available. Picnic tables on grounds.

The only museum in Washington with children as the exclusive focus, the Capital Children's Museum deserves its growing reputation. This "hands-on" museum wants to help children learn through doing, and so it does in many ways. The International Hall features Mexico. Here children try on Mexican outfits, make tortillas and hot chocolate, paint with yarn, dance a Mexican hat dance, and feed a goat.

In the "Changing Environments" area, younger children can operate simple machines with giant levers and gears, and work with a wide variety of puzzles and manipulative games. The "City Room" lets them crawl through under-street pipes, climb on a fire engine, and visit different shops. They can manufacture clothing in "The Factory" and play with the Centimeter Eater computer in "Metricville." Communications is another main theme, with exhibits from cave paintings to a print shop and telecommunications center offering telephone, radio, and electronic communications.

Children are encouraged to feel comfortable with computers. In addition to computers in Metricville and the Pattern and Shapes exhibit, the Future Center offers seminars for children as young as 4 (admission is separate from the rest of the Museum).

Special activities include an annual Halloween party and Children's Day, held in June at the Carter-Barron Amphitheater.

The Capitol

Located at the east end of the Mall on Capitol Hill. Visitors' entrance off First Street at East Capitol Street. Mailing address: United States Capitol Historical Society, 200 Maryland Avenue, NE, Washington, DC 20002 (202-225-6827).

- Open daily, 9 A.M.–4:30 P.M. Extended summer hours set each year.

- Metrorail Red line (Union Station) and Blue and Orange lines (Capitol South).
- Parking is very limited.
- Tourmobile® stop.
- Wheelchair access on east side; elevators inside. Special areas in both galleries for wheelchairs.
- Strollers permitted.
- Tours begin at the Rotunda, daily, 9 A.M.–3:45 P.M., starting every 5–15 minutes.
- Senate restaurant and limited access to cafeterias.

A good way to survey the Capitol is to start with the guided tour, which lasts about 25 minutes (this might be too long for your young child). The tour includes all the areas in the Capitol open to the public: the Rotunda, Statuary Hall, original capitol, Old Senate Chamber, Old Supreme Court Chamber, crypt area, and beautifully decorated Brumidi corridors. The Whispering Gallery is most fun for children. To visit the House and Senate chambers, you must obtain a pass from your Senator or Congressman, except when Congress is not in session. Tours no longer visit the chambers when in session.

After the tour take a leisurely, independent look around. View the familiar paintings in the Rotunda and on the great staircases. Find your state's favorite sons in the Statuary Hall. The Capitol has two wings, the Senate (north) and the House of Representatives (south). Walk or take the Capitol subway to your senator's or representative's office to obtain passes to the House and Senate visitors' galleries. Sit in on a committee hearing. You can check which hearings are open to the public from the morning newspaper. Most offices and hearing rooms are in the office buildings — those of the Senate to the north, of the House to the south of the Capitol.

Special activities include military concerts held on the West Front steps of the Capitol from June through August, Monday, Tuesday, Wednesday, and Friday evenings at 8 P.M. Come early with a picnic to get a good seat.

Eastern Market

7th and C Streets, SE, Washington, DC 20003

- The outdoor Farmer's Market is open all day Saturday. The inside Market is open Tuesday–Thursday, 7 A.M.–6 P.M. and Friday and Saturday 6 A.M.–7 P.M. On Sunday there is an Outdoor Flea Market.
- Metrorail Blue and Orange lines (Eastern Market, walk north on 7th street until you see the market).
- Limited parking available in front of the Market.
- Limited wheelchair access.
- Strollers are allowed and can get through the aisles, but it is crowded during the summer and on Saturdays.

This farmer's market, built in 1871, is still a lively produce market. Children will most enjoy the outdoor event on Saturdays; there's lots to look at and goodies to buy. A good number of vendors sell an array of fruits, vegetables, and flowers, and other colorful stalls are crowded with jewelry, cotton clothing, wooden toys, African American art, pottery, and more. Inside, the market building houses tasty food counters downstairs, but the lines can be very long. This could try children's patience and yours! (There are some casual food establishments across the street.) Art exhibits are shown upstairs.

Folger Shakespeare Library

201 East Capitol Street, SE, Washington, DC 20003
(202-544-7077).

- Open Monday–Saturday, 10 A.M.–4 P.M. Closed Sunday and Federal holidays.
- Metrorail Blue and Orange lines (Capitol South).
- Wheelchair access in rear of buildings, between 2nd and 3rd Streets.
- Strollers permitted.
- Walk-in tours 11 A.M., Monday–Saturday. Special activities for children's groups can be arranged through the docent program.

The Folger Shakespeare Library houses a unique collection of rare books and manuscripts relating to the humanities of the Renaissance and focusing on Shakespeare. Although the specialized exhibits are of limited appeal to small children, visiting the Elizabethan exhibition hall, with its oak paneling, vaulted ceiling and striking tile floor, can be an exciting experience. Don't miss the Elizabethan theater, used throughout the year for plays, lectures, concerts, and poetry readings. The gift shop emphasizes the Renaissance period with stuffed unicorns, puzzles, note cards, T-shirts, games, coloring books, and children's books.

Special activities include the Elementary and High School Shakespeare Festivals held each spring. The dramatizations, acted by children, last 20 minutes and are usually scheduled in half-day segments. Admission is free. Youngsters 8 years and above would certainly enjoy watching these performances or even participating in them through their schools.

Library of Congress

1st and East Capitol Streets, SE, Washington, DC 20540 (202-707-8000).

- Madison Gallery, Madison Foyer, and Current Events Corridor open weekdays, 8:30 A.M.–9:30 P.M.; Saturday and Sunday, 8:30 A.M.–6 P.M. All other exhibit areas open weekdays, 8:30 a.m to 5 P.M. Closed Federal holidays.
- Metrorail Blue and Orange lines (Capitol South).
- Tourmobile® stop.
- Wheelchair access at 1st and 2nd Street entrance; ramp on Independence Avenue.
- Strollers permitted.
- Tours weekdays, 10 A.M.–3 P.M., leaving on the hour from 1st Street side of building. Slide presentation 15 minutes before each tour (shown from 9:45 A.M.–2:45 P.M.). Tours last about 45 minutes each. Call 202-707-5458 to make advance arrangements for large groups.

The Library of Congress, the biggest literary treasure house in this country, is a splendid example of Italian Renaissance architecture, with its domed main reading room and beautiful exhibit hall. In its three buildings are housed 90 million books, maps, manuscripts, photographs, prints, motion pictures, microfilms, and documents. Permanent exhibits of interest to older children include a Gutenberg Bible and a 15th century illuminated Bible manuscript. Public exhibitions drawn from the collections change frequently. The reading rooms are open to persons of college age and above and to high school students with letters from their principals.

Sewell-Belmont House

144 Constitution Ave., NE, Washington, DC 20002
(202-546-3989).

- Open Tuesday–Friday, 10 A.M.–3 P.M.; Saturday, Sunday, and holidays, noon–4 P.M. Closed Monday, Thanksgiving, Christmas, and New Year's Day.
- Metrorail Red line (Union Station) and Orange line (Capitol South).
- No wheelchair access.
- Strollers permitted, but must be carried up and down stairs.
- Groups of 15 or more by appointment.

This 1800s Capitol Hill townhouse provides displays related to the suffragist movement of the early 1900s. Pictures, statues, and memorabilia from the period are attractively displayed. The memorial to Alice Paul, a leader in the movement, highlights the tour. Much of the house was recently restored.

Supreme Court

First Street and Maryland Avenue, NE, Washington, DC 20543
(202-479-3000).

- Open weekdays, 9 A.M.–4:30 P.M. Closed weekends and Federal holidays.

- Metrorail Red line (Union Station) and Blue line (Capitol South).
- Tourmobile® stop.
- Wheelchair access at Maryland Avenue entrance.
- Strollers are not permitted.
- Free lectures offered every hour on the half-hour, 9:30 A.M.–3:30 P.M., except during Court sessions. Visitors information line, 202-479-3030, provides current Court sitting information.
- Cafeteria, snack bar, and gift shop on ground floor.

This dazzling white marble building houses the highest court in the land. The spectacle of the Court in session is most impressive. Nine justices, robed in black, are seated on a raised platform against a backdrop of red curtains, listening to attorneys plead cases. The Court hears oral argument from the first Monday in October through the end of April. Thereafter, it takes the bench every Monday through the end of June to release orders and opinions (this takes about 10 minutes).

Visitors must wait on line to be admitted to the Courtroom. There are two lines: one for the full session, and one for a three-minute stop, which might be more suitable for your children.

Around Town

After covering the Mall and Capitol Hill, there's still a great deal more to see in Washington. The White House, the FBI, the Bureau of Engraving and Printing, the Kennedy Center, the Washington Cathedral, and the National Zoo are the best-known. There are dozens of historical buildings and small museums as well. Some favorites include the Phillips Collection, National Geographic's Explorer's Hall and the Washington Doll's House and Toy Museum. Check maps carefully to plan excursions that include sights close to one another.

Anacostia Neighborhood Museum

1901 Fort Place, SE, Washington, DC 20020 (202-287-3369). Take Southeast Freeway from Capitol Hill, then cross the 11th Street Bridge; take Martin Luther King Avenue exit to Morris Road; left to Fort Place.

- Open daily, 10 a.m–5 P.M. Closed Christmas.
- Ample off-street parking.
- Wheelchair access. Call to make arrangements for tours for blind or hearing-impaired persons.
- Strollers permitted.
- Monthly programs; call for schedule.
- Tours weekdays at 10 A.M., 11 A.M., and 1 P.M.
- Large picnic area with benches and tables.

This unusual museum, run by the Smithsonian Institution, maintains close ties with the local community. Exhibits focus on the culture and heritage of African-Americans, contemporary urban problems, art, and crafts. Films, slides and touchable artifacts often accompany exhibits and make for a stimulating museum experience for all.

Exhibitions change frequently and include a variety of projects and activities which stress participation from preschool to adult groups. Walk-in tours are available on weekends. Pre-tour materials are provided for scheduled groups, and teaching kits are available to educators.

Special activities include a month-long Kwanzaa celebration in December.

B'nai B'rith Klutznick Museum

1640 Rhode Island Avenue, NW, Washington, DC 20036 (202-857-6583).

- Open Sunday–Friday, 10 A.M.–5 P.M. Closed Saturday and holidays.
- Metrorail Red line (Farragut North) and Blue line (Farragut West).

- Wheelchair access on Rhode Island Avenue.
- Strollers permitted.
- Docents available for walk-in tours of the permanent collection. Call 202-857-6583 to arrange guided tours for groups of 10 or more.

This museum encompasses a wide range of Jewish cultural, artistic, historical, and traditional ritual and ceremonial items. Life-cycle events and holidays are featured. Rotating special exhibitions are of particular interest. The gift shop offers a variety of adult and children's books as well as high-quality ritual and gift items (the shop closes at 4:30 P.M.).

Bureau of Engraving and Printing

14th and C Streets, SW, Washington, DC 20228
(202-447-0193).

- Open weekdays, 9 A.M.–2 P.M. Closed weekends and Federal holidays.
- Metrorail Orange and Blue lines (Smithsonian).
- Limited parking is available around the Tidal Basin.
- Tourmobile® stop.
- Wheelchair access. Some wheelchairs available.
- Strollers are not permitted.
- Tour of facility takes about 25 minutes. Expect at least a half-hour wait (sometimes as long as two hours) during peak tourist season.

Millions of dollars are printed here daily. The number of $1s, $5s, $10s, and other denominations printed depends on orders from Federal Reserve Banks throughout the country. The Bureau also prints stamps and other official government financial papers. Visitors watch all the processes involved in producing currency: printing and cutting sheets of special papers, and most impressive, stacking and counting the bills. A guide escorts you and will answer questions. A recording gives explanations and background information.

Corcoran Gallery of Art

17th Street and New York Avenue, NW, Washington, DC
20006 (202-638-3211).

- Open Tuesday–Sunday, 10 A.M.–5 P.M.; Thursday until 9 P.M. Closed Monday and Christmas and New Year's Day.
- Admission charged for certain special exhibitions. Call 202-638-3211 for information on special events.
- Metrorail Blue line (Farragut West) and Red line (Farragut North).
- Commercial parking lot nearby; limited on-street parking.
- Wheelchair access on E Street; call prior to visit.
- Strollers permitted.
- Walk-in tours daily at 12:30 P.M. Special tours for children's groups can be arranged.

The Corcoran Gallery is the oldest and largest private museum of art in the nation's capital. Founded in 1869 by William Wilson Corcoran, the museum is dedicated to encouraging American excellence in the fine arts. The gift shop sells quality toys and children's books in addition to books on American art and artists, jewelry, and posters.

Spacious entrance atriums and a grand staircase welcome visitors to this museum famous for its American art collection, with outstanding examples from the Colonial period to present times. Gilbert Stuart's famous portrait of George Washington, well-known landscapes of the Hudson River School, and monumental historical paintings appear familiar to many children. In the European galleries look for the fine selection of French Impressionist paintings. The museum is also known for its extensive collection of modern photography.

The museum's studio classes for children ages 4–11 highlight a variety of media from drawing, painting, and sculpture to American crafts. The Education Office, 202-638-3211, can provide more information. The Corcoran School of Art, the only professional art school in Washington, offers classes for teenagers and adults.

Special activities include exhibitions emphasizing contemporary art, photography, and Washington regional art. Special events, dance performances, concerts, and story-telling are frequently scheduled in conjunction with these exhibitions. Contact the Office of Special Events, 202-638-3211, for specific information.

Daughters of the American Revolution Museum

1776 D Street, NW, Washington, DC 20006 (202-879-3254).

- Gallery open weekdays, 8:30 A.M.–4 P.M.; Sunday, 1–5 P.M. Period rooms open weekdays, 10 A.M.–3 P.M.; Sunday 1–5 P.M. Closed Saturday and most holidays.
- Metrorail Red line (Farragut North) and Blue and Orange lines (Farragut West).
- Commercial parking lot; limited on-street parking.
- Wheelchair access on C Street; call prior to visit.
- Strollers permitted.

The Museum, located in DAR headquarters, features a gallery with changing exhibitions of American decorative arts up to 1830 and 33 American period rooms. Ask your docent to take you to the New Hampshire Attic, where dolls, toys, and children's furniture from the 18th and 19th centuries are displayed. Then, visit the parlors, kitchen, and dining rooms furnished with fine period objects. The Museum offers a special tour for elementary school classes. Teachers should call 202-879-3239 at least six weeks in advance to schedule a visit. A Sunday program for 5–7 year-olds, "Colonial Adventure," is offered twice a month. Limited spaces are available, so call ahead for reservations.

Decatur House

748 Jackson Place, NW, Washington, DC 20006 (202-842-0920).

- Open Tuesday–Friday, 10 A.M.–2 P.M.; Saturday, Sunday, and holidays, noon–4 P.M. Closed Thanksgiving, Christmas, and New Year's Day.

- Adults, $3; senior citizens and students, $1.50. Student group rates available.
- Metrorail Red line (Farragut North) and Blue and Orange lines (Farragut West).
- Partial wheelchair access.
- Strollers permitted.
- Call in advance for group tours, which can be tailored to particular interests.

This elegant, Federal-style townhouse faces Lafayette Square across from the White House. It was designed by Benjamin Henry Latrobe for Commodore Stephen Decatur, an early American naval hero. Decatur and his wife moved into this home in 1819, but they were to live here only 14 months before the Commodore was mortally wounded in a duel. There followed a succession of distinguished residents. In 1871 General Edward Fitzgerald Beale and his wife moved into the house and introduced a number of Victorian features. The first floor, in the Federal style, is furnished as it might have been during the Decaturs' residency. The second floor is furnished in the Victorian manner, and includes parquet flooring in the drawing room, where the California state seal is depicted with various woods. Children might enjoy seeing the set of dueling pistols.

The Decatur House also sponsors Young People's Tours of the house and of Lafayette Square, for third, fourth, and fifth-graders, scouts, church groups, and so on.

Frederick Douglass Home (Cedar Hill)

1411 W Street, SE, Washington, DC 20020 (202-426-5961). Take South Capitol Street from the Capitol to the Southeast Freeway; then cross the 11th Street Bridge; go south on Martin Luther King, Jr. Avenue; east on W Street.

- Open daily, 9 A.M.–4 P.M.; April to mid-October, until 5 P.M. Closed Thanksgiving, Christmas, and New Year's Day.
- Donation box available for contributions.
- Wheelchair access to first floor may be arranged.

- Strollers permitted.
- Groups need to make reservations well in advance.
- Films about Douglass' life are shown on the hour, followed by guided tours of grounds and home by National Park Service rangers.
- A small sales area offers publications and other items pertaining to Douglass.

The noted black leader and anti-slavery editor Frederick Douglass spent the later years of his life at Cedar Hill. The character of the fervent abolitionist is reflected in the furnishings of the house and in information given on regular tours which cover 14 of 21 rooms. One point of interest is the "Growlery," a small, one-room structure separate from the house that Douglass often retreated to. Most of the furniture and artwork is original to the house and is typical of that found in any upper middle class white or African-American home of the late 19th century. The handsome brick house with its commanding view of the Federal City is spacious and comfortable by the standards of the late 19th century, but not elaborate.

Special activities include an annual Christmas open house and events in commemoration of Frederick Douglass' birthday and Black History Month in February. The Annual Oratorical Contest for area students is held in mid-January.

Dumbarton Oaks Gardens and Museum

3101 R Street, NW, Washington, DC 20007 (202-342-3200). Museum entrance at 1703 32nd Street, NW.

- Museum open Tuesday–Sunday, 2–5 P.M. Closed Sunday. Gardens open daily, 2–5 P.M., except holidays and inclement weather. Gardens open until 6 P.M. from April 1 to October 31.
- Suggested $1 donation at museum. Admission to gardens April–October: adults and children over 12, $2; senior citizens, $1; children under 12, free. No admission charge to gardens from November–March.
- On-street parking generally available.

- Wheelchair access to museum. (Call to see if a museum wheelchair is available if you need one.) The gardens are partly accessible, and there is a wheelchair garden tour.
- Strollers permitted.
- Nearby Montrose Park has many pleasant picnic spots.

Dumbarton Oaks Gardens, an oasis in bustling Georgetown, is spectacular in the spring, beautiful in the fall, and pleasant in the winter. The estate's 10 acres of terraced hillsides, formal and informal plantings, and curving footpaths are artfully landscaped, expertly maintained, and enjoyed by children and adults. There are places to look carefully, as well as places to romp.

Part of the main building is devoted to a museum featuring Pre-Columbian and Byzantine art. Postcards, notecards, slides, and books about the gardens are available at the museum sales desk. See Chapter 5, Nature, for more information on the gardens.

Explorer's Hall, National Geographic Society

17th and M Streets, NW, Washington, DC 20036 (202-857-7000).

- Open Monday–Saturday, 9 A.M.–5 P.M.; Sunday, 10 A.M.–5 P.M. Closed Christmas.
- Metrorail Red line (Farragut North) and Metrorail Blue and Orange lines (Farragut West).
- Commercial parking lots nearby.
- Wheelchair access at M Street entrance.
- Strollers permitted.
- For general and schedule information, call 202-857-7588.
- Arrangements can be made for globe demonstrations. Call 202-857-7689.
- Groups larger than 20 should reserve seats by calling 202-857-7689.

Explorer's Hall has been dramatically renovated and has great appeal to children of all ages. An interactive learning center called Geographica fills the north end of the hall. Through modern technology, powerful images, and a sense of fun, Geographica teaches about earth and its wonders. Visitors can explore at their own pace such topics as anthropology, astronomy, oceanography, and other aspects of geography. Other favorites (the giant Olmec head, Henry the macaw, and hominid skeletons) are situated within Geographica. The 11-foot globe is the heart of Explorers Hall. Surrounded by a 72-seat amphitheater called Earth Station One, the globe is the terrestrial star of interactive, multi-media shows. "Travelers" participate in the program by answering questions posed by the narrator Captain. Adults and children alike enjoy testing their geographic knowledge in this setting. Programs run several times an hour. The south end of the hall is used for temporary shows. Explorers' Den displays and sells the Society's excellent maps, publications, and videos in a Victorian parlor setting.

Federal Bureau of Investigation

J. Edgar Hoover Building, E Street between 9th and 10th Streets, NW, Washington, DC 20004 (202-324-3447).

- Open weekdays, 8:45 A.M.–4:15 P.M. Closed weekends and holidays.
- Metrorail Red line (Metro Center).
- Wheelchair access.
- Strollers permitted.
- Tours beginning every 15–20 minutes, until 4 P.M. (No access to building except on tour.)
- Reservations can be made in advance through your Congressman or Senator or other government agency.

The FBI tour is one of the most popular shows in town. It includes exhibits on crime and crime detection, fingerprinting, unusual firearms, and blood typing. There are mementos of Dillinger and other notorious criminals, and a demonstration of target shooting on the indoor target range. Tours last about an hour, and there may be as long as a two-hour wait on busy summer days.

Ford's Theater/Lincoln Museum/ Petersen House

511 10th Street, NW, Washington, DC 20004 (202-426-6924).

- Open daily, 9 A.M.–5 P.M. Closed Christmas. Theater closed to visitors during matinee performances (Tuesday, Thursday, Saturday, Sunday). Call to verify museum hours on matinee days.
- Metrorail Red, Blue, and Orange lines (Metro Center); Yellow line (Gallery Place).
- Wheelchair access to theater but not to the museum, balcony, or house where Lincoln died.
- Strollers permitted but must be carried up and down stairs.
- Talks once each hour from 9:20 A.M. to 4:20 P.M. by National Park Service rangers in the orchestra of theater. When the theater is closed talks are held in the museum.

Completely restored, Ford's Theater now looks as it did on April 14, 1865, the night Lincoln was shot. The museum, located in the basement of the theater, provides a self-guiding tour which follows Lincoln's career as a lawyer, campaigner, President, and finally as the victim of an assassin's bullet. Among the memorabilia on display are the clothes Lincoln was wearing that fatal night. Talks by Park Service rangers describe the events that led up to the assassination. A museum shop, maintained by the Park and History Association, highlights books, posters, and postcards about Lincoln and the Civil War period.

To complete the picture of the assassination, visit the Petersen House directly across the street at 516 10th Street, NW (202-426-6830). The wounded President was carried into the bedroom of the house and died there the next morning.

Franciscan Monastery

14th and Quincy Streets, NE, Washington, DC 20017 (202-526-6800). Take North Capitol Street to Michigan Avenue. Go east on Michigan past Catholic University, then right on Quincy Street. Monastery is at top of the hill.

- Open daily, 9 A.M.–5 P.M.
- Metrorail Red line (Brookland/Catholic University).
- Wheelchair access.
- Strollers permitted.
- Hourly tours Monday–Saturday, 9 A.M.–4 p.m (no tour at noon); Sunday, 1–4 P.M.

Called the Memorial Church of the Holy Land, this unusual church is located in a 44-acre woodland. The grounds include one of the largest rose gardens in the country. Along the garden walks are the 14 Stations of the Cross with replicas of shrines at Bethlehem and Lourdes. Children like the catacombs beneath the church.

Interior Department Museum

C Street, between 18th and 19th Streets, NW, Washington, DC 20240 (202-208-4743).

- Open weekdays, 8 A.M.–5 P.M. Closed weekends and Federal holidays. All adult visitors must show photo identification at the building entrance.
- Metrorail Blue and Orange lines (Farragut West, 18th street exit).
- Wheelchair access at E Street entrance.
- Strollers permitted.
- Reasonably priced cafeteria open to the public, 7:30 A.M.–2:45 P.M.
- Gift shop open 8:30 a.m–4:30 P.M.

The diversity of the Interior Department's activities is evident in the variety of the exhibits here. American Indian artwork, historic documents, dioramas, and natural history specimens help to tell the Department's story. National Parks, mining, geological research, and Indian pottery are among the topics explored in the museum's well-crafted displays. Newly installed exhibits, featuring hundreds of photographs and historic and contemporary artifacts, present an overview of the Department's past and current activities. They are the first phase of a major renovation planned for the museum in the 1990s. The Indian crafts shop, across the hall from the museum, sells authentic articles from various reservations, including silver jewelry, rugs, pottery, baskets, moccasins, and Kachina dolls.

Islamic Center

2551 Massachusetts Avenue, NW, Washington, DC 20008 (202-332-8343).

- Open daily, 10 A.M.–5 P.M.; closed Friday 12:30 A.M.–2:00 P.M. for prayer.
- Wheelchair access.
- Strollers permitted.
- Call in advance for groups.

The mosque, the largest and most ornate in the United States, is the only part of the Islamic Center open to the public. Guides explain the religious service and point out the rich decorations of the building. The rugs, mosaics, and art objects are outstanding examples of Islamic design and craftsmanship.

John F. Kennedy Center for the Performing Arts

New Hampshire Avenue and F Street, NW, Washington DC (202-467-4600, general information; 202-416-8000, Concert Hall; 202-467-4600, Opera House). Located on the Potomac River upstream from the Lincoln Memorial.

- Building open daily, 10 A.M.–midnight.
- Commercial parking garage.
- Tourmobile® stop.
- Wheelchair access to all theaters. Call 202-416-8340 two hours in advance to arrange for a wheelchair. Free listening system for the hearing-impaired in the Eisenhower and Terrace Theaters and the Opera House.
- Strollers permitted.

- Tours of the center are given by Friends of the Kennedy Center daily 10 A.M.–1 P.M., beginning every 15–20 minutes. Tours start in lobby of Parking Level A. For special tour arrangements call 202-416-8341.
- Restaurants and cafeteria.

Performances of music, opera, dance, theater, and film from the United States and abroad are presented on the stages of the Kennedy Center. There are five main theaters: the Concert Hall, Opera House, Eisenhower Theater, Terrace Theater, and Theater Lab. The first three of these theaters are separated by two great parallel halls, one decorated with the flags of the 50 states, the other with the flags of the nations of the world. Many children enjoy these. The theater of the American Film Institute is located off the Hall of States. The center has been decorated with a dazzling array of gifts from many nations.

The 53-minute film *JFK, In His Own Words* is shown on Saturdays at 11 A.M. and 1 P.M. in the American Film Institute theater. Admission is free for this moving biography, which uses Kennedy home movies and television footage to tell the story of JFK's life from childhood through his presidency.

Don't miss seeing the renowned bronze sculpture of President John F. Kennedy in the Grand Foyer and the view from the rooftop terrace; these are worth a trip even if you don't see a show.

Special activities include performances for children and families throughout the year and an annual open house. See Chapter 7, Arts and Entertainment, for more information.

Martin Luther King Memorial Library

901 G Street, NW, Washington, DC 20001 (202-727-1248, children's division).

- Open Monday–Thursday, 9 A.M.–9 P.M.; Friday–Saturday, 9 A.M.–5:30 P.M. During school year also open Sunday, 1–5 P.M. Call 202-727-0321 for specific hours for different rooms.

- Metrorail Red, Blue, and Orange lines (Metro Center); Yellow, Red, and Green lines (Gallery Place).
- Wheelchair access.
- Strollers permitted.
- Group tours can be arranged by calling the librarian, 202-727-1221, weekdays, 9 A.M.–5:30 P.M. Call well in advance.

This modern facility, the main branch of the DC Public Library System, has special collections on Washingtoniana and Black Studies, as well as a 56-foot-long mural of the life and times of Dr. Martin Luther King, Jr. Young children like to watch the AP ticker in the lobby. Teenagers are attracted to "The Other Place," the brightly decorated young adult room furnished with bean bags, and featuring books, records, cassettes, video tapes, filmstrips, and computers. Group tours of the library are designed for the ages and interests of the visitors, and talks on specialized subjects can be arranged.

The DC Public Library operates Dial-a-Story (202-638-5717) which presents recorded tales lasting about 3 minutes. It also provides a monthly calendar, *This Month*, and a seasonal guide to classes and programs at the DC Public Library. Both are available at this and all library branches.

National Aquarium, Washington

U. S. Department of Commerce Building, 14th Street and Constitution Avenue, NW, Washington, DC 20230 (202-377-2825, general information recording; 202-377-2826, office).

- Open daily, 9 A.M.–5 P.M. Closed Christmas.
- Adults, $2; senior citizens and children 4–12, 75¢; children under 4 and Aquarium members, free.
- Metrorail Blue and Orange lines (Federal Triangle).
- On-street parking on 14th and 15th Streets and Constitution Avenue.
- Wheelchair access.
- Strollers permitted.

- Cafeteria next to the Aquarium in lower lobby of Commerce Building open weekdays, 9 A.M.–3 P.M. Closed Saturday and Sunday.
- Gift shop open daily, 9 A.M.–5 P.M.

It's an unlikely spot, but you'll find the oldest aquarium in the United States on the lower level of the U. S. Department of Commerce Building. Over 1,200 creatures of the deep reside there in 70 tanks, ranging in size from 50 to 6,000 gallons. Included are rare sea turtles, American alligators, and tropical clownfish. Children really enjoy the "Touch Tank" where they can hold hermit crabs, sea urchins, and horseshoe crabs. You can also see a slide show in the Mini Theater. A real draw for your child may be the shark feedings on Monday, Wednesday, and Saturday at 2 P.M., or the Piranha feedings, Tuesday, Thursday, and Sunday at 2 P.M. Even though some tanks are a bit high for the younger ones to peer into by themselves, this small aquarium is a fun outing for all ages. While you're in the Commerce Building, check out the census clock in the lobby and the seismograph machine that registers vibrations of earthquakes.

Special activities include Shark Day held in late July, a celebration of the most feared denizen of the sea.

National Building Museum

Pension Building, Judiciary Square, 401 F Street NW, Washington, DC 20001 (202-272-2448).

- Open daily, 10 A.M.–4 P.M.; Sunday, noon–4 P.M. Closed Thanksgiving, Christmas, and New Year's Day.
- Metrorail Red line (Judiciary Square, F Street exit)
- Parking in commercial lots.
- Wheelchair access.
- Strollers permitted.
- Tours conducted (no reservations required) weekdays at 12:30 P.M.; Saturday, Sunday, and holidays at 12:30 and 1:30 P.M. Call ahead to schedule a group tour. Guided tours of the

museum's Chinatown neighborhood are offered on selected days each month. Call ahead for information and reservations.
■ Gift shop on first floor.

As soon as you step off the Metrorail escalator, you will be awed by this massive and beautiful brick structure. Adapted from palace plans of the Italian Renaissance, it was designed in 1881 to be a modern office building for the Pension Bureau. Now it serves as a museum celebrating American achievements in building. As you approach the museum, look up at the buff-colored terra cotta frieze. It shows six Civil War military units encircling the building on an endless march. You will be inspired again, entering the museum, as you go into the Great Hall, a space large enough to enclose a 15-story building. Children love this space (it may be hard to keep them from running around) as well as the fountain at its center. Exhibition galleries are in interconnecting rooms off the Hall, and upstairs.

Make sure to go upstairs. Anyone who wants to know how Washington and its buildings got the way they are must visit the permanent exhibit "Washington: Symbol and City." It has hands-on appeal to families, with touchable, large-scale models and objects from the Capitol, White House, Washington Monument, and Lincoln Memorial. It follows the building of Washington over the past 200 years. Exhibit games ask questions that are answered by pushing a button. This is a fun introduction to the city's history.

Other permanent and temporary exhibits interpret the building trades, urban planning, architecture and engineering, and historic preservation. There are exciting school programs for children from elementary through high school. Call 202-357-2700 for details.

Special activities include a May Festival of Building Arts featuring building craft demonstrations and hands-on activities for all ages.

National Museum of American Art

8th and G Streets, NW, Washington, DC 20560
(202-357-2700).

- Open daily, 10 A.M.–5:30 P.M. Closed Christmas.
- Metrorail Red and Yellow lines (Gallery Place, 9th street exit).
- Wheelchair access through garage or ramp at 9th and G Streets.
- Strollers permitted.
- Free walk-in tours weekdays at noon; Saturday and Sunday, 2 P.M. Call in advance for groups, 202-357-3111.
- Cafeteria service; courtyard tables available, weather permitting. Sandwiches, soups, and salads are made to order in "Patent Pending," an excellent restaurant. Eat them indoors or, in good weather, outside in the courtyard.

Although off the Mall, this member of the Smithsonian family is worth a side trip. The impressive Greek Revival building, completed in 1867, once housed the U.S. Patent Office. Now it serves as permanent home for the Smithsonian Institution's National Museum of American Art and National Portrait Gallery (see listing below). This museum offers a panorama of American painting, sculpture, photographs, folk art, and graphics, from earliest times to the present. Winslow Homer, George Catlin, 19th-century landscape artists, American Impressionists, and 20th-century painters are all well represented in these halls.

National Museum of Women in the Arts

1250 New York Avenue, NW, Washington, DC 20005
(202-783-5000)

- Open daily, 10 A.M.–5 P.M.; Sunday noon–5 P.M. Closed Thanksgiving, Christmas, and New Year's Day.
- Suggested contributions: adults, $3, senior citizens and students, $2.
- Metrorail Red, Blue, and Orange lines (Metro Center, 13th & G Streets exit).

- Wheelchair access. A limited number are available.
- Strollers permitted.
- Walk-in tours conducted if a docent is available. Special guided tours for children and adults are also available: call the Education Department.
- Palette Cafe in museum. Soups, salads, and other light entrees. McDonald's across the street.
- Small, pleasant gift shop with interesting and beautiful items for children and adults.

This is a super small museum for children and adults. Just after entering, children are immediately drawn into the elegant and huge Martin Marietta Hall, a great room with marble floors, large crystal chandeliers, and two grand staircases. These take you to the art galleries on the upper levels. The permanent collection surveys art by women from the 16th Century to the present. Included are works by Mary Cassat, photographs by Louise Dahl-Wolfe, and sculpture by Camille Claudel. Special exhibits present international women's accomplishments. The galleries in which works are displayed are not too large, so children can wander through them without feeling lost.

The museum opened in 1987 after being beautifully renovated in an award-winning Renaissance Revival style. It was originally built in 1907 as the Masonic Grand Lodge of the National Capital.

During the school year the museum's Education Department offers Sunday children's programs. They relate to the current exhibition or aspects of the permanent collection. Special tours geared to children ages 6–12 are offered and are often followed by a related hands-on experience. Call for details.

National Portrait Gallery

8th and F Streets, NW, Washington, DC 20560
(202-357-2700).

- Open daily, 10 A.M.–5:30 P.M. Closed Christmas.
- Metrorail Red and Yellow lines (Gallery Place, 9th street exit).
- Wheelchair access at 9th and G Streets entrance.

- Strollers are not permitted.
- Walk-in tours begin at Information Desk weekdays, 10 A.M.–3 P.M.; Saturday and Sunday, 11 A.M.–2 P.M. Call in advance for groups (202-357-2920).
- Cafeteria and restaurant (Patent Pending) shared with National Museum of American Art (see above).

Located in the old U.S. Patent Office Building, the Portrait Gallery examines American history by focusing on the individuals who have aided in the development of our nation. The collection includes paintings, sculptures, prints, drawings, and photographs of prominent American statesmen, artists, writers, scientists, Indians, and explorers. Works such as Lansdowne's portrait of George Washington and portraits of every American president through George Bush highlight the works currently on view.

Basilica of the National Shrine of the Immaculate Conception

4th Street and Michigan Avenue, NE, Washington, DC 20017 (202-526-8300). The shrine is adjacent to Catholic University.

- Open daily, May–October, 7 A.M.–7 P.M.; November–April, 7 A.M.–6 P.M.
- Metrorail Red line (Brookland/Catholic University).
- Wheelchair access.
- Strollers are not permitted.
- Tours beginning every half-hour, Monday–Saturday, 9–11 A.M. and 1–3 P.M.; Sunday, 1:30–4 P.M.
- Cafeteria and gift shop.

The largest Roman Catholic church in the United States, the Shrine was started in 1920 and is now essentially complete. Its style, an adaptation of Byzantine and Romanesque, is described on the tour, which includes the upper church and small chapels.

Special activities include a summer organ recital series and periodic concerts. Call for more information.

National Zoological Park

Rock Creek Park entrances at Adams Mill Road, Beach Drive, and 3000 Block of Connecticut Avenue, NW, Washington, DC 20008 (202-673-4717; call Zoo Police in the event of extreme weather, 202-673-4731).

- Buildings open daily May 1–September 15, 9 A.M.–6 P.M.; September 16–April 30, 9 A.M.–4.30 P.M. Grounds open daily April 15–October 15, 8 A.M.–8 P.M.; October 16–April 14, 8 A.M.–6 P.M. Closed Christmas.
- Metrorail Red line (Woodley Park-Zoo — a 7-minute, uphill walk; Cleveland Park — a 6-minute, level walk).
- Parking fees: If you come and go before 10 A.M., $1; 10 A.M.–4:30 P.M., $3–7 depending on length of stay; after 4:30 P.M., $2.
- Wheelchair access; a limited number of wheelchairs are available — first-come, first-served. Handicapped parking available on Lot B near the Elephant House and on Lot D near the lower duck ponds.
- Strollers and wagons are available for rent in winter, 9:30 A.M.–3 P.M., in summer, 9:30 A.M.–4 P.M. $5 per stroller, $6 per wagon (holds two children).
- Call in advance for group tours and special information.
- Restaurants and snack bars are scattered throughout the grounds; picnicking permitted; no fires, bicycling, or skateboards.

The 165-acre National Zoo has long been acclaimed as one of the best and most attractive facilities of its kind in the country. Particularly delightful to view are the white tigers and, of course, Ling-Ling and Hsing-Hsing, the pandas from China. The pandas are best seen at their 11 A.M. and 3 P.M. feeding times. The new wetlands exhibit around the birdhouse is a treat for younger children. Other favorites include the giraffes, lions and tigers, hippos, and elephants. Monkeys constantly entertain visitors with their playful antics behind glass in their remodeled homes, and the Great Ape House allows a look at the residents "nose to nose." A trip to Beaver Valley will reveal otters, beavers, seals, and bears. Some of these animals live in specially designed houses that permit underwater viewing, and the beavers and otters even have a video monitor peeking into their nest.

The Education Building (open 9 A.M.–5 P.M. year round) has an auditorium which shows movies on weekends every hour on the half hour; first showing 10:30 A.M., last showing 4:30 P.M. While waiting for the movie to start, the Book Store Gallery and Gift Shop is a nice place to browse, and nearby is the Zoolab, a children's learning center. This is a place you must stop with children ages 3–7. It is equipped with touch and feel areas that allow children to examine animal's nests, skins, feathers, antlers, etc. Books and art objects are available. There are two other, smaller labs at the zoo: the Bird Lab (or Bird Resource Center) located in the Bird House, and the Herp Lab, in the Reptile House. Both feature hands-on activities; Herp Lab is best for

children 6 and over since many of the activities require some reading. All Labs are open in the summer, Friday 10 A.M.–1 P.M.; Saturday and Sunday, 10 A.M.–2 P.M. During the school year, Zoolab is closed on Fridays. During January and February, only the Zoolab is open, and only on Fridays.

The feeding and waking times for animals vary according to the season and their keepers' schedules. Planning to attend a specific feeding time can often disappoint a youngster, since exact feeding times are unpredictable. Note that the public is not permitted to feed the animals. Gift and souvenir shops feature a wide array of zoo-related paraphernalia.

The Zoo is very crowded on weekends and holidays during good weather, and the parking lots fill up fast. Try to go early in the day during the week, or go later in the day and stay for a picnic dinner. Public transportation is highly recommended, but

remember if little ones are along, it's a 6-minute walk from the nearest Metrorail stop to the Connecticut Avenue entrance.

Special activities include a summer evening concert series and many events sponsored by Friends of the National Zoo (FONZ). Call for more information.

The Octagon

1799 New York Avenue, at 18th Street, NW, Washington, DC 20006 (202-638-3105, TDY 202-638-1538).

- Open Tuesday–Friday, 10 A.M.–4 P.M.; Saturday and Sunday, noon–4 P.M. Closed Monday and major holidays.
- Suggested donations: adults, $2; senior citizens and students, $1; children, 50¢. Call in advance for group reservations.
- Metrorail Blue and Orange lines (Farragut West; 18th and I Streets exit).
- Commercial parking garages nearby; on-street, metered parking.
- Wheelchair access at garden entrance.
- Strollers are not permitted.
- The tour is recommended for children 12 years of age and older.

The Octagon was built by Colonel John Tayloe III in 1800 to serve as his winter townhouse. During the War of 1812, the building served as the temporary White House for President and Mrs. Madison, and here the Treaty of Ghent was signed on February 17, 1815, ending that war. The Octagon served as the headquarters for the American Institute of Architects between 1889 and 1949 and is today owned by the American Architectural Foundation. Trained docents discuss the early history of Washington, DC, the Tayloe family, the architecture of the house, and its decorative arts furnishing. There are changing architectural exhibitions in the second floor galleries.

Special activities include children's events held in September and December. Call for specific dates and admission fees.

Old Post Office Tower, Nancy Hanks Center

1100 Pennsylvania Ave., NW, Washington, DC 20004
(202-523-5691).

- Pavilion open daily March–Labor Day, 8 A.M.–11 P.M.; after Labor Day–March, 10 A.M.–6 P.M. Closed Thanksgiving, Christmas, and New Year's Day.
- Metrorail Blue and Orange lines (Federal Triangle).
- Wheelchair access.
- Strollers should be left outside or in the lobby.
- Tours to Congress Bells and the Old Post Office Tower start every 5–7 minutes; Labor Day to mid-April, 10 A.M.–5:45 P.M.; mid-April–Labor Day, 10 A.M.–10:30 P.M. Tours are first-come, first-served for 10 people at a time. They begin at the glass-enclosed elevator on the stage level. Congress Bells tours are not held during the weekly practice ringing on Thursday, 6:30–9:30 P.M., or when ringing for national holidays or the opening and closing of Congress.

Frequently threatened with demolition since it was completed in 1899, the Old Post Office was restored and rededicated in 1983. Its large interior courtyard houses a wide and lively variety of shops and food kiosks (see Chapter 9, Shopping, and Chapter 10, Restaurants) and is the setting for concerts and other arts programs. Take a tour of the 315-foot tall clock tower, which offers a breathtaking view of Washington from the observation deck and is a particularly wonderful place to see sunsets in the summer. Well-timed for children, the tour includes a look at the 10 Congress Bells and a recording of the ringing bells.

Old Stone House

3051 M Street, NW, Washington, DC 20007 (202-426-6851, 202-426-0125, TDY).

- Open Wednesday–Sunday, 8 A.M.–4:30 P.M. Closed Monday and Tuesday and Federal holidays.

- Metrorail Blue and Orange lines (Foggy Bottom). It's a long walk for children; check your map.
- Wheelchair access limited to ground floor.
- Strollers permitted in the garden, but not in the house.
- Picnicking allowed in the garden.

The Old Stone House is believed to be the oldest and only surviving pre-Revolutionary building in Washington. This was the modest home and shop of a Colonial cabinet-maker and is representative of a middle-class dwelling of the period. Its small size makes it seem cozy and comfortable to children.

   Special activities include numerous programs and demonstrations of period crafts and history. There is also a Christmas candlelight program in December. Call for further information.

Phillips Collection

1600 21st Street, NW, Washington, DC 20009 (202-387-2151).

- Open Monday–Saturday, 10 A.M.–5 P.M.; Sunday, noon–7 P.M. Closed July 4th, Thanksgiving, Christmas, and New Year's Day.
- Admission on weekends: adults, $5; senior citizens and full time students, $2.50; children under 18 and members, free. Suggested contributions on weekdays are same as weekend fees.
- Metrorail Red line (Dupont Circle, Q Street exit).
- On-street parking available but scarce; commercial lots nearby.
- Wheelchair access below main entrance.
- Strollers permitted.
- Regular tours Wednesday and Saturday, 2 P.M.; special tours for children or adults by arrangement, 202-387-7390.

This outstanding art collection of mainly 19th- and 20th-century European and American painting and sculpture, with a sprinkling of old masters, is tastefully displayed in the former home of the Phillips family. It is America's first museum of modern art.

The relatively small size makes it a pleasant museum stop for families. Visitors who come to the Phillips especially to see "Renoir's Luncheon of the Boating Party" should not overlook the fine selections of Bonnard, Braque, Daumier, Cezanne, Klee, Rothko, and Jacob Lawrence. There is a looking and learning pamphlet for parents and children to use together while touring the museum; particular emphasis is placed on the Music, Renoir, and Rothko rooms. Special children's guides are sometimes available for special exhibits. The sales shop includes books, posters, reproductions, post cards, and note cards. Cafe available.

Special activities include chamber music concerts (free with museum admission) performed in the gallery from September to May, Sunday at 5 P.M. Occasional parent-child workshops are planned. Call 202-387-7390 for information.

Renwick Gallery

17th Street and Pennsylvania Avenue, NW, Washington, DC 20560 (202-357-2700, 202-786-2424, TDY).

- Open daily, 10 A.M.–5:30 P.M. Closed Christmas.
- Metrorail Blue line (Farragut West, Farragut Square exit).
- Wheelchair access, corner of Pennsylvania Avenue and 17th Street. Wheelchairs are available.
- Strollers are not permitted.
- Call 202-357-2531 in advance to arrange tours.

Designed in 1859 by architect James Renwick, Jr. to house the collection of William Corcoran, this building was Washington's first private art museum. Due to the growth in his collection, Corcoran moved his paintings and sculpture to their present location. The U.S. Court of Claims moved into the original gallery. Now the gallery is a showcase for contemporary American crafts.

The Highlight Tour gives a general overview of the whole gallery including the history of its two period rooms, the Grand Salon and the Octagon Rooms, and a quick showing of the current exhibits. Some of the exhibits may be of more interest to children than others. Exhibits are often supplemented with films, demonstrations, and lectures. The museum shop usually has craft items for sale, as well as an extensive selection of books on cooking, weaving, rugmaking, pottery, and other crafts.

Tech 2000, Gallery of Interactive Multimedia

Techworld Plaza, 800 K Street, NW, Washington, DC 20001 (202-842-0500). Located two blocks north of Chinatown across from the Washington Convention Center.

- Open Tuesday–Sunday, 11 A.M.–5 P.M. Closed Monday and Thanksgiving, Christmas, and New Year's Day.
- Adults, $5; students, $4; senior citizens and children under 12, $3; handicapped visitors, free.
- Metrorail Red and Yellow lines (Gallery Place, Chinatown exit).
- Commercial parking nearby. Very limited on-street parking.
- Wheelchair access.
- Strollers are not permitted.
- Most appropriate for school-age children.
- Guided tours for up to 15 individuals are available by appointment. School groups of 15 to 35 also can arrange for tours in advance.

Adults and children can explore the many uses of interactive multimedia (the integration of audio, video, and computer graphics under the control of a computer program) in education, business, and the home. There are more than 60 hands-on exhibits featuring different configurations of computers, videodiscs, CD-ROM, and other components. You can view paintings from Wyeth's Helga collection, study art history, review the life of Martin Luther King, Jr., learn defensive driving techniques, or assess your individual learning style. This is one place where your computer literate children can bring you up-to-date on state-of-the-art technology.

Textile Museum

2320 S Street, NW, Washington, DC 20008 (202-667-0441).

- Open Monday–Saturday, 10 A.M.–5 P.M.; Sunday 1–5 P.M. Closed holidays.
- Admission free, but contributions accepted.
- Metrorail Red line (Dupont Circle).
- Commercial parking lot nearby.
- Visitors with special needs can call the Education Department, 202-667-0441. Wheelchairs are available.
- Strollers are not permitted.
- Drop-in tours available mid-September–May, Wednesday, Saturday, and Sunday at 2 P.M. Reserved tours offered Monday, Tuesday, Wednesday, Friday, and Saturday, 10 A.M.–4 P.M.; Thursday, 1–4 P.M. Call Education Department, 202-667-0441.
- Garden available for picnic lunches.

The Textile Museum features outstanding permanent collections of Oriental rugs, American Indian rugs, and Coptic and Pre-Columbian textiles. With the museum's emphasis on gaining insight into other cultures, the carefully and dramatically displayed exhibits of tapestries and weaving will be particularly interesting for children. Each Saturday, the museum sponsors a "Rug/Textile Appreciation Morning," when patrons can bring in rugs and textiles from their homes. These sessions emphasize conservation, history, and other special topics. There is a museum shop with an unusually good selection of materials related to stitchery. The museum also sponsors lectures and workshops. Exhibits change often so call ahead for information on current displays.

Special activities include Celebrations Day, held the first Saturday in June, with many hands-on activities for children and free favors. There are also frequent museum-sponsored lectures and workshops.

Washington Dolls' House & Toy Museum

5236 44th Street, NW, Washington, DC, 20015 (202-244-0024).
One block west of Wisconsin Avenue between Jennifer and
Harrison Streets.

- Open Tuesday–Saturday, 10 A.M.–5 P.M.; Sunday, noon–5 P.M.
  Closed Monday and Thanksgiving, Christmas, and New Year's
  Day.
- Adults, $3; children under 14, $1; senior citizens, $2.
- Metrorail Red line (Friendship Heights).
- On-street parking and commercial parking lots nearby.
- Wheelchair access for one wheelchair at a time.
- Strollers are not permitted.
- Guided tours available for 12 or more. Reservations required.

Children and adults enjoy the enchanting displays of this carefully researched collection of doll houses, dolls, toys, and games,
most of them Victorian and all of them antique. Each peek into
this tiny fantasy world reveals something new. There are lavishly
furnished Victorian houses that include furnishings such as a
wall telephone that rings, a sewing machine, and even a squirrel.
Beautifully carved animals fill the cages of miniature zoos and
circuses. A turn-of-the-century quintet of Baltimore row houses
and a 1903 New Jersey seaside hotel have special appeal for
visitors. A detailed exhibit of an elaborate Mexican house with an
aviary, a working elevator, and a garage complete with a model
vintage automobile fascinates old and young alike. And a small
Lionel train from the 1930's can be operated upon request.

This remarkable collection, assembled to provide a glimpse
into the way people lived in the past, is the work of museum
founder Flora Gill Jacobs. The items are invitingly displayed and
easy for children to see. Arrangements can be made for birthday
parties in the Edwardian tearoom. One museum shop contains
supplies for doll house collectors and a variety of items for
children; the other provides an assortment of building and wiring
supplies, kits, and books for doll house builders. An enlarged

consignment shop has a selection of antique toys and dolls for sale.

Special activities include an annual Christmas display high-lighted by a revolving musical tree. Other exhibits salute base-ball, Easter, Halloween, and the changing seasons.

Washington National Cathedral

The Cathedral Church of St. Peter and St. Paul, Massachusetts and Wisconsin Avenues, NW, Washington, DC 20016 (202-537-6200, 202-537-6211, TDY).

- Open daily in winter, 10 A.M.–4:30 P.M.; in summer, 10 A.M.–9 P.M.
- Parking on grounds is limited. Some on-street parking in surrounding neighborhood.
- Wheelchair access. Wheelchairs are available.
- Strollers are not permitted.
- Tours approximately once per hour, Monday–Saturday, 10 A.M.–3:15 P.M.; Sunday, 12:30–2:45 P.M.; no tours during ser-vices.
- Maps for self-guided tours are available upon request.
- Observation gallery and gift shop.

This splendid Episcopal 14th century gothic-style cathedral, started in 1907, was completed in September 1990. The tour of the main cathedral, small chapels, and crypts is especially inter-esting to children. They feel comfortable in the Children's Chapel, a room scaled down to their size, and are most impressed with the stained glass, stonework, and other cathedral-related crafts. A visit to the Pilgrim Observation Gallery is also exciting. It begins with an elevator ride to the enclosed gallery, which is at the roof level of the cathedral. The gallery affords an excellent view of Washington as well as the gargoyles, flying buttresses, and gardens of the cathedral. Don't miss the gardens and the herb cottage.

The Cathedral Medieval Workshop, open to the public on

Saturday, is a hands-on workshop where parents and children can work with stones to see how cathedrals are built. There are also hands-on demonstrations of the other art forms involved.

Cathedral acoustics are excellent. Many church music programs are fine for older children, while the annual Christmas Eve pageant is especially designed for the very young.

Special activities include the annual Open House, usually held the last Saturday of September. Featured are demonstrations of stone carving, flower arranging, needlepoint, stained glass, tours, and music and special activities designed for children. This is the one day a year when the bell tower is open to the public to climb (ages 9 and up). Balloons and food are for sale. The Cathedral's Flower Mart, usually held the first Friday and Saturday in May, features an antique carousel and an excellent selection of herbs and garden plants to purchase for your garden.

Washington Navy Yard

Main entrance to complex at 9th and M Streets, SE, Washington, DC (202-433-2218, Public Affairs Office). Mailing address: NDW, Public Affairs, Building 1, Washington Navy Yard, SE, Washington, DC 20374.

Plenty of parking is available in the Navy Yard. There are several places you may want to see within the complex. Begin with a stop at the Visitors' Center to get a map of the Navy Yard's Historic Precinct, and check to see if any ships are docked and open to the public. The Visitors' Center is open weekdays, 8 A.M.–3:30 P.M.

The Combat Art Gallery

Building 67 (202-433-3815).

- Summer hours (Memorial Day–Labor Day), Wednesday–Saturday, 10 A.M.–5 P.M. Winter hours, Wednesday–Friday, 9 A.M.–4 P.M.; Saturday and Sunday, 10 A.M.–5 P.M. Special hours during summer Navy pageant season, Wednesday, 7–10 P.M. Closed Thanksgiving, Christmas Eve, Christmas, and New Year's Day.

- No wheelchair access.
- Strollers permitted.

The gallery features paintings of ships, battles, and famous officers; there are also changing exhibits.

Display Ship Barry

Pier 2, 202-433-3372

- Open in summer, daily, 10 A.M.–5 P.M.; in winter, daily, 10 A.M.–4 P.M.;
- No wheelchair access.
- Strollers must be parked at pier.
- Call 202-433-3381 to arrange a school program.

The former United States Navy Destroyer Barry (DD-933), the third ship of the Force Sherman class of destroyers, was decommissioned after 26 years of service. The Barry is permanently moored at the Washington Navy Yard as a display ship for the Nation's capital and as a lasting memorial to the Navy. School-age children and adults alike love going on board the Barry, but it is extremely important to remember to obey your tour guide, follow all safety signs, and stay on the designated tour route.

The Marine Corps Museum and Historical Center

Building 58 (202-433-3534).

- Open Monday–Saturday, 10 A.M.–4 P.M.; Sunday and holidays, noon–5 P.M. Closed Christmas.
- Wheelchair access.
- Strollers permitted.

Housed in the 19th century building formerly used as a Marine barracks, this museum provides a chronological review of the Marine Corps' role in American history. Included are two flags flown over Iwo Jima, military dioramas as well as special exhibits. The museum would be of most interest to older children. Call 202-433-6060 to find out about the Summer Sunset Parade.

The Navy Museum

Building 76 (202-433-4882 or 202-433-2651, recording).

- Summer hours (Memorial Day–Labor Day), weekdays 9 A.M.–5 P.M. Winter hours, weekdays, 9 A.M.–4 P.M.; Saturday, Sunday, and holidays, 10 A.M.–5 P.M. Closed Thanksgiving, Christmas Eve, Christmas, and New Year's Day.
- Wheelchair access.
- Strollers permitted.
- Call 202-433-4882 to arrange for a school program appropriate for 1st through 12 grades.

Families will enjoy self-guided tours of this museum. Scavenger hunt booklets are available for 5–7 year-olds visiting with their families; there is also a booklet for children ages 8 and older. There are workbooks for students about World War II.

This museum has great appeal to youngsters. Exhibits are devoted to the U.S. Navy from the Revolutionary War to the Space Age. There is also an excellent display of model ships. What children really want to see is the weaponry. They can climb on the cannon, operate the barrels of anti-aircraft weapons, and turn submarine periscopes.

Special activities include free family entertainment entitled "An American Sailor Pageant" held on Wednesday evenings from May 29–September 4. The U.S. Navy Band plays during an hour-long skit about the Navy's past and present. Call 202-433-2219 for information. Not to be missed is the Seafaring Celebration on the first Saturday in November. It is a day full of hands-on activities about maritime traditions like shipbuilding, signal flag making, scrimshaw, etc.

The White House

1600 Pennsylvania Avenue, NW, Washington, DC 20500 (202-456-2200 or 202-456-6213, TSD).

- Open Tuesday–Friday, 10 A.M.–noon; Saturday until 2 P.M. Closed Sunday, Monday, Thanksgiving, Christmas, and New Year's Day.
- Metrorail Blue and Orange lines (McPherson Square).
- Tourmobile® stop.
- Wheelchair access at north east gate. Wheelchairs are available.
- Strollers must be parked before going on the tour.

During the off season (November through late March) this is a continuous tour and all who are in line by noon are assured of seeing the White House. Entrance for the tour is through the Visitors' Entrance on East Executive Avenue.

During the busy season (late March through October) tickets are necessary and may be obtained from the ticket booths on the Ellipse (the park area south of the White House) the day of the tour only. The booths open at 8 A.M. and tickets are issued on a first-come, first-served basis. For family groups, one member of the family may pick up tickets for the group at the blue ticket booth. For larger groups, one representative may fill out a voucher for up to 60 tickets at the white ticket booth. If the group is larger than 60, several representatives will be required. When the full group assembles for their tour, a Park Ranger will issue tickets to each member.

Early morning tours with a tour guide can be arranged through your congressman or senator. These tickets are available on an extremely limited basis. Write at least a month in advance and give specific dates. Occasionally the White House is closed for official Presidential events. Notice may not be given. Call 202-456-7041 to confirm tours.

The White House has been the home of our President since John Adams moved from Philadelphia in 1800. The private family quarters upstairs are not open to the public, but most adults and older children find the visit to the handsome state rooms in the main residence rewarding. Call 202-456-7041 for a recorded message describing the current status of White House tours.

Special activities include the annual Easter Egg Roll on the White House lawn, held the Monday after Easter from 10 A.M. to 2 P.M. and open to children under age 8 with accompanying adult. One weekend in October and one in April are set aside for tours of the gardens and the house. Candlelight tours are held in the evenings following Christmas. Specific dates are determined each year.

Woodrow Wilson House

2340 S Street, NW, Washington, DC 20008 (202-387-4062).

- Open Tuesday–Sunday, 10 A.M.–4 P.M.; closed Monday and major holidays.
- Adults, $4; senior citizens and students, $2.50; children under 7, free.
- Metrorail Red line (Dupont Circle).
- Limited wheelchair access.
- Strollers should be parked downstairs.
- Call in advance for group tours and group rates.

Immediately following the inauguration ceremonies for President Harding, Woodrow Wilson and his wife moved from the White House to this stately townhouse and lived there until his death. The only former President's house open to the public in Washington, it still reflects the presence of this scholarly and idealistic man. Children with a penchant for collecting like to see the drawing room and library, which have souvenirs from all over the world. Children might also be interested in the well-stocked kitchen of the 1920s, the 1915 elevator, the graphoscope, and an early version of a film projector.

Special tours and outreach programs for elementary and secondary classes are available. These emphasize using primary source documents and artifacts to learn about daily life in the Wilson home (elementary classes) and about World War I and League of Nations issues confronting Wilson (secondary classes). Call for details.

3 Main Sights And Museums In Maryland and Virginia

Maryland and Virginia offer more sites and museums for good family outings. This chapter is arranged alphabetically by city under Maryland and Virginia. Use this chapter with a nature or park choice from Chapters 5 or 6 for a full day outing.

In Nearby Maryland

Clinton

Historic Surratt House

9110 Brandywine Road, Clinton, MD 20735 (301-868-1121). Take the Beltway (Route 495) to Exit 7A (Branch Avenue/ Route 5); go south for 3½ miles to right turn on Wood-yard Road (Route 223 west); continue for a short distance to left turn on Brandywine Road; house is on the left, immediately after the turn.

- Open March 1st–mid-December, Thursday and Friday, 11 A.M.–3 P.M.; Saturday and Sunday, noon–4 P.M. Closed mid-December–February.
- Adults, $1; children, 50¢.
- Wheelchair access on the first floor only.
- Strollers are not permitted in historic house.

- Last tour 30 minutes before closing. Call about frequency of tours.
- Group tours Wednesday, by appointment.
- The museum has a small gift shop with books and intriguing toys.

This two-story frame house was a tavern, post office, polling place, and the home of the first woman executed by the U.S. government, Mary Surratt. In July 1865, she was hung for her alleged role in the assassination of President Abraham Lincoln. John Wilkes Booth stopped briefly at the house the evening of April 14, 1865, as he tried to escape after shooting the President. Today, costumed docents give visitors tours of the home and discuss the continuing question of whether or not Mary Surratt was a co-conspirator in the plot to assassinate President Lincoln.

The home is a typical middle class home of the Victorian period. The well-rounded displays include Victorian furniture, rugs, lace curtains, clothing, and kitchen implements. Those who have always wondered what's in the closed attics of museums can step into this attic and see where guns were hidden in the house.

Special activities and exhibits focus on 19th century life, including the Victorian Christmas in December and a February exhibit of 19th century valentines and crafts. Call for further information.

College Park

College Park Airport and Museum

6709 Corporal Frank Scott Drive, College Park, MD (301-864-1530). Take the Beltway (Route 495) to Kenilworth Avenue south towards Bladensburg; turn right on Calvert Road; then right at the second traffic light on Corporal Frank Scott Drive (sign will say College Park Airport); continue to the airport and museum.

- Museum open for tours Wednesday–Friday, 11 A.M. to 3 P.M.; Saturday and Sunday, 11 A.M. to 5 P.M.
- Wheelchair access.
- Strollers permitted.
- Group tours available by appointment (301-864-1530).

The College Park Airport is the world's oldest continuously operated airport and serves as a general aviation airport for small, privately-owned aircraft. The airport was the site of many aviation firsts, including the first army flying school, the first regularly scheduled commercial airmail service, and the first controlled helicopter flight.

The airport museum commemorates the historic importance of the airport. Displays include airplane models, uniforms, equipment, and early photos and watercolors. Several films, including a 1909 film of Orville Wright flying his aircraft, are available for viewing upon request. Visitors can compare the present site to the past by examining the photos and a diorama of the army aviation school as it appeared in 1912.

Special activities include a two-day Air Fair in September.

Glenn Dale

Marietta

5626 Bell Station Road, Glenn Dale, MD 20769 (301-464-5291). Take the Beltway (Route 495) to Annapolis Road east (Route 450); left on Route 193, Glenn Dale Boulevard; first left on Bell Station Road; Marietta is the first driveway on the left.

- Open March–December, Sunday, noon–4 P.M. Closed January and February.
- Adults, $1; students, 50¢; senior citizens, 75¢; children under 5, free.
- Parking available.
- No wheelchair access.

- Strollers should be left at the door.
- School and other group tours available, 301-464-5291.
- Picnicking on the grounds.
- A variety of children's books, toys, antiques, and handcrafted gifts in the shop.

Gabriel Duvall, a Justice of the U.S. Supreme Court, built this Federal style country home between 1812 and 1813. The home is the current headquarters of the Prince George's County Historical Society and the Society's library.

Children are intrigued by the piano and butler's desk hidden inside cabinets. The four-poster beds are especially interesting because of the mattresses made of straw which crackle to the touch. An unusual canopied cradle on tall legs is also on display, an heirloom from the Duvall family.

The 25 acres of land surrounding Marietta was a working farm where the Duvall family raised tobacco and grain crops. Today visitors can walk around the grounds to see a root cellar, which is being restored, the Judge's law office, and a cemetery with family gravestones. Visitors have seen deer disappear into a grove of trees as they walked out the front door.

Special activities include a Mad Hatter's Tea Party in March with tea and stories for the children. Reservations are required and a fee is charged. Candlelight tours take place during two weekends in December. Other special events which may be repeated include: Family Outing Day, with children's games on the extensive lawn; a quilt exhibit, a doll show, and a period clothing exhibit.

Glen Echo

Clara Barton National Historic Site

5801 Oxford Road, Glen Echo, MD 20812 (301-492-6245). From outer loop of the Beltway (Route 495), take exit 40 and follow signs to Glen Echo Park, about 3 miles from exit. You will be on MacArthur Boulevard. Turn left on Oxford Road Drive just past Glen Echo Park. House is at the end of the road. From inner loop of the Beltway (Route 495), exit at Clara Barton Parkway east for 2 to 3 miles, then follow signs to park and proceed as above. From Washington, DC, take Massachusetts Avenue till it ends at Goldsboro Road. Turn left, then follow to MacArthur Boulevard. Turn right, then left on Oxford Road.

- Open daily, 10 A.M.–5 P.M. Closed Thanksgiving, Christmas, and New Year's Day.
- Wheelchair access by prior arrangement so that appropriate accommodations can be made. There are six steps in the house. Staff will help carry a child in a wheelchair up those steps.
- Strollers are not permitted in the house..
- Groups of more than 10 need to make reservations. Special group tours, including tours for the deaf and the elderly, may be arranged. Special programs are available for school and social groups. These include slide presentations and movies. Call in advance.
- Picnic area at adjacent Glen Echo Park.

Clara Barton, the Civil War heroine known as the "Angel of the Battlefield" and founder of the American Red Cross, had this structure built in 1891. It originally served as a warehouse for relief supplies for the Red Cross. In 1897 it was modified for her living quarters and also served as national headquarters for the American Red Cross from that date until 1904. Unique features of the house include the many concealed closets used for supply storage and the topmost room which bridges over the central well. The National Park Service maintains this site.

Glen Echo Park and Carousel

MacArthur Boulevard at Goldsboro Road, Glen Echo, MD 20812 (301-492-6282, recording; 301-492-6663, carousel). From outer loop of the Beltway (Route 495), take exit 40 and follow signs to Glen Echo Park, about 3 miles from exit. From inner loop of the Beltway (Route 495), exit at Clara Barton Parkway east for 2 to 3 miles, then follow signs to park. From Washington, DC, take Massachusetts Avenue till it ends at Goldsboro Road. Turn left, then follow to MacArthur Boulevard. Turn left to park.

- Open daily, 6 A.M.–1 A.M. (These hours allow artists access to their studios. Most events for the public occur during the day and evening hours.)
- Limited wheelchair access.
- Strollers permitted in park only.
- The 1921 Dentzel carousel is open May–September, Saturday and Sunday, noon–6 P.M.; Wednesday and Thursday, 10 A.M.–2 P.M. 50¢ per ride. Group bookings are possible.

Many Washingtonians remember riding the trolley to swim in the large outdoor pool and ride the bumper cars. The pool is long closed and the bumper car pavilion is now an open-air pavilion, but Glen Echo still has a lot to offer visitors. The National Park Service has converted this former amusement park into an arts center with classrooms for adult and children's courses. Glen Echo sponsors over 500 art classes per year, covering such topics as fine arts, crafts, stained glass, sculpture, and theater. Free children's art workshops Sunday afternoons in spring and summer are very popular. There are free artists' demonstrations on site.

The carousel is a special treat. Riding the multi-colored, hand-carved animals to the rhythm of the 1926 Wurlitzer band organ is pure joy for kids. When Glen Echo Park closed and the carousel was about to be shipped to California, a group of concerned citizens raised money, bought it back and presented it to the National Park Service. It operates rain or shine (it's covered) and is the best carousel in the area.

Special activities include dance, folk music, and storytelling on weekends from May into October. The Washington Folk Festival is held here in late May or early June and the Irish Festival takes place at Glen Echo, usually on the weekend before Memorial Day.

Greenbelt

NASA/Goddard Space Flight Center

Visitors' Center, Greenbelt, MD 20771 (301-286-8981). Take the Beltway (Route 495) to the Baltimore-Washington Parkway; go north and follow signs to NASA.

- Open Wednesday–Sunday, 10 a.m–4 P.M. Call for special summer hours. Closed Thanksgiving, Christmas, and New Year's Day.
- Parking available.
- Wheelchair access.

- Strollers permitted.
- Tours are held Wednesday–Saturday, 11:30 A.M. and 2:30 P.M. Walking tours are held on the 1st and 3rd Sunday of the month at 11 A.M. Bus tours are held on the 2nd and 4th Sunday of the month at 11 A.M. and 2 P.M.
- Picnicking is permitted. Refreshments may be purchased from vending machines on site.
- Memorabilia and souvenirs for sale at the gift shop.

School children of all ages will find something to fascinate them on this self-guided tour. Real and model rockets and satellites are on exhibit both outside and inside. Dock the Manned-Maneuvering Unit Simulator with a satellite by manipulating the controls. Use the computer system to build your own satellite and rocket system. The computer will alert you to any mistakes. Sunspots and solar flares can be witnessed as they happen with the solar telescope. Watch as weather maps of the earth are transmitted here from space. View a giant TV screen showing recent footage of NASA's space ventures. Many additional exhibits highlight the space program's contribution to fields such as communications, navigation, and aeronautics.

On the first and third Sunday of each month from 1–2 P.M., you can watch small home-made rockets being launched by members of local rocket clubs and the general public.

Special activities are listed in a quarterly calendar of events. Call above phone number to request a copy.

Greenbelt Museum

10-B Crescent Road, Greenbelt, MD 20770 (301-474-1936). Take the Beltway (Route 495) to Kenilworth Avenue north; turn right on Crescent Road and continue to the museum, on the left just past the library parking lot.

- Open Sunday, 1–5 P.M., and by appointment.
- Wheelchair access to the home is limited.
- Strollers permitted, but the house is very small and it is best to leave them outside.

- Group tours available.
- Playground and lake nearby.

Greenbelt is one of three "green towns" built by the U.S. government in an effort to provide jobs during the Great Depression. It is one of America's earliest planned towns and much of the city is on the National Register of Historic Places. The Greenbelt Museum is located in an original home, one half of a duplex building, built by the Federal government. The home appears much as it did in 1937 when the first residents were selected by the government to move into the town of the future. The collection includes early photographs of the town, Art Deco pieces, and furniture.

The home is located adjacent to many of the revolutionary planning features of the town: a playground, inner walkways, a pedestrian underpass, and a town center. The nearby Greenbelt Center School is considered one of the best examples of Art Deco architecture in the area. Children can let off steam at the playground or the nearby lake after listening to grandparents describe life in the Great Depression.

Kensington

Noyes Library

10237 Carroll Place, Kensington, MD 20895 (301-949-3780). Take the Beltway (Route 495) to Exit 33 or 33 A (Connecticut Avenue north) towards Kensington. At the sign "Welcome to Kensington" be in the right lane so you can continue straight ahead on University Boulevard. (Connecticut Avenue veers to the left.) At stop sign turn right on Baltimore Street, then immediately bear left to get on Carroll Place. The library is straight ahead, a beige building with sycamore trees in front.

- Open Tuesday, Thursday, and Saturday, 9 A.M.–5 P.M.
- Limited on-street parking.
- No wheelchair access.

- Strollers permitted.
- Most appropriate for children ages infant–6 years.
- Call in advance for groups.
- Picnicking permitted outside the building.

This charming one-room library, Montgomery County's oldest, is now an historic landmark. It sits on its own triangular island surrounded by old trees and turreted Victorian homes. Once inside, children immediately sense the intimacy of this library, which is just for them. Basically, the programs offered here are like those of any other Montgomery County library: movies, penny theaters, and special events. However, many special programs which turn up at other libraries had their beginnings at Noyes. The hours permit Noyes' librarians to accommodate groups. Grandparents can borrow special "grandparent kits," with toys and books centered on a particular theme, to have on hand for visiting youngsters. For more information about the services offered by the Montgomery County libraries, contact the Children's Services Division of the Montgomery County Public Libraries, 301-217-3837.

Washington Temple
(Known as the "Mormon Temple")

9900 Stoneybrook Drive, Kensington, MD 20895 (301-587-0144). Take the Beltway (Route 495) to exit 33 or 33 A (Connecticut Avenue north), towards Kensington. Turn right at second light on Beach Drive and follow to end. Turn left on Stoneybrook Drive. The Visitor Center is ¼ mile on left.

- Visitor Center and gardens open daily, 10 A.M.–9 P.M. No access to the Temple.
- Wheelchair access.
- Strollers permitted.

The Visitor Center has films and exhibits describing the construction of the temple and the programs of the church.

Special activities include, at Christmas, the live nativity scene, 300,000 Christmas lights which cover trees and bushes on the grounds, and inside the Visitor Center, 14 ten-foot Christmas trees decorated by different congregations. Exhibit and holiday entertainment continue from December until the first week in January.

Laurel

Montpelier Mansion

Muirkirk Road and Route 197, Laurel, MD 20708 (301-953-1376). Take the Beltway (Route 495) to Baltimore-Washington Parkway north; exit at Route 197 north toward Laurel; turn left on Muirkirk Road; entrance is immediately on the right.

- Open March–first weekend in December, Sunday, noon–4 P.M. (last tour starts at 3:15 P.M.). Closed for the rest of December–February.
- Adults, $1.50; children, 50¢; senior citizens $1.00.
- Wheelchair access to the first floor only. Please call in advance so assistance can be provided.
- Strollers should be left at the door.
- Group tours available; call for information.
- A separate gift shop on the grounds has many unusual children's items for sale. Open March–first weekend in December, Wednesday, Saturday, and Sunday, noon–4 P.M.

Completed in the 1780s by Major Thomas Snowden, Montpelier is a masterpiece of Georgian architecture. The expansive grounds (75 acres) include a boxwood maze and one of the two remaining 18th century gazebos in the nation that is still on the original site. Interesting features of the interior include the intricate carvings and offset central hall staircase. Children enjoy seeing the Quaker classroom and secret staircase.

The Montpelier Cultural Arts Center is located in a modern barn on the property. It is open seven days a week from 10 A.M.–5 P.M. (except holidays). The Arts Center features artists in residence, art galleries, and classes. For information on Arts Center programs, call 301-953-1993.

Special activities include Christmas candlelight tours, George Washington musicale, Montpelier Spring Festival, and Colonial Day. Call for more information on these and other events.

Rockville

Beall-Dawson House and Stonestreet Medical Museum

111 West Montgomery Avenue, Rockville, MD 20850 (301-762-1492 or 301-340-9853). Take 270 north to Route 28 towards Rockville. Turn right on Montgomery Avenue (Route 28). Jog left at the second traffic light. Turn left on North Adams Street, then left on Middle Lane. Parking lot is on left.

- Open Tuesday–Saturday, noon–4 P.M.; first Sunday of the month, 2–5 P.M. Closed major holidays.
- Adults, $2; students and senior citizens, $1. Members and children 12 and under, free.
- Metrorail Red line (Rockville).
- Free parking in back of house on Middle Lane and Adams.
- No wheelchair access.
- Strollers are not permitted.
- Especially appropriate for 4th graders.
- Tours on-going during hours of operation. Call to arrange special tours.
- Picnicking allowed on lawn.
- Small museum shop with toys and children's books.

The enthusiastic volunteers at the Beall-Dawson House are not only excited about the renovations and furnishings of this 19th century home but also about helping children understand this historical period. The tour guides take a special interest in very young visitors and point out features of the home that may interest them. These features include absence of electrical light fixtures, techniques to marble the staircase, fireplaces in each room, and a card table with extensions for candles. Children enjoy detecting the differences between the brick on the formal entrance and the less expensive brick on the sides.

Because of the Montgomery County fourth grade history curriculum, the Beall-Dawson House has become an integral part of many fourth grade historical field trips. The special exhibits are often geared to this age, with past exhibits of wedding dresses, sewing accoutrements, funeral attire, and African American history artifacts.

If you call ahead, the guides may be able to provide age-appropriate period dress-up costumes and period toys to play with.

On the grounds of the Beall-Dawson House is the Stonestreet Medical Museum. It is the original one-room office used by Dr. Stonestreet in the late 1800's. Set up to suggest a 19th century country doctor's office, the Museum contains displays of medical, surgical, dental, and apothecary equipment. The collection contains such unusual items as a Civil War amputation kit and an 1850 stethoscope.

Special activities include an annual community open house on the second Sunday in December. For information about other special events call the numbers listed above.

Silver Spring

National Weather Service Science and History Center and the National Marine Fisheries Service Exhibit

1325 East West Highway, Silver Spring, MD, 20910. (301-713-0692). Take the Beltway (Route 495) to Georgia Avenue south (Route 97). Turn right on Colesville Road. The National Weather Service is on the left corner of Colesville Road and East-West Highway.

- Open weekdays, 8:30 A.M.–5 P.M. Closed Federal holidays.
- Metrorail Red line (Silver Spring).
- Nearby public parking.
- Wheelchair access and facilities.
- Strollers permitted.
- Weather exhibit suitable for older children. Fisheries exhibit appropriate for all ages.
- Call ahead for an introductory film and guided tour of the weather exhibit.
- Eatery on-site.
- NOAA gift shop.

A quick detour if you happen to be at the Silver Spring Metrorail Station is the National Oceanic and Atmospheric Administration (NOAA) complex. Even though the weather service exhibit center has received much publicity, the real gem of the NOAA exhibits is in the National Marine Fisheries Service. This one-room lobby museum contains glass cases of ship models from early times to the present used in commercial fisheries management. In these times of ecological studies and awareness, this exhibit is particularly relevant because the service monitors fish catches, enforcing our laws on the catching of baby seals, dolphins, and whales. One case of particular interest contains a "floating" replica of Aquarius, an undersea dwelling and laboratory from which scientists study oceans and their inhabitants.

The National Weather Service Science and History Center is a one-room exhibit also, but the exhibit is geared for junior high and high schoolers who have an interest in meteorology history. In the exhibit is a full-scale replica of a weather office of 1895, equipped with instruments, furniture and weather records. Younger children enjoy listening to the weather reports on the exhibit telephones.

A fountain is situated in the courtyard between the two NOAA buildings. Obtain food from the Bromax Express eatery, entrance on the courtyard, or from the Giant Foods shopping center across the street and enjoy a picnic by the fountain.

In the same vicinity as these mini-centers, NOAA plans to

open a large museum to be completed by the Spring of 1993. This museum will house artifacts such as the first topographical survey of the United States and the first computer used by the United States government. Outdoor exhibits are also planned.

Wheaton
National Capital Trolley Museum

1313 Bonifant Road, Wheaton, MD 20914 (301-384-6088). Take the Beltway (Route 495) to Georgia Avenue north (Route 97); turn right on Layhill Road (Route 182); after 2 miles turn right on Bonifant Road to museum on left.

- Open January–November, Saturday and Sunday, noon–5 P.M., July–August also open Wednesday, 11–3 P.M.; open Memorial Day, July 4, and Labor Day, noon–5 P.M.; open December, Saturday and Sunday, 5–9 P.M. for Holly Trolley illuminations.
- Admission free. Trolley fares for adults, $2; children 2–18, $1.50; children under two, free.

- No wheelchair access.
- Strollers permitted.
- Picnic grove available for lunches.
- The museum has a small gift shop featuring inexpensive railroad-related gifts.
- Trolley charters can be arranged for birthday parties.

This suburban Maryland museum features a picturesque collection of antique Washington streetcars and European trams. Visitors can take a 20-minute trolley ride through the countryside and listen to the staff relate historical, mechanical, and anecdotal information about the cars. Occasionally old films or slide shows on subjects related to transportation are shown in the auditorium. Children particularly enjoy operating the model trolley layout.

Special activities usually take place each month, including "Santa on the Streetcar" in December and parade days in April and September when all the trolley cars are brought out for display or use. There is an annual Open House in the fall. Call for information on these events.

In Nearby Virginia

Alexandria

Alexandria, George Washington's hometown, has many sights that make history come alive for children as well as adults. The town, which originated with a tobacco warehouse in 1732, was a major Virginia port. Freighters filled with imported goods for local specialty shops still unload here, and younger children who get bored with antiques and architecture are always happy to sit and watch the river traffic. Older children and their parents have a good time shopping in modern Alexandria for quality items or knickknacks. There are many good restaurants in all price ranges. Start out at the Alexandria Convention and Visitors' Bureau and plan the tour according to the age, interests, and stamina of family members.

The Metrorail Yellow line, King Street stop is the closest to Old Town Alexandria, where many of the historic sites are located. Be prepared for a 15 to 20 minute walk from the subway stop to the corner of King and Washington Streets. If you choose to drive to Alexandria, take the George Washington Memorial Parkway south (which becomes Washington Street) to the center of Old Town Alexandria, King and Washington Streets. There are public parking lots and limited street parking throughout the area.

Alexandria Archaeology (located in the Torpedo Factory)

105 North Union Street, Studio 327, Alexandria, VA 22314 (703-838-4399).

- Open Tuesday–Friday, 10 A.M.–3 P.M.; Saturday, 10 A.M.–5 P.M.; Sunday, 1–5 P.M. Closed Easter, Thanksgiving, Christmas, and New Year's Day.
- Wheelchair access.
- Strollers permitted.
- Most appropriate for school-age children.
- School groups can arrange to visit the lab/museum to interpret artifacts, maps, and other archival information. Programs are directed to 3rd–6th graders.
- Picnicking permitted in the two parks located on either side of the Torpedo Factory.
- A food court behind the Torpedo Factory has a variety of foods to eat inside or outside on the extensive docks along the Potomac River.

Alexandria Archaeology was formed to preserve and interpret archaeological information from the city of Alexandria and to involve the public in archaeological preservation. At the lab/museum children can observe volunteers working with artifacts, cleaning, and categorizing. Visitors also see a life-size model of an archaeologist at work. The favorite part of the exhibit for many children is the exhibit of animal skeletal remains. The organization encourages participation in field trips to archaeological digs during the summer. Call for specific information.

One visitor reported that she knew the museum's message was effective because her children began excavating the backyard as soon as they returned from visiting Alexandria Archaeology.

Special activities include Virginia Archaeology Week, held during the first week in October. During this event, visitors to the lab/museum may tour sites as well as explore a special hands-on artifact exhibit. Further information about special programs is available from the education coordinator, 703-838-4399.

To learn more about the Torpedo Factory Art Center see the listing in this chapter.

Alexandria Convention and Visitors' Bureau

Ramsay House, 221 King Street, Alexandria, VA 22314 (703-838-4200 or 703-838-5005 for 24-hour recorded information on events).

- Open daily, 9 A.M.–5 P.M. Closed Thanksgiving, Christmas, and New Year's Day.
- Bureau will make available parking passes for out-of-town visitors.
- No wheelchair access.
- Strollers permitted, but must be carried up steps.
- Orientation video to Alexandria.
- Translation services in 18 languages.
- Bureau will make hotel and restaurant reservations.

This visitors' center is the restored home of William Ramsay, Scottish merchant and city founder. Stop here first to receive information on Alexandria since its founding in 1749. You can also receive annotated maps, lists of galleries and shops, and other helpful services for tourists.

Boyhood Home of Robert E. Lee

607 Oronoco Street, Alexandria, VA 22314 (703-548-8454).

- Open Monday–Saturday, 10 A.M.–4 P.M.; Sunday, 1–4 P.M. Closed December 15–February 1 and Thanksgiving, Christmas, and Easter.
- Adults, $3; children 11–17, $1; children under 10, free. Reduced rates for groups of 10 or more.
- No wheelchair access.
- Strollers are not permitted. They can be left at the door.
- Group tours by appointment. Special activities for school tours when advance notice is given.
- Across the street at 614 Oronoco Street, the Lee-Fendall House features a collection of doll houses on the third floor.

Lighthorse Harry Lee brought his family to this house in 1812, when young Robert was only 5. Robert grew up here on this tree-lined street, and when he enrolled in West Point he gave this house as his home address. The Lees rented the house, built in 1795 during the boom that accompanied the establishment of the Federal City. The Lafayette Room is so named because the famed General visited Robert's mother here. In this house, George Washington Parke Custis, adopted son of George Washington, was married. Children enjoy seeing the nursery with its "pint-sized" furniture and the kitchen with early cooking implements.

Carlyle House

121 North Fairfax Street, Alexandria, VA 22314
(703-549-2997).

- Open Tuesday–Saturday, 10 A.M.–5 p.m; Sunday, noon–5 P.M. Closed Thanksgiving, Christmas Eve, Christmas, and New Year's Day.
- Adults, $3; children 11–17, $1; children 10 and under, free. Group tours for 10 or more, $2 per adult.
- Wheelchair access to two floors.

- Strollers permitted on the first floor only.
- Tours on the hour and half-hour; the last tour begins at 4:30 P.M.

This restored mansion, home of John Carlyle, was the place where General Edward Braddock and five British governors met to devise a taxation plan to raise money for the French and Indian War. This "taxation without representation" was to have far-ranging consequences. The house contains furnishings and artifacts of the era, and cutaway sections illustrate how it was built.

Special activities include an annual Christmas celebration.

Christ Church

118 North Washington Street, Alexandria, VA 22314 (703-549-1450).

- Open Monday–Saturday, 9 A.M.–4 P.M.; Sunday, 2–4:30 P.M.
- Sunday Services at 8, 9, and 11:15 A.M. and 5 P.M. Visitors should plan for unexpected closings for weddings, funerals, and special church services because this is an active Episcopal church.
- Wheelchair access (one-step barrier; assistance provided).
- Strollers permitted.

This lovely colonial Georgian church, in continual use since its completion in 1773, is the oldest in Alexandria and one of the oldest on the East Coast. Visitors can sit in the boxed-in pews belonging to George Washington and Robert E. Lee. Look for the little brass tablet that marks where Lee knelt at the altar rail to be confirmed. Children enjoy the raised "wine-glassed" pulpit with its winding staircase.

Children find the greatest fascination, however, in the adjacent graveyard, where searching tombstones for dates and inscriptions is an adventure in this peaceful setting. See also Fort Ward Park in Chapter 6, Parks and Recreation.

Special activities include The Greening of the Church which occurs the Sunday before Christmas. This activity is especially ap pealing to both visitors and residents as the "Holiday Spirit" is captured by the fresh greens, holly, boxwood wreaths, and candles.

Fort Ward Museum

4301 West Braddock Road, Alexandria, VA 22304 (703-838-4848). Take Route 395 to Seminary Road east; after about 1 mile turn left on North Howard Street; then right on West Braddock to entrance.

- Open Tuesday–Saturday, 9 A.M.–5 P.M.; Sunday, noon–5 P.M. Closed Monday and Thanksgiving, Christmas, and New Year's Day.
- Park open daily, 9 A.M. to sunset.
- There is a parking lot directly behind the museum and other parking lots throughout the park.
- Wheelchair access to the museum. The path to the historic fort does have hilly terrain.
- Strollers permitted.
- There are picnic areas throughout the park.

Of special interest to Civil War buffs, this museum exhibits weapons, uniforms, musical instruments, and other memorabilia of the period, in addition to rotating exhibits. Visitors may tour the preserved earthwork walls of Fort Ward as well as the restored northwest bastion. See also Fort Ward Park in Chapter 6, Parks and Recreation.

Special activities include living history events that occur throughout the year, in particular, a special weekend of activities in the summer.

Gadsby's Tavern Museum

134 North Royal Street, Alexandria, VA 22314 (703-838-4242).

- Open Tuesday–Saturday, 10 A.M.–5 P.M.; Sunday, 1–5 P.M. Closed Thanksgiving, Christmas, and New Year's Day.
- Adults, $3; children 11–17, $1; children under 11, free with paying adult.

- Group rates available upon request.
- Limited wheelchair access.
- Strollers are not permitted.
- Gadsby's Tavern (restaurant open for lunch and dinner).

Gadsby's Tavern actually consists of two tavern buildings. One is the 1770 City Tavern and the other is the 1792 City Hotel. The buildings were named for John Gadsby, an Englishman who operated them from 1796 until 1808. The present museum includes a taproom, ice well, bedrooms, and the ballroom in which George Washington's birthday dances were held.

Special activities include a recreation of an 18th century market fair held in September.

George Washington Masonic National Memorial

101 Callahan Street, Alexandria, VA 22301(703-683-2007).

- Open daily, 9 A.M.–5 P.M. Closed Thanksgiving, Christmas, and New Year's Day.
- Metrorail Yellow line (King Street).
- No wheelchair access.
- Strollers can be checked as they are not practical for the tour.
- Tours every 35 minutes, May–October (last tour at 4:10 P.M.); tours every 70 minutes, November–April (last tour at 3:35 P.M.).

This monument to George Washington towers over the Alexandria skyline, affording a good view of the area. Memorabilia displayed include George Washington's bible, a clock that was stopped at the time of his death, and other Washington artifacts. Children enjoy the large mechanical model of a Shriner's parade complete with platoons of brightly-clad nobles marching to recorded band music.

The Lyceum, Alexandria's History Museum

201 South Washington Street, Alexandria, VA 22314
(703-838-4994).

- Open Monday–Saturday, 10 A.M.–5 P.M. (Thursday until 8 P.M.);
  Sunday, 1–5 P.M. Closed Thanksgiving, Christmas, and New
  Year's Day.
- Wheelchair access to the lecture hall and facilities.
- Strollers permitted.
- The Lyceum Museum Shop features books, puzzles, and
  games.

An impressive example of Greek Revival architecture, the Lyceum
was built in 1839 as a cultural center for Alexandria history. The
building served as a military hospital during the Civil War and
later as a private residence, office building, and bicentennial
center. Since 1985 The Lyceum has been Alexandria's History
Museum.

Special activities for families include concerts, exhibitions,
and the annual Scottish Preview held the Saturday after Thanksgiving.

Market Square/Alexandria City Hall

300 block of King Street, Alexandria, VA 22314 (703-838-4000).

- Wheelchair access.
- Strollers permitted.

During the original survey of Alexandria in 1749, two half-acre
lots were set aside to be used for a market place and town hall.
In the course of the town's history, this site has held schools,
jails, whipping posts, and a private fire company. The earliest
town court house was erected here in 1752. The building burned
down in 1871 and was replaced, through contributions of private
citizens, by the current building, which is an exact replica of the
clock tower originally designed by Benjamin Latrobe. It is still the

home, on Saturday mornings, of the oldest continuously operating market in the country.

Special activities include weekday lunchtime concerts, an annual Christmas lighting ceremony, and other events. For a calendar of events, call the Alexandria Convention and Visitors' Bureau, 703-838-4200.

Stabler-Leadbeater Apothecary Shop and Museum

105 and 107 South Fairfax Street, Alexandria, VA 22314 (703-836-3713).

- Open Monday, Tuesday, and Thursday–Saturday, 10 A.M.–4 P.M. In winter, closed both Tuesday and Wednesday. Closed Thanksgiving, Christmas, and New Year's Day.
- Donations $1.
- No wheelchair access.
- Strollers permitted.

This drugstore was used by George Washington, Robert E. Lee, Daniel Webster, and other historic figures. Original prescription books with their orders and a sampling of pharmaceutical equipment are on display. A recording relates the history of the shop.

Torpedo Factory Art Center

105 North Union Street, Alexandria, VA 22314 (703-838-4565, recording; 703-683-0693, tour information from The Friends of the Torpedo Factory Art Center).

- Open daily, 10 A.M.–5 P.M. Closed Easter, Thanksgiving, Christmas, and New Year's Day.
- Wheelchair access.
- Strollers permitted.
- Tours available through the Friends of the Torpedo Factory. Special demonstration tours can be arranged for groups. Call 703-683-0693 two weeks in advance.

- Picnicking permitted in the two parks located on either side of the Torpedo Factory.
- A food court behind the Torpedo Factory has food available to eat inside or outside on the extensive docks along the Potomac River.

Over 200 professional artists work, exhibit, and sell their art in this renovated World War I munitions plant. Children can see weavers, metal sculptors, painters, stained glass artisans, potters, printmakers, and more. Watching clay undulate and "grow" on the potter's wheel seems to be especially fascinating for children, perhaps because it is so messy. Families may explore the factory on their own. A stroll through the Torpedo Factory, stopping at will, plus lunch at one of the many restaurants in Old Town, can make a pleasant afternoon outing. (See also, Alexandria Archaeology in this chapter, and Chapter 8, Behind the Scenes, Torpedo Factory listing.)

Arlington

Arlington House, the Robert E. Lee Memorial

Arlington National Cemetery, Arlington, VA 22211 (703-557-0613). Walk from Arlington Cemetery Visitor Center parking lot or ride the Tourmobile®.

- Open daily, October–March, 9:30 A.M.–4:30 P.M.; April–September, 9:30 A.M.–6 P.M. Closed Christmas and New Year's Day.
- Metrorail Blue line (Arlington Cemetery).
- Tourmobile® stop.
- Wheelchair lift to the first floor; tours for the visually- and hearing-impaired can be arranged by calling ahead.
- Strollers permitted.
- Guided group tours October–March, by appointment only. An "Everyday Life Program" is offered for 4th-graders, in which they can experience activities that may have occurred when the Lee family lived here.

Robert E. Lee courted and wed Mary Custis in this hilltop mansion. They lived here for 30 years, from 1831–1861, and raised 7 children here. It has been restored with some of the original furnishings and similar pieces of the early 1800s. Don't miss the magnificent view of the Washington skyline from the front portico, which Lafayette described as the "finest view in the world." Show the children the upstairs children's room and playroom. The house is staffed by costumed "interpreters of history." (See also Arlington House.)

Special activities include a St. Patrick's Day open house, a June 30 open house on Robert E. Lee's wedding day, a candlelight open house in October, and a Christmas open house featuring mid-19th century decorations.

Arlington National Cemetery

Arlington, VA 22211 (703-697-2131). Located in Virginia, directly across from Memorial Bridge.

- Open daily, October–March, 8 A.M.–5 P.M.; April–September, 8 A.M.–7 P.M.
- Metrorail Blue line (Arlington Cemetery).
- Parking: $1/hour for first three hours, $2/hour thereafter.
- Tourmobile® stop. Adults, $2.75; children 3–11, $1.25. Stops at Kennedy gravesites, Tomb of the Unknowns, and Arlington House. Without debarking to visit the sites, the ride takes approximately 40 minutes. See Tourmobile® information in Chapter 1, Starting Out.
- Wheelchair access.
- Strollers permitted.
- School and group tours of 20 or more, call 202-554-7022.
- Bookstore in Visitors' Center with some children's tour books.
- Changing of the Guard occurs April–September, twice per hour; October–March, once per hour. An average of 18 funerals occur per day.

To bring the subject of war down to a comprehensible level for both children and adults, there is no better place than the

Arlington National Cemetery. The sheer expanse of the cemetery, with its vast number of graves spanning the time period between the American Revolution and the Persian Gulf War, brings a sense of the finality and devastation of our wars. At the information center one can ask about the location of the burial site for any individual buried here. In addition to soldiers' graves, sections of the cemetery are dedicated to veterans who were astronauts, chaplains, and nurses.

Children enjoy the hike up the hill to the Kennedy gravesites, where they can see a panoramic view of Washington with airplanes flying overhead. (Even if you plan to walk through part of the cemetery, it is advisable to buy a ticket at the Tourmobile®

booth at the Visitors' Center so that you can board a bus at any of the Tourmobile® stops.) At the Tomb of the Unknowns, the changing of the guard ritual is fascinating because of the soldiers' special taps clicking as they march and their rifle maneuvers. Across from the site of the Unknown Soldiers is the actual mast of the U.S.S. Maine; the sinking of the Maine began the Spanish American War.

Because Robert E. Lee left his home and estate to become the leader of Virginia's Confederate Forces, and Mrs. Lee could not pay her taxes in person, their estate became this military cemetery. Information such as this is provided by the Tourmobile® guides in an informative manner. Even younger children can follow the history of the cemetery on a Tourmobile® ride: older parts of the cemetery have various sizes of headstones, pointed headstones designate soldiers from the Confederate armies, and the more recent gravestones are arranged to look like soldiers standing at attention while on parade. (See also Arlington House.)

Special activities include services held in the amphitheater for Easter Sunrise, Memorial Day, and Veterans Day.

Chantilly

Sully Historic Site

Route 28, Chantilly, VA, 22021 (703-437-1794). Take the Beltway (Route 495) to Route 66 west; then take Route 50 west to right turn on Route 28 north, Sully Road. Sully is ¾ mile from the intersection of Routes 50 and 28.

- Open March–December, Wednesday–Monday, 11 A.M.–5 P.M. Open January–February, weekends only, 11 A.M.–4 P.M. Closed Tuesday and Thanksgiving and Christmas.
- Adults, $3; children 3–12, $1; senior citizens, $1.50 on weekdays; no group rates.
- Wheelchair access.
- Strollers are not permitted in the house, but they can be stored at the door.

- School tours available with reservations.
- Picnic area.
- There are usually special Sunday activities for the general public.

Sully Historic Site is one of several restored Lee family houses in Virginia. Sully was built in 1794 by Richard B. Lee, first congressman of northern Virginia and uncle of General Robert E. Lee. Relatively modest compared to some other plantations, it is a family-oriented place in which children can easily imagine themselves living. An upstairs room furnished as a schoolroom will capture their imaginations. After touring the house and dependencies, children can do cartwheels on the extensive lawn and watch the jets coming in to land at close-by Dulles airport.

For school groups, there are special programs such as the ones on textiles, where students can learn spinning and weaving, on food preparation, where beaten biscuits are made from an old Lee recipe, and on school life, where children use slates, quill pens, and the McGuffey Reader. Reservations must be made in advance.

Special activities include Civil War Life in April, an Antique Car Show in June, a Quilt Show with hands-on activities in September, harvesting in October, holiday illumination with bonfire and fireworks in December, and Scout Day, also in December.

Great Falls

Colvin Run Mill Historic Site

10017 Colvin Run Road, Great Falls, VA 22066 (703-759-2771). Take the Beltway (Route 495) to exit at Route 7 west (Tysons Corner). Mill is 7 miles west of Tysons Corner and 15 miles east of Leesburg.

- Open March–December, Wednesday–Monday, 11 A.M.–5 P.M.; January and February, weekends only, 11 A.M.–4 P.M. Closed Tuesday.

- Free admission to grounds. Admission for tours of the mill and the miller's house, adults $3; children 3–12, $1.
- Limited wheelchair access.
- Strollers permitted.
- Tours of the mill and the miller's house are given every hour on the hour. The tours are usually informal and uncrowded.
- The original general store sells cornmeal and flour ground in the mill and "penny" candy.
- Picnicking is permitted on the grounds with picnic tables provided. Save some bread crumbs from your picnic to feed the resident ducks.
- Weather permitting, grinding takes place on Sundays from noon to 2 P.M.

Colvin Run Mill, built in the early 1800's, is a working grist mill which produces whole grain products to sell in the on-site general store. Children of all ages are fascinated by the huge grinding stones, the movement of the grain from one level to the next, and the outside water wheel.

The historic site also includes the original miller's house, with hands-on exhibits such as a grain elevator that can be manipulated, the original general store, and a recreated dairy barn with typical period farming equipment of the community and a scale model of the mill.

Special activities include "Independence Day Celebration," with entertainment and a children's parade; "Autumn Traditions," usually the first Sunday in October, with hands-on exhibits; and a "Country Christmas," approximately the third weekend in December, with Victorian decorations, Santa Claus, and family crafts. Admission to the grounds is charged during these events.

Leesburg

Morven Park

Route 3, Box 50, Old Waterford Road, Leesburg, VA 22075 (703-777-2414). Take the Beltway (Route 495) to exit at Route 7 west (Tysons Corner); continue through the town of Leesburg; then right to Morven Park Road; left to Old Waterford Road (Route 698); then right to main entrance. From Maryland, take the Beltway (Route 495) to Route 192, Old Georgetown Pike. At Route 7 go west (right turn) through the town of Leesburg, then follow above directions.

- Open Memorial Day weekend–Labor Day, Tuesday–Saturday, 10 A.M.–5 P.M., Sunday 1–5 P.M.; October–May, open weekends only. Open on Mondays when they are Federal holidays.
- Adults, $4; children 6–12, $2; children under 6, free.
- Wheelchair access to the carriage museum and lower level of the mansion; some additional wheelchair access available with prior notice.
- Strollers are not permitted inside any of the buildings.
- Tours of the mansion and carriage house are by reservation only for groups of 30 or more. A special children's tour is available for the mansion and carriage museum.
- Picnic area.
- Special events are scheduled on some weekends.

This 1,200-acre estate is operated as a memorial to Westmoreland Davis, former Governor of Virginia. Children tend to be most interested in the extensive vehicle collection. In the old carriage house and Carriage Museum there are coaches, breaks, and the gigs driven by turn-of-the-century American society members, plus everyday phaetons, surreys, carts, and sleighs, a funeral hearse, and a charcoal-burning fire engine.

Special activities include an arts and crafts festival in June, a fall steeple chase meet in October, and a Christmas open house the first weekend in December.

Oatlands Plantation

Route 15, Leesburg, VA 22075 (703-777-3174). Take the Beltway (Route 495) to exit at Route 7 west (Tysons Corner); continue to Leesburg; then south on Route 15 for 6 miles.

- Open late March–late December, Monday–Saturday, 10 A.M.–5 P.M., Sunday, 1–5 P.M.
- Adults, $5; senior citizens and students $4; children under 12, free. Scheduled groups of 15 or more, $4 per person.
- No wheelchair access.
- Strollers are not permitted in house tour.
- Tours Monday–Saturday are on the hour and half hour, 10 A.M.–4:30 P.M.; Sunday, 1–4:30 P.M.
- Picnicking permitted.
- Gift shop with some toys.

This hunt-country estate, built by George Carter, dates from the early 1800's. Adults are interested in the Georgian architecture and the decorative and unusual features, such as the octagonal drawing room and a flanking pair of staircases. Children enjoy the terraced 4-acre formal English garden, which is considered one of the finest examples of early Virginia landscape design. There they can explore the tea house and the reflecting pool and look for imaginary dinosaur footprints in the stone slabs around the sundial.

Special activities include point-to-point races in April, Sheep Dog Trials in May, Draft Horse and Mule Day on the Saturday before Labor Day, a Garden Fair in late September, a needlework exhibition in October, and hunter trials in November. During November and December, the mansion is decorated with traditional Christmas decorations, many of which are made at the plantation.

Lorton

Gunston Hall

Gunston Road (Route 242), Lorton, VA 22079 (703-550-9220). Take Route 1 south from Alexandria for 14 miles; then go east on Route 242 for 4 miles to Gunston Hall.

- Open daily, 9:30 A.M.–5 P.M. Closed Christmas, Thanksgiving, and New Year's Day.
- Adults, $4; children grades 1–12, $1; senior citizens, $3; children under 6, free. Call in advance for group tours and rates.
- Wheelchair access can be arranged.
- Strollers permitted on the grounds, but not in the house.
- Picnic area.
- A marked trail wanders through the woods to the river.

This Colonial plantation overlooking the Potomac River is an outstanding example of a great period in the history of Virginia and the nation. Its tasteful interior and the landscaped garden are among the finest in the area. Gunston Hall was the home of George Mason, an author of Virginia's Declaration of Rights, which served as the model for the Federal Bill of Rights. The 18th century furnishings and the intricately carved woodwork are outstanding.

Upstairs are the children's rooms and nursery which contain simpler, small-scale furniture of the period. Children will be interested in the trundle bed and the yarn winders which the daughters of the family were taught to use. A museum features Mason family objects, and a diorama shows how the plantation worked as a whole. Outbuildings on the grounds that children enjoy visiting include the kitchen, dairy, smokehouse, schoolhouse, and laundry. The formal gardens contain 12-foot boxwood hedges, planted by Mason himself.

Special activities include a kite festival in March, George Mason Day with a history re-enactment in May, a car show in September, and caroling by candlelight at Christmas.

Manassas

Manassas National Battlefield Park

Manassas, VA 22110 (703-361-1865). Take the Beltway (Route 495) to Route 66; exit at 11B (Route 234 north/Sudley Road). Park is ½ mile north of exit.

- Open daily in winter, 8:30 A.M.–5 P.M.; in summer, 8:30 A.M.–6 P.M.
- Adults, 17–61, $1. Pass is good for one year.
- Parking lot.
- Wheelchair access.
- Strollers permitted.
- Fast food restaurants in Manassas.

One July day in 1861, wagonloads of sightseers came from Washington to see their boys in blue defeat Johnny Reb on the banks of Bull Run. By evening they were retreating in haste, along with Union troops, as the Confederates won their first major victory of the Civil War. The next summer, the forces met again at Bull Run for another, bloodier Southern victory. The Visitor Center features a map of the battlefield program every 15 minutes, a museum, a slide show on the hour, folders, and booklets. There is also a one-mile walking tour (the Henry Hill Tour). In winter, tours depend on weather and the size of the crowd. A van tour covers the second battle as well.

Mount Vernon

Mount Vernon (George Washington's Home)

Mount Vernon, VA 22121 (703-780-2000). Take the George Washington Memorial Parkway (becomes the Mount Vernon Memorial Highway) south; Mount Vernon is located 8 miles south of Alexandria. (See Chapter 1, Starting Out, for information on the Spirit of Washington and Tourmobile®.)

- Open daily, March–October, 9 A.M.–5 P.M.; November–February, 9 A.M.–4 P.M.
- Adults, $7; children 6–11, $3; senior citizens age 62 and above, $6; children under 6, free. Group rates for students grades 1–12, $3, with one free chaperone per 10 students.
- Wheelchair access to the museum and the lower level of the mansion. Wheelchair accessible rest rooms are located on the estate and at the Mount Vernon Inn.
- Strollers permitted.
- Picnicking is not permitted on the plantation grounds, but good riverside spots are located along the Parkway. There is a snack bar and restaurant, the Mount Vernon Inn, 703-780-0011, just outside the main gate.
- The Museum Shop is located on the estate. A larger shop at the inn, The Mt. Vernon Inn Gift Shop, contains toys, games, and books.
- Scout leaders may contact the education department for information on the scouting trail.

Children of all ages will be interested in this elegant and stately plantation mansion because it was the home of George Washington. The 30-acre estate is also an education in the economic and social life of the South in the 18th century, which centered around the plantation. George Washington spent most of his life in this spacious white pillared mansion overlooking the Potomac. Youngsters not interested in the carved mantels and china tea sets usually enjoy touring the dependencies, the extensive village-like group of flanking service buildings. These include the smokehouse, greenhouse, storehouse, coach house, spinning house, wash house, stable, kitchen, and slave quarters.

Mount Vernon accommodates thousands of tourists each day, and crowds during peak touring seasons can be enormous. To get the most from this visit, try going early in the morning on a weekday. Mount Vernon is owned and operated by the Mount Vernon Ladies' Association.

Special activities have included "Colonial Days at Mt. Vernon" with demonstrations by blacksmiths, coopers, paper

makers, spinners, and military surgeons; "George Washington —
Pleasures of Music and Dance," with 18th century dancers and
musicians; and "General Washington is in residence at Mt.
Vernon," where a costumed actor greets guests and performs as
George Washington.

Woodlawn Plantation/Frank Lloyd Wright's Pope-Leighey House

9000 Richmond Highway (Route 1), P.O. Box 37, Mount Ver-
non, VA 22121 (703-780-4000). Take Route 1 south from
Alexandria 7 miles to Woodlawn; turnoff is near junction of
Route 1 and Route 235.

- Open daily, 9:30 A.M.–4:30 P.M. Closed Thanksgiving, Christmas, and New Year's Day. Woodlawn open weekends only in
  January. Pope-Leighey house open weekends only in January
  and February.
- Adults, $5; senior citizens and students, $3.50; children
  under 5, free. Group rates (for 15 or more): adults $4, senior
  citizens and students, $2.75. Combination ticket for Wood-
  lawn Plantation and the Pope-Leighey house: adults, $8; se-
  nior citizens and students, $6.
- Wheelchair access to the first floor of the mansion only.
- Strollers are to be left in the reception area.
- Special hands-on tours and slide presentation for school
  groups by appointment.
- Picnicking permitted.
- Nature trails, designed by the Audubon Society, wind through
  the woods.
- The fine gift shop sells miniatures, crafts and books.

George Washington gave part of his Mount Vernon estate to his
granddaughter, Nelly Custis, and his nephew, Lawrence Lewis,
as a wedding present. Woodlawn Mansion, designed by Dr.
William Thornton, architect of the U. S. Capitol, was built here.
Adults will appreciate the elegant living room, dining room and
parlor. Youngsters like the children's bedrooms and the collec-

tion of stuffed birds acquired by Nelly Custis' son. A restored garden features roses and boxwood plantings.

Also on the grounds is a Usonian home designed by Frank Lloyd Wright, the Pope-Leighey house. The house reflects Wright's belief that people of moderate means are entitled to well-designed homes. Visitors can pick up a discovery packet to help them compare this 20th century home to the earlier plantation home.

Special activities include a needlework exhibit in March, outdoor events with musical performances in the summer, a quilt show in October, and a Woodlawn Christmas in December. Of particular interest to children is the Annual Woodlawn Heritage Arts and Crafts Festival in late Spring, with storytellers, old-fashioned games, and 19th century craftsmen. For Halloween, ghostly tours are given by costumed guides. One week in August is reserved for a special children's needlework workshop, where boys and girls work with 19th century materials, even making old-fashioned ice cream. Reservations are required.

Reston

U.S. Geological Survey

12201 Sunrise Valley Drive, Reston, VA 22092 (703-648-4748). Take the Beltway (Route 495) to Dulles Toll Road, to Exit 3 (Reston Parkway). Turn left, then right at second light on Sunrise Valley Drive. Turn at the second left.

- Visitor Center open Monday, 1:30 P.M.–4 P.M.; Tuesday and Thursday, 9:30 A.M.–4 P.M.
- Parking available.
- Wheelchair access.
- Strollers permitted.
- School and other group tours: Monday, 1:30 P.M.–4 P.M.; Tuesday and Thursday, 9:30 A.M.–4 P.M. Reservations requested.
- Cafeteria and picnic tables outside on patio.

- Earth Science Information Center is a map store non-pareil. The center also provides numerous free pamphlets and posters. Subjects of the pamphlets include rock collecting, volcanoes, earthquakes, caves, and prospecting for gold. Children can purchase large scale maps of their towns and neighborhoods in the Washington, DC area for less than $3.
- Hispanic, Asian, and Native American exhibits are organized annually.

Visitors to the U.S. Geological Survey will find a wealth of information and numerous activities. In addition to watching videos on subjects like volcanoes, groups may arrange a guided tour of the facility and sightsee along the woodland trail.

On the tour children can place their feet in actual dinosaur footprints in quarry stone taken from a quarry in Culpeper. Another highlight of the tour is the Carbon-14 laboratory, where wood and even cloth can be dated. In the lab is a Rube Goldberg-type set-up where substances bubble and smoke surrounded by glass tubes, flasks, wires, and bunsen burners. Here the scientists demonstrate ways of taking ancient material and estimating the number of years ago that glaciers, avalanches, and so on occurred during the Ice Age. Upstairs, computer experts with state of the art computer mapping equipment demonstrate how the Geographic Information Systems (GIS) operate. On past tours, these experts have shown students how they can even track the migration of a caribou herd in Alaska. A special treat is the tour of the printing plant with the smell of ink and the roar of the huge cutting, folding, and printing machines.

On the trails outside visitors will see native foliage, a groundwater observation well, and large rock samples. A detailed map provided by the visitors' center will delight hikers as they traverse the grounds.

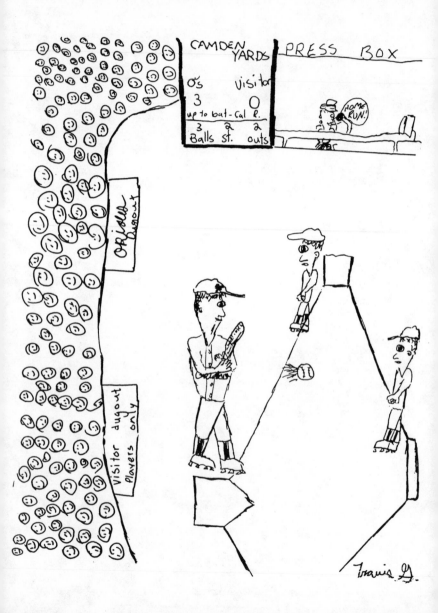

4 Baltimore and Beyond

Baltimore

Baltimore is a city that continues to do an excellent job of updating its image while preserving its historic heritage. There is a wealth of things to do and see in this nearby international port town with its rich cultural texture. Many attractions are within walking distance of the Inner Harbor, but you may want to park your car and take advantage of the trolley service to the heart of Baltimore. The trolley costs a quarter and runs approximately every fifteen minutes, from 11 A.M.–7 P.M., seven days a week. However, it is impossible to explore the rich offerings of Baltimore in one day, so come back often or consider staying the weekend. Spending a night in one of the city's convenient hotels makes a real treat for the entire family. If your visit to Baltimore includes plans to attend an Orioles baseball game, follow directions to downtown Baltimore and look for signs directing you to Orioles Park at Camden Yards (there are plans for MARC connections). To reach Baltimore from Washington, DC, travel north about 40 miles on Route I-95, Route 1, or the Baltimore-Washington Parkway. See Chapter 1, Starting Out, for information on the Baltimore Area Visitors' Center.

Inner Harbor Area

To reach the Inner Harbor area take I-95 north to I-395, which will take you into downtown Baltimore. Then follow the very visible signs to the Inner Harbor. There are many commercial parking lots throughout this part of town. On-street parking is very limited.

Baltimore Maritime Museum, Lightship Chesapeake and U.S.S. Torsk

Pier 3, Pratt Street, Baltimore, MD 21202 (410-539-3854).

- Open daily, 9:30 A.M.–4:30 P.M. Closed Thanksgiving, Christmas, and New Year's Day.
- Adults, $3.00; senior citizens, $2.50; children 5–12, $1; children under 5, free.
- No wheelchair access.
- Strollers must be left on the dock.
- Restaurants and food stalls at adjacent Harborplace.

This is a great favorite for children. They always love the tours of these two vessels, even if they aren't old enough to truly understand the different naval technologies presented.

Baltimore Public Works Museum

751 Eastern Avenue, Baltimore, MD 21202 (410-396-5565).
Take I-95 to the Inner Harbor exit. Turn right on Pratt Street, then right on President Street. Follow President Street through the intersection with Eastern Avenue. A commercial parking lot is located at President and Fleet Streets. The museum entrance is on Falls Way, facing the Inner Harbor. Museum is situated on the edge of Little Italy (a two block walk from the National Aquarium over pedestrian bridges).

- Open mid April–mid October, daily, 10 A.M.–4 P.M.; mid October–mid April, Wednesday–Sunday, 10 A.M.–4 P.M. Closed Good Friday, Thanksgiving, Christmas, New Year's Day, Martin Luther King's Birthday, and other Baltimore City holidays.
- Adults, $1.50; children 5–16, 75¢; children under 4, free. Wednesday admission is free for all visitors.
- Parking in nearby commercial lots.
- Wheelchair access.
- Strollers permitted.
- Recommended for children ages 5 and up.

- Call in advance to arrange tours. Group rates (adults, $1; children, 50¢) apply for 10 or more.
- Restaurants and fast food available at Harborplace.

Here is another hands-on museum with wide age appeal that helps us understand Public Works. It is located in an 80-year-old red brick sewage pumping station. Inside the museum there is a 15 minute child-oriented video and a popular "Construction Site" filled with puzzles, blocks, and books. If weather permits, the outdoor "Streetscape" is compelling, with a two-level exhibit that features a fire hydrant, public telephone, parking meter, manhole, and alarm box, with a "peel back the pavement" look at the network of pipes and connections below. A stairway joins both levels for a closer look.

Harborplace

Corner of Pratt and Light Streets, Baltimore, MD 21202 (410-332-4191).

- Stores open Monday–Saturday, 10 A.M.–9 P.M.; Sunday, noon to 6 P.M. Restaurants close later.
- Parking available in numerous commercial lots.
- Wheelchair access.
- Strollers permitted.
- Many restaurants and food stands.

Harborplace is located in the heart of Baltimore's revitalized financial and business district, overlooking its inner harbor. Its three main buildings offer an exciting range of more than 130 shops, restaurants, stalls, and harborside terraces, as well as easy access to several main attractions such as the National Aquarium. You can take a ride in paddle boats or travel on the Water Taxi to the various sights on the Inner Harbor. The outdoor promenades are perfect for strolling, skipping, pushing a stroller, or people watching. In good weather, you may be lucky and run into street performers who will keep you and your children amused. It is a fun place to spend a few hours.

Special activities include a variety of holiday festivities. Call for further information.

Maryland Science Center

601 Light Street and Key Highway, Baltimore, MD 21230 (410-685-5225).

- Open weekdays, 10 A.M.–5 P.M.; Saturday, 10 A.M.–6 P.M.; Sunday, 10 A.M.–6 P.M. Extended summer hours. Closed Thanksgiving and Christmas.
- Full admission to the Science Center, the Davis Planetarium, and the IMAX Theater is: adults, $7.50; senior citizens, military personnel (with I.D.), and children 4–17, $5.50.
- Group rates available; call 410-685-2370 for reservations.
- Wheelchair access.
- Strollers permitted.
- Live demonstrations daily.
- Science store features a variety of interesting items.
- Friendly's restaurant on site.

You can easily spend a whole day in this excellent museum with its permanent exhibits on energy, the Chesapeake Bay, space, structures, television production, and the Hubble space telescope. Many hands-on exhibits will keep your children involved. Temporary exhibits change every three months, so it is a place you can visit often. The Davis Planetarium, on the second floor, and the IMAX theater (four stories tall and 75 feet wide) are also well worth your time. Both change their offerings. The view in the Planetarium is spectacular, but the dialogue can be quite advanced for young children. IMAX, on the other hand, is an exciting presentation that takes you soaring over the Grand Canyon, plummets down a roller coaster's sloping tracks and explores the depths of the ocean.

The National Aquarium

Pier 3, 501 East Pratt Street, Baltimore, MD 21202 (410-576-3810, recording).

- Open mid September–mid May, weekdays, 10 A.M.–5 P.M., Friday until 8 P.M., Saturday and Sunday, 9 A.M.–5 P.M.; mid May–mid September, Monday–Thursday, 9 A.M.–5 P.M., Friday–Sunday, 9 A.M.– 8 P.M. Closed Thanksgiving and Christmas.
- Adults, $11.50; senior citizens, active military personnel, and students 12–18, $8.75; children 3–11, $6.75; children under 3, free. Advance timed tickets are available through Ticket Center in Washington, DC, 202-432-0200.
- Wheelchair access through member's entrance. Call 410-576-3800 to make arrangements. The rain forest area is not accessible to wheelchairs.
- Strollers are not permitted in the building, but the Aquarium will provide backpacks for babies and toddlers.
- Food stalls and restaurants in nearby Harborplace.
- There is a nice shop featuring "fishy" souvenirs.
- Check out the new marine mammal pavilion, which has its own gift shop.

The National Aquarium in Baltimore is exciting both outside and inside. It is a spectacular, seven-level structure that houses

fascinating and sophisticated aquatic exhibits. Children especially like the children's cove in which they can hold horseshoe crabs, sea stars, and other small animals. The new marine mammal pavilion features beluga whales and bottlenose dolphins, with state of the art video and sound Vidiwalls. In the surrounding educational arcade kids can learn humpback whale songs, create bubbles to help humpbacks engulf their meals, and play "Whales in Jeopardy." The Aquarium is perhaps Baltimore's most popular attraction, so it is best to visit late afternoon or evenings to avoid the crowds. If you think your family will visit the Aquarium more than once in a year you may save money by becoming a member.

reStore at the Chocolate Factory

608 Water Street, Baltimore, MD 21202 (410-752-7588).
Located near the Inner Harbor on Water Street between
Gay Street and Market Place.

- Open weekdays, 10 A.M.–5 P.M.; Saturday, 10 A.M.– 2 P.M. Closed Sunday and most Federal holidays.
- On-street, metered parking on Gay and Market streets, and many commercial lots.
- Wheelchair access.
- Strollers permitted.
- Suitable for all ages but appeals most to children 3–7.
- Tours available for groups; call to make arrangements.

This recycling center provides low-cost creative materials such as buttons, threads, plastic containers, sticky tapes, cones, foam, dowels, and fabric. Children delight in shopping for themselves and filling a bag: large $5.50, medium $3, and small $1.50. Books and pamphlets on how to use creative materials are available. The book store also features inexpensive, high quality paperbacks and resources for parents, teachers, and caregivers. If you plan to go often, consider purchasing a membership, which will entitle you to discounts.

United States Frigate Constellation

Constellation Dock, Pier One, Pratt Street, Baltimore, MD
21202 (410-539-1797).

- Open daily, October 15– April 14, 10 A.M.–4 P.M.; April 15–June
  14, 10 A.M.–6 P.M.; June 15–Labor Day, 10 A.M.–8 P.M.; after
  Labor Day–October 14, 10 A.M.–6 P.M. Closed Thanksgiving,
  Christmas, and New Year's Day.
- Adults, $3; senior citizens, $2; active military personnel, $1;
  children 6–15, $1.50; children under 6, free. Last tickets for
  the day are sold 30 minutes before closing.
- Wheelchair access to display area and shop, but not on board
  the ship.
- Strollers must be left on the pier.
- Group tours available by appointment.

- Food stands and restaurants at nearby Harborplace.
- Live presentations; check dates and time.

The U.S.F. Constellation is another guaranteed favorite for kids. As the first ship commissioned in the U.S. Navy, she was launched in Baltimore in 1797 and is considered to be the oldest American warship continuously afloat. Tours are self guided.

   Special activities include special historical reenactments in the summer, including Will, the ordinary "Jack Tar" sailor who entertains all with tales of life at sea in the 1800's. Check times and dates for reenactments in the "A Living History" series.

Elsewhere in Baltimore

Babe Ruth Museum

   216 Emory Street, Baltimore, MD 21230 (410-727-1539). Take I-95 north to I-395, then follow the signs for Martin Luther King, Jr. Boulevard exit. Turn right at second light on Pratt Street, then right on Emory.

- Open daily, April–October, 10 A.M.–5 P.M.; November–March, 10 A.M.–4 P.M. Closed Easter, Thanksgiving, Christmas, and New Year's Day.
- Adults, $4; children under 16, $1.50; senior citizens, $2.50.
- Call in advance for group rates.
- Parking available in the museum lot on Pratt Street just before Emory Street.
- Wheelchair access to first floor only.
- Strollers permitted.

Here is an opportunity for fans of all ages to visit the house where baseball's number one slugger was born, and to view the numerous mementos and films of Babe Ruth. You will also get a feel for Maryland's baseball heritage and for the history of the Orioles. There are three changing exhibits each year.

In 1993 the Babe Ruth Museum will expand to become the Babe Ruth Birthplace and Baseball Center. The Center, housed across the street, will feature the Baltimore Orioles, Negro Leagues, and amateur baseball as well as a Sportscasters' Hall of Fame and a rooftop restaurant.

Baltimore City Life Museums

Offices at 800 East Lombard Street, Baltimore, MD 21202 (410-396-1806).

The museums in this charming collection are devoted to the history of Baltimore. Included are Museum Row — the Carroll Mansion, the 1840 House, the Center for Urban Archaeology, and the Courtyard Exhibition Center; the Peale Museum; the H.L. Mencken House; and Brewer's Park. Through a wide range of multimedia exhibits, special events, living history programs, and archaeological excavations, each facility tells the story of Baltimore in particular and American urban development in general. Hands-on History is a program for school groups (grades 3–12) that provides a glimpse of life in the 1940s. Call the number above for information on this and other educational programs. Each sight is described below.

H. L. Mencken House

1524 Hollins Street Baltimore, MD 21223 (410-396-7997). Located on Union Square in west Baltimore.

- Open Saturday–Sunday, April 1–October 31, 10 A.M.–5 P.M.; November 1–March 31, 10 A.M.–4 P.M. Closed Easter, Thanksgiving, Christmas, and New Year's Day.
- Adults, $1.75; senior citizens, active military personnel, and college students, $1.25; children 6–18, 75¢; children under 6 free. Families pay no more than $5. No admission charge on Saturday from 10 A.M.–1 P.M. School and youth groups free.
- On-street parking available.

- No wheelchair access.
- Strollers should be left downstairs.
- Most appropriate for children ages 10 and older.

About one mile west of the Inner Harbor is the H. L. Mencken House, home of the famous "Sage of Baltimore" for more than six decades. The house and yard are as he left them, restored with his original furnishings and personal belongings, including his treasured Tonk baby grand piano, which was an integral part of many Saturday evening jam sessions. An audio-visual presentation provides an overview of Mencken's life and career.

Museum Row

800 East Lombard Street, Baltimore, MD 21202 (410-396-3524, general information).

- Open April 1–October 31, Tuesday–Saturday, 10 A.M.–5 P.M.; Sunday, noon– 5 P.M. November 1–March 31, closes at 4 P.M. Closed Easter, Thanksgiving, Christmas, and New Year's Day.
- Admission fees cover all sights in Museum Row. Adults, $4; senior citizens, active military personnel, and college students, $3; children 6–18, $2; children under 6, free. Families pay no more than $12. No admission charge on Saturday from 10 A.M.–1 P.M. School and youth groups free. Fees for individual sites are the same as for the Peale Museum and the H. L. Mencken House.
- Small parking lot and on-street parking available.
- Wheelchair access to all sites; first floor only for Carroll Mansion.
- Strollers permitted.

Surrounding a lovely landscaped courtyard in Museum Row, just east of the Inner Harbor, are the Carroll Mansion, the 1840s House, the Center for Urban Archaeology, the Courtyard Exhibition Center, and Brewers' Park. The **Carroll Man-**

sion, the richly furnished home of Charles Carroll of Carrollton, a signer of the Declaration of Independence, features a superb exhibit on Carroll's life and illustrates the elegant lifestyle of wealthy Baltimore families of the time. Call 410-396-3523 for more information.

In contrast to the luxurious setting of the Mansion, the **1840 House** is a living history museum, designed to simulate life in 1840s Baltimore through dramatic and "hands-on"

programs. The house is furnished mainly with reproductions to encourage children's involvement. This museum offers "Journeys Through Time," unique opportunities for children and adults to travel back in time and enjoy an evening dinner, spend the night, or celebrate a birthday. Call 410-396-3279 for more information.

The **Center for Urban Archaeology** includes a working laboratory and a fascinating exhibit featuring a full-scale excavation pit and artifacts from local digs. Artifacts on display include ceramics and glassware from 18th and 19th century homes, industries, and shops.
Call 410-396-3156 for more information.

The **Courtyard Exhibition Center** houses changing exhibits about the history of Baltimore. Call 410-396-9910 for more information.

Adjacent to the Courtyard, on the site of an 18th century brewery, is **Brewers' Park**, an unusual setting to stop for a picnic lunch. A 40-foot timber sculpture marks the entrance to the park. Other features include the exposed foundations of the malthouse and brewery and a cut-away recreation of the brewery owner's elegant federal-style home.

Peale Museum

225 Holliday Street, Baltimore, MD 21202 (410-396-1149).
From I-95 north, take I-395, then follow signs to the Inner Harbor. The museum is six blocks north of the harbor, near City Hall.

- Open April 1–October 31, Tuesday–Saturday, 10 A.M.–5 P.M.; Sunday, noon–5 P.M.; November 1–March 31, closes at 4 P.M. Closed Easter, Thanksgiving, Christmas, and New Year's Day.
- Adults, $1.75; senior citizens, active military personnel, and college students, $1.25; children 6–18, 75¢, children under 6, free. Families pay no more than $5. No admission charge on Saturday from 10 A.M.–1 P.M. School and youth groups free.

- On-street, metered parking and commercial lots.
- No wheelchair access.
- Strollers are not permitted in exhibit area. They can be stored at the entrance.
- Call 410-396-3279 for group reservations.
- Most appropriate for school-age and older children.
- Mermaids, Mummies, and Mastodons: The Evolution of the American Museum, through June '92. Check for changing special exhibits.

The oldest museum building in the United States, the Peale Museum opened in 1814. Paintings of patriots and local historical figures by Charles Willson Peale, Rembrandt Peale, and Sara Peale are featured. Artifacts from the beautiful to the bizarre include natural wonders and man-made ones that have delighted museum visitors since the 1800s. Older children may be interested in the prints, paints, maps, and photos that trace Baltimore and national history, but visiting with toddlers and young children is not advised.

Special activities include holiday celebrations in December and other events throughout the year. Call for more information.

Baltimore Museum of Art

Art Museum Drive, Baltimore, MD 21218 (410-396-7100). Take I-95 north to I-395, then follow the signs for Martin Luther King, Jr. Boulevard exit. Turn left on Howard Street, continue north (past 29th Street). Veer right at the fork on Art Museum Drive.

- Open Tuesday, Wednesday, and Friday, 10 A.M.–4 P.M.; Thursday, 10 A.M.–7 P.M.; Saturday and Sunday, 11 A.M.–6 P.M. Closed Monday and Thanksgiving, Christmas, and New Year's Day.
- Adults, $3.50; children 18 and under, free. Thursday, free to all visitors.
- Group tours available by appointment, 410-396-6320.
- Metered parking lots on the east and west sides of museum and some metered on-street parking.

- Wheelchair access.
- Strollers permitted.
- Cafe open Tuesday–Thursday, 11 A.M.–9 P.M.; Friday and Saturday 11 A.M.–10 P.M.; Sunday 11 A.M.–8 P.M..
- Children's art classes and workshops throughout the year; call for information about these and special exhibits.

This exceptional museum features the Cone collection of early 20th century art. Matisse and Picasso are particularly well represented. In the American wing you will find arts of Africa, Oceania, and the Americas. The museum cafe is a nice spot for a break from sightseeing.

Baltimore Museum of Industry

1415 Key Highway, Baltimore, MD 21230 (410-727-4808). Take I-95 north to Exit 55 (Key Highway/Fort McHenry National Monument). Turn left at light, go under overpass, then left on Key Highway. Museum is immediately on the right. Look for the big red crane!

- Open after Labor Day until Memorial Day, Thursday, Friday, and Sunday, noon–5 P.M., Saturday 10 A.M.–5 P.M.; Memorial Day–Labor Day, Sunday and Tuesday–Friday, noon–5 P.M., Saturday 10 A.M.–5 P.M. Closed Christmas and New Year's Day.
- Adults, $3; senior citizens and students, $2; children under 7, free. Family rate $10.
- Parking available.
- Wheelchair access.
- Strollers permitted.
- Groups of 10 or more by appointment. Special rates apply.
- Special programs for children.

This hands-on museum, located in the heart of industrial south Baltimore, contains a print shop, a machine shop, a garment loft, and an assembly-line where youngsters learn about the many parts that pass through their hands to become finished products.

Since the Washington area has so little industry, this museum is a great "find." Housed in a harborside cannery that was used during the Civil War to send oysters off to the soldiers, the building itself bears testimony to the working life the museum recreates. On Saturday at 11 A.M. and 2 P.M. and Sunday at 2:30 P.M., children can work in the oyster cannery shucking oysters, making labels, and so on. This program is an extra $1.75 per child. On Sunday at 2 P.M., children can work on the children's motor works assembly line making small cardboard cars. This activity is an extra $1.

Baltimore and Ohio Railroad Museum

901 W. Pratt Street, Baltimore, MD 21223 (410-237-2381). Take I-95 north to I-395. Exit at Martin Luther King, Jr. Boulevard. Go 3 blocks to left turn on Lombard Street. Turn left at first light on Poppleton. Cross over Pratt Street to museum entrance.

- Open daily, 10 A.M.–5 P.M. Closed all major holidays.
- Adults, $5; senior citizens, $4; children 5–18, $3. Children 4 and under, free. The first Tuesday of the month senior citizens are ½ price.
- Parking available on museum grounds.
- Wheelchair access.
- Strollers permitted.
- Call for family and group rates, 410-752-2463.

This old roundhouse contains the world's largest collection of locomotives, cabooses, freights, and other cars dating back to 1829. Children can go through a caboose and the back of a mail car. The large model railroad station always makes a hit. Enter the museum through Mt. Clare Station, the oldest railroad station in the United States. The whole family will have a good time!

Special activities include rides on the Santa Express in November and December and other short train rides from Easter to Labor Day. Train rides are $1 with admission fee.

Baltimore Streetcar Museum

1901 Falls Road (P.O. Box 4881), Baltimore MD 21211 (410-547-0264). Take I-95 north to I-395. Exit at Martin Luther King, Jr. Boulevard to left on Howard Street. Then turn right on North Avenue, right on Maryland Avenue, left on Lafayette Road, then right on Falls Road to museum.

- Open June–October, Saturday and Sunday, noon–5 P.M.; November–May, Sunday, noon–5 P.M.
- Admission to the museum is free. Streetcar rides are adults, $2; children, 4–11, $1; children under 4, free. The second ride is ½ price; an all day pass is $5.
- Parking lot on site.
- Wheelchair access.
- Strollers permitted.
- Group tours by appointment.

A rolling history of the streetcars of Baltimore, the museum houses a collection of Baltimore streetcars, horse-drawn and electric, covering the 104-year history of this type of transportation in the city.

Special activities include a celebration of the museum's birthday the first Sunday in July, Antique Auto Meets three times a year, a Dixieland Concert in August, and Santa Claus Sunday in December. Call the museum for a complete listing of special events.

Baltimore Zoo

Druid Hill Park, Baltimore, MD 21217 (410-396-7102). From I-95 north, take I-695 west towards Towson. Take I-83 south (Exit 25) to Exit 7. Follow signs to the zoo.

- Open daily, 10 A.M.–4:20 P.M. Extended summer hours. Closed Christmas and one Friday in June for an annual fundraiser.
- Adults, $6.50; children 2–15, $3.50. Children are free the first Saturday of each month between 10 A.M. and noon.
- Parking available on site.

- Wheelchair access.
- Strollers permitted; rentals are available.
- Group permits (20% discount) and tours by appointment.
- Call 410-366-LION (5466) for information about special events.

The Baltimore Zoo is home to over 1,200 mammals, reptiles, and exotic birds. Included in this fine zoological park is a naturalistic habitat for African elephants and the largest colony of African black-footed penguins in the United States. In the Children's Zoo kids can experience what it is like to burrow underground like woodchucks or hop on a lily pad like a frog.

Special activities include Easter with the Beasts on Easter and a How-o-ween Spooktacular, held the weekend before Halloween.

The Cloister Children's Museum

10440 Falls Road, Brooklandville, MD 21022 (410-823-2550). Take I-95 north to I-695 west, to Exit 23 B; follow the sign for Falls Road south. Continue to stop light; turn left on Falls Road; look for Cloister sign ½ mile down the road on the right.

- Open Wednesday–Saturday, 10 A.M.–4 P.M.; Sunday noon–4 P.M. Closed all major holidays.
- Adults and children, $4; senior citizens, $3; children under 2, free. Free admission for members.
- Parking available.
- Wheelchair access to first floor and amphitheater.
- Strollers are not permitted in the building.
- Tour rates available.
- Call 410-823-2551 for information on special activities and performances .

The Cloister is a Tudor mansion built in 1930 and donated to the city of Baltimore by Sumner and Dudrea Parker. It contains displays of antique toys, clothing, and tools. Most of the museum is left "out of glass" so little hands and imaginations may wander.

There is a room with trunks of old "dress-up" clothes and a puppet stage with numerous sock puppets. There are also rooms stocked with collage materials and license plates, shoe soles, and tombstones for making rubbings.

Special activities include performances every weekend, usually on Sunday, featuring puppets, plays, music, or storytelling. They also include Bunny Day near Easter time, an annual birthday celebration in November, and a Candlelight Tour in December. Call ahead to find out if there is an additional fee for special events.

Fort McHenry

2400 East Fort Avenue, Baltimore, MD 21230 (410-962-4299). From I-95 north take Exit 55 (Key Highway/Fort McHenry National Monument) and follow the blue and green signs to Lawrence Street. Turn left on Lawrence and left onto East Fort Avenue. Go to the very end where the park is located.

- Open daily, 8 A.M.–4:45 P.M.; summer until 7:45 P.M. Closed Christmas and New Year's Day.
- Free admission to movie and grounds. Admission to historic area: adults 17–61, $1, unless with a school group.
- Ample parking on site.
- Wheelchair access.
- Strollers permitted.

From a ship in the Baltimore harbor, Francis Scott Key saw the "Star Spangled Banner" still flying from the ramparts of Fort McHenry after a 25-hour bombardment by the British in the War of 1812. There is a movie at the visitor's center about the battle and the writing of the national anthem. Children are usually interested in the cannons (no climbing allowed) and really enjoy the soldiers in period uniforms on summer weekends. Your 8–12 year old can become a "junior park ranger."

Special activities include ranger guided activities offered mid-June through Labor Day. Military demonstrations, drills and special ceremonies are presented by "soldiers" dressed in period uniforms, Saturday and Sunday afternoons, mid-June through August. In the evening on Flag Day (June 14) and Defenders' Day (the second Sunday in September) there are commemorative celebrations with band concerts and fireworks.

Lexington Market

400 W. Lexington Street, Baltimore, MD 21201 (410-685-6169). Take I-95 north to I-395, to Russell Street exit; continue on Paca Street 5 blocks north. You can enter the market from Paca or Lexington Streets. There are additional small markets sprinkled throughout downtown Baltimore.

- Open Monday–Saturday, 8:30 A.M.–6 P.M. Closed Sunday and Memorial Day, July 4th, Labor Day, Thanksgiving, Christmas, and New Year's Day.
- Nearby parking garage and limited on-street parking.
- Wheelchair access.
- Strollers permitted.
- Sample food from a variety of food stalls.

This world-famous market has been in continuous operation since 1782 and is the oldest continuously operated market in the United States. Ralph Waldo Emerson referred to it as the "gastronomic capital of the universe." Over 100 merchants, often successive generations of the same family, can be found selling food from all around the world. The market bustles and offers a multitude of sights, sounds, smells, and tastes. A great place to stop for lunch or a snack.

Maryland Historical Society and Darnall Young People's Museum

201 W. Monument Street, Baltimore, MD 21201 (410-685-3750). Take I-95 to I-395; exit at Martin Luther King Jr. Boulevard. Turn right on Druid Hill Avenue, then left on Howard Street. Museum is at Howard and West Monument Streets.

- Open Tuesday–Friday, 10 A.M.–5 P.M.; Saturday, 9 A.M.–5 P.M. April–October, also open Sunday, 1–5 P.M.
- Adults, $2.50; children 5–18, $1; senior citizens, $1.50, families, $5.50.
- On-street parking and several commercial lots.
- Wheelchair access to all except Pratt House and the library.
- Strollers are permitted, but it is preferred that they be left at the door.
- Call in advance for group tours (no charge for school and scout groups).

Museum highlights include dioramas tracing Maryland history with some hands-on material, dolls, dollhouses, toys, and ship models. The original manuscript of the "Star Spangled Banner" is housed here in an exhibit on the War of 1812. A new exhibit focuses on the history of the Civil War in Maryland.

Special activities include seasonal events that vary each year. Call for more information.

Star Spangled Banner Flag House

844 East Pratt Street, Baltimore, MD 21202 (410-837-1793). Take I-95 north to I-395 to downtown Baltimore. Follow signs for Inner Harbor to Pratt Street. Go east on Pratt Street. Cross over President Street (6 blocks from Inner Harbor) to corner of Albermarle. Turn left then make a U-turn to parking spaces in front of the house.

- Open Monday–Saturday, 10 A.M.–4 P.M.; Sunday, 1–4 P.M. Closed major holidays.
- Adults, $2; senior citizens, $1.50; children 13–18, $1; children 6–12, 50¢; children under 6, free.
- Parking available on the street in front of the house. Ask for a parking permit to place on your windshield.
- No wheelchair access.
- Strollers are not permitted.
- Call in advance for group tours.
- Close to Little Italy, where there are many restaurants.

The home of Mary Pickersgill, who stitched the huge flag that inspired the writing of our national anthem, is furnished with antiques of the Federal period. An adjacent museum contains other war-related displays.

Walters Art Gallery

600 North Charles Street, Baltimore, MD 21201 (410-547-9000). Take I-95 north to I-395 to Martin Luther King, Jr. Boulevard north. Continue for one mile, then turn right on Druid Hill Avenue (which becomes Centre Street). After five blocks turn left on Cathedral to museum.

- Open Tuesday–Sunday, 11 A.M.–5 P.M. Closed Monday and Thanksgiving, Christmas, and New Year's Day.
- Adults, $3; senior citizens, $2; students with I.D and children under 18, free. Admission is free on Wednesday.
- Parking in commercial lots or in limited metered, on-street spaces.
- Wheelchair access.
- Strollers permitted.
- Call 410-547-9001 for information on special exhibitions and programs featured throughout the year.
- New cafe open 11:30 A.M.–4:30 P.M.

Considered one of America's great public museums, with a collection that spans 5000 years of artistic achievement ranging from its well-known ancient Egypt collection to Art Nouveau. Young people can participate in many hands-on workshops, attend concerts and storytellings, and take docent-led tours.

Historic Annapolis

To get a true feeling for old Annapolis, walk the narrow streets lined with frame houses and visit the stately brick houses, many of which have been restored and opened to the public. As you walk recall a time when Annapolis was the Nation's Capital. Older children may appreciate the fact that there are 64 pre-revolutionary buildings here, more than Williamsburg, Philadelphia, or Boston! Plan to take a look at St. John's College and the Naval Academy. Stop first at the Historic Annapolis Foundation, 410-267-8149, located in the Old Treasury Building next to the State House at State Circle, and pick up a walking tour map. Guided tours are available from September to May, Monday through Friday at 10 A.M. and 1:30 P.M.; June through August, daily at 10 A.M., 1:30 P.M., and 3 P.M. Groups of 10 or more persons require reservations. A number of tours are available and prices vary.

To reach Annapolis from Washington, DC, take Route 50 east about 40 miles.

United States Naval Academy

King George Street, Annapolis, MD 21402 (410-263-6933 or 410-267-3363). Come through the gate and park your car. If no spaces remain, you will be directed elsewhere.

- Grounds open daily, 9 A.M.–4:30 P.M. Museum open Monday–Saturday, 9 A.M.–4:30 P.M.; Sunday, 11 A.M.–4:30 P.M. The gift shop opens at 10 A.M. Closed Thanksgiving, Christmas, and New Year's Day.
- Adults and children above 6th grade, $3; 6th graders and under, $1.
- Parking available.
- Wheelchair access to most areas.
- Strollers permitted.
- Guided tours are offered hourly from March–Thanksgiving weekend. At other times it is necessary to make reservations in advance.

- Groups should call ahead to make arrangements for their visit.

This is the part of Annapolis that many youngsters really want to see. Favorites are the museum, John Paul Jones' tomb, and the bust of Tecumseh. At noon on some days you may be lucky to see the midshipmen line up in front of Bancroft Hall and march to lunch to the accompaniment of bugles and drums. Best of all is the dress parade. Call for specific dates — they are held on four Wednesdays each semester at 3:45 P.M. It is best to plan your visit for some time other than graduation, as it is extremely crowded during this week.

William Paca House and Garden

186 Prince George Street, Annapolis, MD 21402 (410-263-5553, house; 410-267-6656, garden).

- Open April–October, daily, 10 A.M.–5 P.M.; Sunday, noon–5 P.M. Call for winter hours.
- House and garden, adults, $5; children, 6–18, $3.50. Garden only, adults, $2; children, 6–18, $1. Children under 6, free.
- Parking in garage off Main Street or on-street parking in historic district.
- Wheelchair access to garden.
- Strollers are not permitted in the house.

This 37-room, five-part mansion was built by William Paca, a signer of the Declaration of Independence and the third elected governor of Maryland. When local gentlemen saw the grandeur of Governor Paca's house they paid him the highest compliment by building their own houses in a similar style. The two-acre terraced garden behind the house, hidden for many years, was uncovered when archaeologists found Paca's plans for the garden. The garden includes roses, boxwoods, flower beds, hollies, a Chinese trellis bridge, domed pavilion, and fish-shaped pond.

State House

State Circle, Annapolis, MD 21401 (410-974-3400).

- Open daily, 9 A.M.–5 P.M. Closed Christmas. No guides on Thanksgiving and New Year's Day.
- Parking on street.
- Wheelchair access from the back of the building.
- Strollers permitted.
- Tours take place at 11 A.M., 2 P.M., and 4 P.M.. Tours are also occasionally scheduled at 11 A.M. and 3 P.M. on weekends.

The white-pillared State House is the oldest state capitol still in use. You can spot the original building before expansion as the two story portion topped by the four tiered dome. Once inside don't overlook the small Old Senate Chamber where George Washington came to resign as Commander in Chief of the Continental Congress. The best time to visit is from January to March, when the assembly is in session. Maryland school groups should arrange meetings with members of their county's legislative delegations.

Special activities include State House by Candlelight tours in December.

Victualling Warehouse Maritime Museum

77 Main Street, Annapolis, MD 21402 (410-268-5576).

- Open Monday–Saturday, 11 A.M.–5 P.M.; Sunday, noon–5 P.M. Closed holidays.
- Adults, 50¢; children, free.
- On-street parking.
- Wheelchair access.
- Strollers permitted.
- Self-guided tours for individuals. Group tours available by appointment.

Housed in the old Victualling Warehouse, this museum offers an interesting diorama of the port of Annapolis 200 years ago, when

Annapolis was the principal seaport of the Upper Chesapeake Bay. Trade and commerce are featured in the other exhibits.

Waterfront Annapolis

The city dock area is the center of activity. Here you can take advantage of the Annapolis yachting facilities, water tours, restaurants, summer theater, specialty shops, galleries, Market House, and water strolling areas. For a look at the harbor, short boat tours as well as day trips operate from May to September. Schedules and fees are posted at the dock, or call Chesapeake Marine Tours, 410-268-7600. The Annapolis Sailing School, 410-267-7205, has 2-hour sailing cruises as well as sailing lesson packages.

Special activities include the Annapolis Arts Festival in June, and the United States Sailboat and Power Boat Shows in October.

Frederick, Maryland

From the Beltway (Route 495) take Route 270 north approximately 50 miles.

Antietam Battlefield

P.O. Box 158, Sharpsburg, MD 21782 (301-432-5124). Take Route 270 north to Route 70 west (in Frederick). Exit at Route 65 south (Sharpsburg exit) just outside Hagerstown. Follow Route 65 for 11 miles to Battlefield on left.

- Open daily, 8:30 A.M.–5 P.M. Summer hours are slightly longer. Closed Thanksgiving, Christmas, and New Year's Day.
- Adults 17–61, $1; senior citizens and children are free. Families pay no more than $3.
- Ample parking available.
- Wheelchair access.

- Strollers permitted.
- Group tours available; call for reservations.
- There are restaurants in Shepherdstown, West Virginia, about five miles away.

A good place to begin is at the Visitor Center, where there is a small museum with period artifacts and a 25-minute film shown hourly that describes the battle of Antietam. For a more thorough understanding of the battle, rent the self-guided tour tape for $4 at the bookstore and drive around the battlefield. The 8½ mile drive, with the tape, takes about two hours and includes 11 stops along the way. These stops often have additional recordings to enhance the experience.

Special activities include Living History Demonstrations (artillery, infantry, and encampment) by National Park Service volunteers. In early December an annual 4½ mile long Memorial Illumination commemorates those lost, killed, and wounded at the Battle of Antietam. Call for more information.

Frederick Keys Baseball

P. O. Box 3169, Harry Grove Stadium, Frederick, MD 21701 (301-662-0013). Take Route 270 north to exit 31A (Route 85), to Market Street. Turn left on Market, continue through 2 traffic lights, then turn left on Adventist. Turn right on New Design Road and park on the stadium grounds.

- Open spring and summer with games scheduled evenings at 7:05 P.M. and Sunday at 2:05 P.M. Call for a schedule.
- General admission is on a first-come, first-served basis: adults, $4; children 17 and under, $2; reserved box seats, $6.
- Easy parking.
- Wheelchair access in general admission.
- Strollers permitted.
- Group rates; call for information.
- Food served at the stadium (great lemonade). There are also plenty of places to eat in Frederick.
- Souvenir stand.

The Frederick Keys baseball team are a Class A affiliate of the Baltimore Orioles. They are considered a high quality farm team in the Carolina League, with some players destined to become Orioles. The Keys play 70 home games a season so you have a good chance of finding a game scheduled when you are planning to visit the Frederick area.

Rose Hill Manor Children's Museum

1611 North Market Street, Frederick, MD 21701 (301-694-1646)
Take 270 north to Route 15 north; take Motter Avenue exit; left onto Motter and left onto 14th Street; turn left again on North Market Street and again at Rose Hill Manor Park.

- Open April 1–mid December, Monday–Saturday, 10 A.M.–4 P.M.; Sunday 1–4 P.M. Open weekends only in March. Closed January and February.
- Adults, $3; senior citizens and children 2–17, $1.
- Ample parking on site.
- Wheelchair access to first floor.
- Strollers permitted.
- Group tours are available; call for information, 301-694-1646.
- Many special events but call for information because activities are tentative due to volunteer participation.

This delightful children's museum is located on a 43-acre historic park and is operated by the Frederick County Parks and Recreation Commission. The staff prides itself on making the 19th century come to life for its visitors. Children and adults are invited to touch and see many exhibits in the manor house, carriage museum, blacksmith shop, log cabin, herb and flower gardens, and the farm museum. Costumed guides conduct tours through exhibits and encourage children to make stitches on a quilt, card wool, and operate a beaten biscuit machine and cream separator.

Special activities include colonial craft demonstrations throughout the year, a fall festival, and the Children's Christmas Open House.

Sugarloaf Mountain

Stronghold, Incorporated, 7901 Comus Road, Dickerson, MD 20842 (301-874-2024). Take 270 north to Exit 22 (Hyattstown); turn right on Route 109 west toward Comus; continue 2 miles and turn right at the Comus Inn; continue on Comus Road for 2½ miles. See sign at entrance.

- Visitors admitted daily, 8 A.M.–1 hour prior to sunset. All visitors must leave by sunset.
- Park at the base of the mountain or take your car part of the way up the mountain and stop at various overlooks.
- Picnic tables, but no fires (cookouts) allowed.

A visit to Sugarloaf is a pleasant way for the family to enjoy nature. This privately owned mountain is known for its lovely foliage and vistas. The auto road goes almost to the top, and there are plenty of good walking and climbing trails and picnic spots. The view from the top of Sugarloaf Mountain is wonderful. Five-year-olds and older can make the climb to the top from the highest car park area.

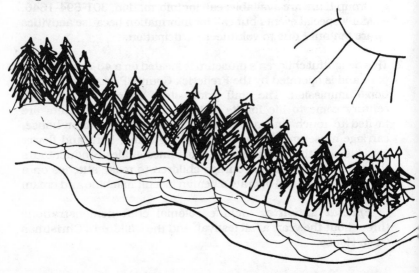

Harpers Ferry

Situated at the junction of the Potomac and Shenandoah Rivers near where Maryland, Virginia, and West Virginia meet, Harpers Ferry is best known as the site of John Brown's raid on the Federal arsenal in 1859. The town played a significant role during the Civil War when the largest number of Union troops surrendered to the Confederates led by "Stonewall" Jackson. Harpers Ferry offers visitors a real sense of history and a beautiful location to explore. In addition to landmarks, such as John Brown's fort, the Stone Steps, and the gun emplacements used by Union and Confederate troops, a living history is presented in the restored shops and offices of the village. Harpers Ferry is also the site of the former Storer College, one of the first institutions of higher education for African Americans.

The local area also boasts a number of hiking trails of varying difficulty. Some are suitable for smaller children. Check at the Visitor Center for more information on the trails. Of special interest are the Appalachian Trail and C & O Canal, which criss-cross in the 2000-acre park.

Information on lodging, dining, and other area attractions can be obtained from the Jefferson County Tourist Information Center, 304-535-2482.

To reach Harpers Ferry, take the Beltway (Route 495) to Route 270 north. At the outskirts of Frederick, go west on Route 340 and follow the signs to Harpers Ferry National Historical Park. The trip takes about 1 hour and 15 minutes from Washington, DC.

Special activities include an active calendar of events sponsored by the National Park Service, which administers the park within Harpers Ferry. These include tours, gun demonstrations, evening campfires, and interpretations of African-American history. The Olde Tyme Christmas program presented by the town of Harpers Ferry runs the first full week of December. "A Civil War Christmas" is held on the first weekend in December.

Harpers Ferry National Park Visitor Center and Information Center

Shenandoah Street, Harpers Ferry, WV 25410 (304-535-6029 and 304-535-6298). Follow signs on Route 340 to the National Historical Park entrance where you will find the Visitor Center parking lot and shuttle buses to take you to the Information Center and to the restored town.

- Visitor Center open daily, 8 A.M.–5 P.M.; Memorial Day–Labor Day until 6 P.M. Closed Christmas and New Year's Day.
- Entrance fee of $5 per vehicle secures a 1-week pass to everything offered by the National Park Service. For those entering the park on foot, bicycle, or tour bus, the entrance fee is $2 per person, but adults over 62, children 16 and under, and bus drivers and escorts are free. A variety of annual passes can be purchased at the Visitor Center. Passes for seniors and handicapped persons are free.
- Park maps available at the Visitor Center.
- Some wheelchair access and facilities including rest rooms, parking, water fountains, and captioned movie. Wheelchairs are available for loan.
- Strollers permitted, but the ride is bumpy.
- Public walking tours are offered Memorial Day to Labor Day. During the rest of the year tours are available by reservation only. Be aware that the streets are stone and narrow and there is local traffic.
- There are places to eat within walking distance of the park area.
- Call for information about special events like the 1860 Election, when 300 living history volunteers recreate the time before the Civil War (usually the second weekend in October).

As you begin your tour, look for the **Stagecoach Inn**, built during the 1820's, when you reach lower town. It serves as an Information Center and bookstore. A wall exhibit shows the four main park themes: local industry, John Brown's raid, the Civil War, and African American History.

African-American History Exhibit

Plans are to open a new African-American history museum in early 1992 devoted to the history of slaves and free blacks before the Civil War and afterwards. Currently, there is an African-American exhibit focusing on Storer College, a predominantly black school which served students from its founding in 1867 to 1955.

John Brown's Fort

This was the armory's fire-engine house, used by John Brown as a refuge during his 1859 raid. Located on the corner of Shenandoah and Potomac Streets.

John Brown Story Museum

On Shenandoah Street, look for this theater and museum relating the events of John Brown's raid. A mural in the lobby depicts the town in 1859. Other exhibits provide brief biographies of John Brown and others involved in the raid. A 10-minute slide program will give you an overview of the town's history and a 26-minute film describes the events leading to the raid and its immediate effects on the country.

Civil War Museums

Located on High Street, these museums house Civil War exhibits relating the soldiers' view of life in occupied Harpers Ferry. During the war the town was constantly occupied by either the Union or Confederate Armies.

Dry Goods Store, Provost Marshall's Office, Blacksmith Shop

On Shenandoah Street, there are good places to visit to appreciate the social and economic history of the times. In the summer they are staffed with people in period clothing.

Harper House

This oldest surviving structure in the park is reached by climbing the stone steps leading uphill from High Street. It is a good example of the crowded conditions of a tenant house in the 1850s.

Master Armorer's House

The house on Shenandoah Street was built in 1858 as the home for the chief gunsmith of the Armory. Contemporary display cases explain the establishment and production of the United States Armory, a Federal gun factory located in Harpers Ferry before the Civil War. Many of the guns made at the factory are on display. Texts describe the manufacturing processes and technological advances.

SUN

5 Nature

Farms, nature centers, and public gardens can provide busy families with a wonderful break from their hectic daily lives. Children can pick strawberries at their own pace (one in the bucket and two in the mouth), listen for woodpeckers on a guided nature walk, participate in daily chores at a working farm, take a brisk walk along a snowy trail, or just enjoy a leisurely stroll through a blooming azalea garden.

Washington, DC

Constitution Gardens

Between the Washington Monument and the Lincoln Memorial on Constitution Avenue, NW, Washington, DC. Mailing address: National Park Service Mall Operations, 900 Ohio Drive, SW, Washington, DC 20242 (202-426-6841).

- Open daily dawn to dusk.
- Park on Ohio Drive along the river. On weekends and holidays parking is available on Constitution Avenue.
- Wheelchair access.
- Strollers permitted.
- Picnicking allowed.

A large mall area, on which temporary government buildings once stood, has been transformed into a sylvan park. The informal design includes a 6-acre lake with a landscaped island, the site of the 56 Signers' Memorial dedicated to the signers of the

Declaration of Independence. The unusual design was intended to create the effect of a park within a park. This is a pleasant place to stop and feed the ducks and seagulls, enjoy a break from sightseeing, or give the children a chance to stretch their legs.

Dumbarton Oaks Gardens

3101 R Street, NW, Washington, DC, 20007 (202-342-3200).
From Georgetown, follow Wisconsin Avenue north and turn right on R Street. Entrance to gardens is at 32nd and R Streets, NW.

- Open daily, 2–5 P.M.; April 1–October 31, until 6 P.M. Closed holidays.
- Admission April–October, adults and children over 12, $2; children under 12, free. No admission charge to gardens November–March.
- On-street parking generally available.
- The gardens have partial wheelchair access and there is a wheelchair garden tour.
- Strollers permitted.
- Tours available by appointment for groups of 12 or more.
- Nearby Montrose Park has many pleasant picnic spots. See listing in Chapter 6, Parks and Recreation.

Dumbarton Oaks Gardens, an oasis in bustling Georgetown, is spectacular in the spring, beautiful in the fall, and pleasant in the winter. The estate's 10 acres of terraced hillsides, formal and informal plantings, and curving footpaths are artfully landscaped and beautifully maintained. After viewing the gardens, follow Lover's Lane (on the east border of the gardens) to Dumbarton Oaks Park, a 27-acre wooded, natural area best known for its pools, waterfalls, and spring wildflowers. See also Dumbarton Oaks listing in Chapter 2, Main Sights and Museums in Washington, DC.

Glover-Archbold Parkway

This park runs from MacArthur Boulevard and Canal Road, NW to just south of Van Ness Street and Wisconsin Avenue, NW, between 42nd and 44th Streets, NW (202-426-6833). There are several places to enter the park including, New Mexico Avenue at Massachusetts Avenue and along 42nd Street. Mailing address: Rock Creek Park, 5000 Glover Road, NW, Washington, DC 20015 (202-426-6833).

- Open daily, dawn to dusk.
- On-street parking in surrounding neighborhoods.
- Limited picnic facilities.

Leave the hustle and bustle of the city behind as you enter this serene, heavily wooded park to wander its nature trails, bird watch, or daydream. This 100-acre park, about 2 miles long and ½ mile wide, wanders through the valley of the Foundry Branch, a small stream. Trails follow the stream from south to north and cross the stream from east to west. There are Victory Gardens, planted and tended by local residents, in the section of the park closest to Whitehaven Park. Call to request a map of Rock Creek Park, including Glover-Archbold Parkway.

Kenilworth Aquatic Gardens

1900 Anacostia Avenue, NE, Washington, DC 20020 (202-426-6905). Located in Anacostia Park across the Anacostia River from the National Arboretum, at Douglas Street and Anacostia Avenue. Take Route 50 south to Kenilworth Avenue exit. Follow brown signs to Aquatic Gardens.

- Gardens open daily, 7 A.M.–5 P.M.; Visitor Center open until 4 P.M. Winter hours may vary. Mornings are the best time for viewing.
- Metrorail, Orange line (Deanwood).
- Transportation available for handicapped persons. Please call in advance.
- Strollers permitted.

- Evening walks by arrangement. Garden walks on summer weekends (Memorial Day through Labor Day) and holidays at 9 A.M., 11 A.M., and 1 P.M.
- Group tours by appointment.
- Picnic area.

More than 100,000 flowering water plants thrive in the pools of the 12-acre Kenilworth Aquatic Gardens, a National Park Service site. Children love the irises, lotuses, and lilies, find the frogs and turtles amusing, and enjoy running along the narrow paths that separate the ponds. The gardens are at their best if you go early in the morning to see night-bloomers before they close and day-bloomers as they open. Plants start blooming in spring. Water lilies start blooming in May and can be seen throughout the summer. A park naturalist is on site every day. Check periodically for scheduled events. See also Anacostia Park listing in Chapter 6, Parks and Recreation.

Rock Creek Nature Center and Planetarium

5200 Glover Road, NW, Washington, DC, 20015 (202-426-6829). Take Connecticut Avenue north to Military Road, turn right. Make another right turn at Glover Road to the Nature Center.

- Nature center open daily, 9 A.M.–5 P.M. Closed Federal holidays.
- Planetarium open for shows Saturday and Sunday at 1 P.M. for children 4 and older (4–7 years-olds must be accompanied by adults); and at 4 P.M. for children 7 and older. Wednesday afternoons at 3:45 P.M. there are after-school shows. Closed Federal holidays.
- Tickets for planetarium shows must be picked up at information desk which opens 30 minutes before show time.
- Parking lot available.
- Wheelchair access.
- Strollers permitted in Nature Center, but not in Planetarium.

- Special programs available by reservation for groups of 10 or more Wednesday–Friday only. Call at least two weeks in advance.
- There are several picnic tables near the parking lot. No food or drink in the nature center.

One of the best in the area, this nature center offers many exhibits of the flora and fauna of its surrounding woodland. Children find the live reptiles and beehive especially interesting. There are also two self-guided nature trails. The weekend schedule includes a film at 11 A.M. and a nature walk at 3 P.M. Birdfeeding workshops and other special programs are scheduled occasionally. A schedule is available from the center.

An exciting part of your visit to the Nature Center is the planetarium show. The room darkens, stars appear, and the audience is transported outdoors on a clear night. The show for the younger children concentrates on the identification of major constellations and the movement of the heavenly bodies through the night sky. The later show, for older children, is divided into a study of the sky as it will appear that night and an in-depth astronomy presentation. Evening stargazing sessions, run in conjunction with the National Capital Astronomers, are held approximately monthly, May through October. See also Rock Creek Park listing in Chapter 6, Parks and Recreation.

United States National Arboretum

3501 New York Avenue, NE, Washington, DC 20002 (202-475-4815). Take the Beltway (Route 495) to Route 50 west; Route 50 turns into New York Avenue; at first intersection turn left onto Bladensburg Road; go 3 blocks, then turn left on R Street; go 300 yards to the entrance.

- Open weekdays, 8 A.M.–5 P.M.; Saturday and Sunday, 10 A.M.–5 P.M. Bonsai collection and Japanese garden open daily, 10 A.M.–2:30 P.M. Closed Christmas.
- Parking available.

- Wheelchair access.
- Strollers permitted.
- Picnicking is permitted in designated areas.
- Guided tours available for grades 5 and above. Call in advance.

Enjoy the varied shrubs and trees, gardens, overlooks, and ponds as you explore this 444-acre museum of living plants by road or footpath. It is most colorful in the spring when thousands of azaleas are in bloom, but is equally enjoyable all year round, as there is always something blooming and plenty of "stretching space" for children to expend a little excess energy. Favorite sections include the Dwarf Conifer collection, about 1,500 specimens attractively planted and separated by grassy areas and walks; the Fern Valley Trail, a natural wooded area planted with ferns, wildflowers, and native trees and shrubs; and the Aquatic Garden, featuring tropical and local aquatic plants. The superb Bonsai collection, a bicentennial gift from Japan, now includes a collection of Chinese and American Bonsai. The National Herb Garden, approximately 2 acres, includes 3 sub-gardens: a formal "knot" garden with plants arranged in intricate patterns resembling various kinds of knots; a historic rose garden; and a specialty garden which contains 10 different "rooms" or plots, each featuring a different area of herb gardening. New areas include the American and Friendship Gardens, featuring perennials and ornamental grasses. The Asian Collections includes a variety of exotic oriental plants.

A recent addition to the Arboretum are 22 of the original 24 National Capitol Columns that once formed the east central portico of the Capitol. The columns were in storage for many years before private funds were raised to finance their removal and reuse. The columns are placed in a nearly square configuration, with a water stair, fountain, and reflecting pool.

The Arboretum provides land for the "Washington Youth Gardens" where children learn and practice the fundamentals of gardening. The administration building hosts horticultural demonstrations, lectures, exhibits, and films. It is often used by local groups to hold flower shows.

Maryland

Nutshell News, a monthly publication of the Maryland National Capital Park and Planning Commission, is available at public libraries or by calling 301-495-2525. This publication lists programs offered by area nature centers.

Audubon Naturalist Society (Woodend)

8940 Jones Mill Road, Chevy Chase, MD 20815 (301-652-5964). Take Rock Creek Parkway to Beach Drive to Jones Mill Road.

- Grounds open daily, dawn-dusk. Building open weekdays, 10 A.M.–5 P.M.; Thursday until 8 P.M. Building closed weekends. Bookshop open weekdays, 10–5 P.M.; Thursday until 8 P.M.
- Parking lot.
- Wheelchair access.
- Strollers permitted in mansion, but not on trails.
- Call 301-652-5964, extension 3007, to schedule a school program at Woodend.
- Call 301-652-5964, extension 3006, for general information on classes and events for children and families.
- Call 301-652-1088, The Voice of the Naturalist, to hear a recording describing the location of area bird sightings.

Woodend, the Audubon Society's tranquil 40-acre estate, serves as its headquarters as well as a wildlife sanctuary. Inside the main house is the Wilbur Fisk Banks Memorial Collection of Birds, consisting of 594 specimens, mostly of eastern North America. A self-guided nature trail is available for enjoyment of the grounds. The bookshop at Woodend includes a large selection of books and other related materials for children (see Chapter 9, Shopping).

Special activities include a number of programs that center around conservation and environmental issues. After-school and summer programs are run for children ages 4 and up, with a few programs for the 2–3 year old age group. Additionally, they offer a variety of family activities, including day and weekend trips, available at a reduced rate to members, as well as a lovely Earth Fair in April and a Holiday Fair in December. An environmental education brochure is published quarterly.

Black Hill Regional Park Visitor Center

20926 Lake Ridge Drive, Boyds, MD 20841 (301-972-3476). From the Beltway (Route 495) take Route 270 north; exit at Boyds-Clarksburg (Route 121); turn left on Clarksburg Road; continue for 2½ miles then take a sharp left on Old Baltimore Road; continue for 1 mile to park entrance on right.

- Open April–October, Monday–Saturday, 9 A.M.–sunset; Sunday, noon–sunset. Open November–March, Saturday, 9 A.M.–sunset; Sunday, noon–sunset. Call to check hours before your visit.
- Parking available.

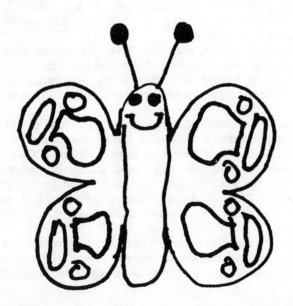

- Wheelchair access.
- Strollers permitted.
- Picnicking in the park.

This visitor center has several displays of wood carvings, stained glass, and the habitat of the Little Seneca Lake. A very popular feature is their collection of 29 videos, 9 of which are directed towards children. Visitors can select a video and view it immediately in the center's auditorium. A variety of nature programs — star search, hawk watch, family hikes, cornhusk basketry — are offered for preschoolers through adults. These programs are listed in *Nutshell News*. See Chapter 6, Parks and Recreation, for a complete listing on the Black Hill Regional Park.

Brookside Gardens

Wheaton Regional Park, 1500 Glenallan Avenue, Wheaton, MD 20902 (301-949-8230). Take the Beltway (Route 495) to Georgia Avenue north to Randolph Road; right on Randolph Road for 2 blocks, right on Glenallan Avenue; ½ mile to entrance on right.

- Grounds open daily, 9 A.M.–dusk. Conservatory open 10 A.M.–5 P.M. Closed Christmas.
- Parking available.
- Partial wheelchair access.
- Strollers permitted.
- Picnic at Wheaton Regional Park (see Chapter 6, Parks and Recreation).

This 50-acre public garden has outdoor plantings landscaped in formal and natural styles. In addition to the well-known azalea, rose, formal, and early American herb gardens, there are aquatic and Japanese gardens. The Japanese teahouse and lake are home to water snakes and fish. Geese and ducks are to be found near the aquatic gardens and butterflies are indeed attracted to the butterfly garden. Inside the two conservatories are colorful annuals and perennials and exotic plants. A stream with stepping stones wandering through the greenhouse is a delight for little ones.

The garden boasts a 2,000 volume horticultural library, some of which are children's books (for use on-site only). There are self-guided, recorded, and staff-guided interpretations of the garden. A self-touring cassette is available free-of-charge. A calendar, Garden Notes from Brookside, lists all the scheduled lectures, workshops, and programs.

Seasonal activities include Christmas, Easter, and autumn displays.

Brookside Nature Center

Wheaton Regional Park, 1400 Glenallan Avenue, Wheaton, MD 20902 (301-946-9071). Take the Beltway (Route 495) to Georgia Avenue north to Randolph Road; right on Randolph Road for 2 blocks; right on Glenallan Avenue; ½ mile to entrance on right..

- Open Tuesday–Saturday, 9 A.M.–5 P.M.; Sunday, 1–5 P.M. Closed Monday and Federal holidays.
- Parking available.
- Wheelchair access.
- Strollers permitted.
- Picnic area in the woods across from service road.

This small nature center in the woods offers mounted specimens of Washington area animals, a diorama of local birds, a beehive, a turtle aquarium, and a large terrarium of carnivorous plants! Outside there is an 1850 cabin and smokehouse, nature trails leading into Wheaton Regional Park (see Chapter 6, Parks and Recreation), and a duck pond. A Nature Center aide program and Conservation Club are also available. *Nutshell News* lists all of the programs offered by the center.

Butler's Orchard

22200 Davis Mill Road, Germantown, MD, 20876 (301-972-3299). Take the Beltway (Route 495) to Route 270; take Damascus exit north; follow signs to Damascus 1½ miles to Butler Orchards sign on your right.

- Open May–Christmas; call to check exact days and hours. Closed Monday except during Strawberry Season, Labor Day, and Columbus Day.
- Parking available.
- Wheelchair access.
- Strollers permitted.
- Call 301-972-3299 to hear a recorded message about the availability of your favorite crops.

Families visiting the 300-acre Butler family farm will get an appealing and instructive view of fruits and vegetables growing in

the orchards and fields and have an opportunity to pick their own produce. Crops during an eight-month growing season include strawberries, blackberries, blueberries, peas, pumpkins, and Christmas trees. Bring your own baskets, which will be weighed before picking, or purchase them at Butler's for a small fee. Fresh seasonal produce is also for sale at the stand.

Seasonal activities include Pumpkin Festivals every weekend in October with free hayrides through the pumpkin fields. Nominal parking charge. School groups and other organizations with reservations are welcome in October for pumpkin harvest tours and hayrides. During December there are unusual ornaments, fresh wreaths, and cut-your-own Christmas trees.

Carroll County Farm Museum

500 South Center Street, Westminster, MD 21157 (410-848-7775). Take the Beltway (Route 495) to Georgia Avenue, north; continue about 40 miles to left turn on Route 140; follow for 1 mile to left on Center Street; continue 1 mile to entrance on right.

- Open for group tours during April, weekdays, 10 A.M.–4 P.M. In May, facility open to general public weekends, noon–5 P.M. Additional hours, July and August, Tuesday–Friday, 10 A.M.–4 P.M. Open for tours about 9 days during Christmas season. Call for schedule. Closed Monday and some holidays.
- Adults, $3; children 6–18, $2; over 60, $2; under 6, free. Groups of 20 or more $2 per person.
- Parking available.
- Wheelchair access.
- Strollers permitted outside, but not in the farm house.
- Picnic area.

This is the way a prosperous northern Maryland farm looked back in 1850. It had a comfortable farmhouse, barns, spring house, smithy, wagon shed, gardens, field crops, and pastures. Families get an idea of this kind of life on visits to the restored 140 acre farm. Demonstrations of such skills as potting, quilting, chair caning, weaving, candlemaking, and blacksmithing are scheduled throughout the season. There's plenty of run-around space for younger children and a general store that sells nickel candy, old-fashioned bonnets, and handcrafted items made by the resident artisans.

Seasonal activities include a celebration and fireworks for Fourth of July, a Fiddlers' Convention, and Harvest Day.

Cedarvale Farm

2915 Coale Lane, Churchville, MD 21028 (301-734-7467). Take the Beltway (Route 495) to Route 95 north towards Baltimore. Take the Route 22 exit in Aberdeen towards Churchville. Turn left on Route 136 and follow for ½ mile to left turn on Coale Lane. Look for the sign with a bison.

- Open to public Sundays, 1–5 P.M.
- Parking available.
- Wheelchair access.
- Strollers permitted.
- School groups may call ahead to arrange for a tour.

This farm features a herd of 17 bison raised primarily to educate school children about native heritage. Bring your rotten apples and stale bread to feed the bison.

Cider Mill Farm

5012 Landing Road, Elkridge, MD 21227 (410-788-9595). Take the Beltway (Route 495) to Route 29 north towards Columbia. Turn right on Route 108, then left at Old Montgomery Road (which becomes Montgomery Road). Turn left on Landing Road to Cider Mill Farm on the left.

- Open September–December, daily, 10 A.M.–6 P.M.; January–May, Friday–Sunday, 10 A.M.–6 P.M. Closed June–August.
- Parking available.
- Wheelchair access.
- Strollers permitted.

- A variety of group tours and workshops are available for preschoolers through adults. Call for more information and to make reservations.

The 59-acre Cider Mill is a functioning apple cider mill and farm on the Howard County Inventory of Historic Places. There are plenty of farm animals to pet and feed — goats, pigs, horses, sheep, chickens, turkeys. Activities at the farm vary according to the season. For example, highlights on different weekends in the fall include seeing fresh cider pressed (and tasting the results), hayrides, apple butter making, making scarecrows, and pumpkin carving. Other events include a St. Patrick's Day festival (making scarecrows and planting potatoes), Civil War encampments, and Colonial Days (First Maryland Regiment encampment, living history, crafts, and frontier days interpreter). Throughout the year families will enjoy music, crafts, storytelling, games, and face painting activities. A variety of tours and workshops are offered to educate children and adults in traditional cider making, farming, and rural crafts in an informal, hands-on atmosphere. Call the farm for more information about scheduled events and to receive a copy of their weekend activities schedule.

Clearwater Nature Center

Cosca Regional Park, 11000 Thrift Road, Clinton, MD, 20735 (301-297-4575). Take the Beltway (Route 495) to Route 5 south to Woodyard Road (Route 223). Turn right (west) and continue to Brandywine Road (Route 381), then left (south) to Thrift Road. A right turn here will lead you to the park.

- Open weekdays, 8:30 A.M.–5 P.M. Easter–Thanskgiving, open Sunday also, 11 A.M.–4 P.M. Closed some holidays.
- Parking available.
- Wheelchair access.
- Strollers permitted.
- Picnicking permitted in the park.

The nature center features an attractive indoor fish and turtle pond and a wetland beaver lapidary exhibit. Hiking trails criss-cross the park and a variety of interesting guided theme hikes, including creek hikes, night hikes, and insect hikes, are planned. Boats are available to rent during the summer. Other activities include workshops, arts and crafts, films, outdoor explorers (ages 4–7), hiking club (ages 8–10), and ecology club (ages 11–14). See also Cosca Regional Park listing in, Chapter 6, Parks and Recreation.

Jug Bay Natural Area, Patuxent River Park

Park is composed of a number of properties on the river along the eastern boundary of Prince George's County. Mailing address: 16000 Croom Airport Road, Upper Marlboro, MD 20772 (301-627-6074).

- Open daily, 8 A.M.–dusk. Closed Thanksgiving, Christmas, and New Year's Day.
- All parklands are considered "limited use natural areas" and require a permit or reservation. Call above number for more information on permits.
- Parking available.
- Activities accommodate senior citizens and physically handicapped visitors.
- Historic sites.
- Primitive group camping by advance reservation.
- Fishing, boating, and canoeing. April–October, by reservation, interpretive boat tours on Jug Bay for groups.
- Equestrian trails.
- Nature study.

If you are planning a visit to this scenic 2,000 acre natural area you will need to plan ahead. Much of the parkland is open to the public; however, visitors need special permits and groups need reservations. The following describes the many natural attractions this park has to offer.

Chesapeake Bay Critical Area Driving Tour is a four-mile, self-guided, one-way drive connecting the Jug Bay Natural Area with the Merkle Wildlife Sanctuary. As you drive along the Patuxent River shore line you may see osprey, Canada geese, bald eagles, and other sights. The tour includes educational displays, observation towers, and a 1,000 foot bridge across Mattaponi Creek. The drive is open for private cars on Sunday from noon to 3 P.M. and at other times in the Park's own vehicles. Several times a year the road is open for bicycle tours. Call for more information.

The Black Walnut Creek Nature Study Area is dedicated to nature study and environmental education. You can walk out on boardwalks through the marsh and swamp and on woodland trails for an up-close view of the wetlands. Free nature hikes are available by reservation.

River Ecology is explained on interpretive tours of the Patuxent River on a pontoon boat, the "Otter." Visitors can get close enough to really observe the river's ecology, wetlands, and wildlife. An Annual Jug Bay Regatta takes place here in August. Bring your own home-made raft and compete for prizes as you float down the Patuxent River.

At **Patuxent Village**, a living history exhibit, visitors see a smoke house, a tobacco packing shed, a 150 year old log cabin, and other exhibits depicting life along the river. Children and parents can learn how to strip tobacco and pack it for shipment on sailing ships and steamboats and how to smoke fish and meat. Tours and demonstrations are available for groups by reservation.

The **W. H. Henry Duvall Tool Collection** contains over 1,000 19th-century tools, domestic items, and farm implements. The tool museum is open Sunday afternoon and by reservation for groups.

Outdoor Recreation activities include group and primitive camping, fishing, canoeing (canoes can be rented at Jug Bay), boating, and horseback riding (bring your own horse!).

Locust Grove Nature Center

Cabin John Regional Park, 7777 Democracy Boulevard, Bethesda, MD 20817 (301-299-1990). Take the Beltway (Route 495) to Old Georgetown Road; go north to left on Tuckerman Lane; park is at corner of Westlake Drive. Nature Center is located next to the tennis courts.

- Open Tuesday–Saturday, 9 A.M.–5 P.M. Closed Sunday, Monday, and holidays.
- Parking available.
- Wheelchair access.
- Strollers permitted.
- Specially designed programs for schools, camps, and other groups, by reservation.
- Scheduled programs for children and families, by reservation.
- Picnic tables and grills in Cabin John Park.

This recently renovated nature center has a small library of nature books, games, and puzzles. New exhibits and displays are being designed and will be installed shortly. The center sponsors a variety of nature programs such as night hikes, camp fires, hikes with a special theme, craft workshops, storytimes, and more. *Nutshell News* lists all of the programs offered by the center. See Cabin John Regional Park listing in Chapter 6, Parks and Recreation.

Meadowside Nature Center

Rock Creek Regional Park, 5100 Meadowside Lane, Rockville, MD, 20853 (301-924-4141). Take the Beltway (Route 495) to Georgia Avenue, north; continue to left turn on Norbeck Road; turn right on Muncaster Mill Road, then left on Meadowside Lane.

- Open Tuesday–Saturday, 9 A.M.–5 P.M.; Closed Monday and Federal holidays.
- Parking available.
- Wheelchair access.

- Strollers permitted.
- Picnic area for bag lunches.

This nature center is surrounded by 350 acres, including 7½ miles of nature trails, a lake, a marsh, a pond, two butterfly gardens, an herb garden, a raptor cage (with live owl, hawk, and turkey vulture), and a mid 1800s farmstead. Inside the center is a reference library, a curiosity corner with a microscope table, a touch bin, and other exhibits. Snakes and fish are there to view, as is a mock wigwam. "Legacy of the Land" is a diorama of the Maryland habitat. Kids love crawling into and sliding out of the cave and enjoy looking at an underground cross-section of the earth showing tree roots and a view into the bottom of the pond. A Summer Conservation Club, adult volunteer program, and Junior Naturalist program are available. See *Nutshell News* for a calendar of events. More information on Rock Creek Regional Park and Lake Needwood can be found in Chapter 6, Parks and Recreation.

The National Colonial Farm

Piscataway National Park, 3400 Bryan Point Road, Accokeek, MD 20607 (301-283-2113). Take the Beltway (Route 495) to Exit 3A south, Indian Head Highway (Route 210). Proceed south on Indian Head Highway for 10 miles. Turn right at Bryan Point Road. Follow for 4 miles to farm parking lot on right.

- Open Tuesday–Sunday, 10 A.M.–5 P.M. Closed Monday, Thanksgiving, Veteran's Day, Christmas, and New Year's Day.
- Adults $2, children under 12, 50¢; not to exceed $5 per family.
- Parking lot.
- A vehicle for handicapped persons is available. Call 301-283-2113 during the week to make arrangements.
- Scheduled group tours by reservation, Tuesday–Friday. Guided tours for individuals and families, Saturdays at 12:30 and 2:30 P.M.
- Picnic tables in Saylor Grove parking area.

At this beautiful site on the Potomac opposite Mount Vernon, the Accokeek Foundation, in cooperation with the National Park Service, has re-created a working farm. It features demonstration gardens and animals of a middle-class tobacco plantation in the mid 18th century. Seasonal farm work goes on every day, as well as daily domestic activities. On the interpretive tours, children of all ages have the chance to observe the farming methods and family lifestyle characteristic of the period. Bird enthusiasts will be pleased to know that the farm is home to three pairs of bald eagles. See Piscataway Park listing in Chapter 6, Parks and Recreation.

Seasonal activities include a militia muster (held in late April) — a re-enactment of colonists being trained by the British to protect their homes from the French and Indians — and a Fall Festival in late September, featuring demonstrations of a variety of colonial crafts.

Old Maryland Farm

R.M. Watkins Regional Park, 301 Watkins Park Drive, Upper Marlboro, MD 20772 (301-249-7077). Take the Beltway (Route 495) to Central Avenue (Route 214) east. Turn right at Enterprise Road (Route 193). Turn right at the marquee, right at the stop sign, then left immediately into the park. After the next stop sign, park in the lot on the left (across from the train station). Walk down the path behind the train station to Old Maryland Farm.

- Open Tuesday–Friday, 10 A.M.–4 P.M.; Saturday, 11 A.M.–4 P.M. Closed Sunday, Monday, Thanksgiving, Christmas, and New Year's Day.
- Parking available.
- Wheelchair access.
- Strollers permitted.
- Group programs for adults and children by reservation.
- Arrangements to hold birthday parties at the farm can be made in advance. Fee is $3 per child.
- Picnicking permitted in the park.

This demonstration farm features livestock, agricultural antiques, an indoor exhibit room, and organic theme gardens in raised beds. A tree bank houses thousands of saplings for use in land reclamation projects. In April and May volunteers can help plant the saplings. Weekend volunteers can work in the gardens or serve as tour guides. Training is provided. Children enjoy seeing the livestock fed each Saturday at noon. See R.M. Watkins Regional Park listing in Chapter 6, Parks and Recreation.

Seasonal events include Farm Day Camps in June, July, and December, a Harvest Day Festival on the last Saturday of October, October pumpkin tours, and a December campfire, sing-along, and hayride.

Howard B. Owens Science Center and Planetarium

9601 Greenbelt Road, Lanham-Seabrook, MD, 20706 (301-577-8718). Take the Beltway (Route 495) to Exit 22A, Greenbelt Road; continue for 3 miles to entrance on right.

- Planetarium open to public, Friday at 7 P.M. Other showings upon special request for scout groups, civic and/or fraternal organizations and non-public school groups.
- Adults, $2; senior citizens and students in kindergarten through grade 12, $1; group rates available.

This modern science center emphasizes participatory exhibits and interactive programs. The Summer Science Enrichment Program is open to preschool through high school students on a first-come, first-served basis. Serves primarily students of the Prince Georges County Public Schools.

Oxon Hill Farm

6411 Oxon Hill Road, Oxon Hill, MD 20745 (301-839-1177). Take the Beltway (Route 495) to Indian Head Highway, Exit 3A (south); then go right at end of ramp to Oxon Hill Road; make immediate right into farm.

- Open daily, 8:30 A.M.–5 P.M. Closed Thanksgiving, Christmas, and New Year's Day.
- Parking available.
- Wheelchair access.
- Strollers permitted.
- Groups are welcome but there are no tours.
- Picnic area.
- Cow milking at 10:30 A.M. and 4 P.M., and chicken feeding and egg gathering at 2 P.M.

Oxon Hill is a working farm with daily demonstrations of farm chores, animals, crops, and equipment typical of those on farms in the early 1900s. It is administered by the National Park Service. Younger children like petting the animals; older children are interested in the animal care, farming methods, and craft demonstrations. There is also a natural spring, a self-guided nature walk that explains how farms utilized the surrounding woods, and an additional bonus — a most spectacular view of the Potomac River, Washington, DC, and Virginia.

Special activities include sheep-shearing, gardening, threshing, cider pressing, corn harvesting, and sorghum syrup cooking. Call for specific dates.

Albert M. Powell State Trout Hatchery

Route 61, Box 180, Hagerstown, MD 21740 (301-791-4736).
Take the Beltway (Route 495) to Route 270 north. Near Frederick take Route 70, west to Route 66. Continue north on Route 66 for about 100 yards to the hatchery on the left.

- Open daily, 9 A.M.–4 P.M.
- Parking available.
- Wheelchair access and stroller use is limited due to safety considerations.

Visitors are welcome to watch the trout swimming in the outdoor ponds. Other attractions in the area are Greenbriar State Park for boating, picnicking, camping, and hiking, and Washington

Monument State Park where you can climb to the top of a 35-foot tower and enjoy a panoramic view of Maryland, Virginia, and West Virginia.

Summit Hall Farm Park

502 South Frederick Avenue, Gaithersburg, MD 20877 (301-258-6350). Take the Beltway (Route 495) to Route 270 north. Exit at Shady Grove Road. Turn right on Shady Grove Road to left turn on Frederick Avenue (Route 355) for about 1½ miles; the Farm Park is on your left.

- Park offices open weekdays, 8:30 A.M.–4:30 P.M. Garden plots accessible through entry road off Frederick Avenue.
- Picnicking allowed and two pavilions are for group rental.
- Call City of Gaithersburg office number above to reserve a plowed garden plot.

The park is the site of a future major (57-acre) regional City of Gaithersburg recreational facility. Now it is the site of local recreation offices and individual garden plots available to City and non-City residents in April of each year. Walk among the individual garden plots or stroll down to view the geese which settle by the pond gracing the City-owned, privately-occupied, Manor House. There is a large public swimming pool, 301-258-6445, and a miniature golf course will be built in the near future.

University of Maryland Observatory

University of Maryland Observatory, Metzerott Road, College Park, MD 20742 (301-405-3001, Department of Astronomy). Take the Beltway (Route 495) to University Boulevard east to left turn on Metzerott Road.

- Open the 5th and 20th of every month, 8 P.M. Eastern Standard Time, 9 P.M. Daylight Savings Time.
- Parking available.
- Wheelchair access.

- Call in advance for special or group programs for 15 or more individuals.
- Interesting and educational for older children, but not recommended for primary school children.

A visit to the observatory begins with a slide talk on a topic of popular interest in astronomy. The topics range from archaeo-astronomy to quasars. Topics change frequently, so call in advance for details. A short film is shown and, weather permitting, everyone looks at the sky through the observatory's four telescopes. The program coordinator is available to answer questions and provide assistance with the telescopes.

Watkins Nature Center

R. M. Watkins Regional Park, 301 Watkins Park Drive, Upper Marlboro, MD 20772 (301-249-6202).

- Open weekdays, 9 A.M.–5 P.M.; Saturday, 9 A.M.–4: 30 P.M.; Sunday 11 A.M.–4 P.M. Closed Sunday in January and February.
- Memorial Day–Labor Day there is a park admission fee on weekends.
- Parking available.
- Wheelchair access.
- Strollers permitted.
- Picnic sites in the park.

Located in the 300 acre Watkins Regional Park, this nature center has a number of exhibits and displays including live birds of prey (owls and hawks), snakes, turtles, frogs, and toads. Groups can call to schedule a nature program tailored to their interests and needs. In addition, a variety of scheduled programs are available for families by reservation. See R. M. Watkins Regional Park listing in Chapter 6, Parks and Recreation.

The Wild Bird Center

7687 MacArthur Boulevard, Cabin John, MD 20818 (301-229-3141). Take the Beltway (Route 495) to River Road; go north to Seven Locks Road; turn left; turn left on MacArthur Boulevard to 77th street.

- Open daily, 10 A.M.–6 P.M. Closed July 4th, Christmas, and New Year's Day.
- Parking available.
- No wheelchair access.
- Strollers permitted.
- Call for information about bird programs. Children's in-store programs are scheduled several times a year.
- School programs available by reservation.

There are several Wild Bird Centers in Maryland and Virginia, but this one is the original. Located in one of the few original "Sears Catalog" houses still standing, the building sits on a busy suburban street corner less than a mile from the Potomac River. Outside, the dozen or more feeders and houses host birds you're likely to see in your backyard: hummingbirds, pileated woodpeckers, purple martins, cardinals, goldfinches, and other songbirds. Inside, the store carries the Washington area's largest selection of bird feeders, houses, seeds, binoculars, books, and gifts — everything for the backyard birdwatcher. Call for a free subscription to *Wild Bird News,* the Wild Bird Center's newsletter. If it's about birds, this shop has it. Items ranging from bird mailboxes to T-shirts, children's books and stationery, all with a bird theme, are available in addition to the traditional items which compliment the hobby of birdwatching. The Center has an education program available for schools, scout groups, community centers, and so on. Teachers and group leaders may also schedule in-store visits for up to 10 children.

Each Wild Bird Center maintains its own schedule of events. Centers are located in the following areas:

Annapolis, MD	(410-280-0033)
Columbia, MD	(301-596-2990)
Gaithersburg, MD	(301-330-WILD)
Glen Dale (Lanham), MD	(301-805-4858)
Severna Park, MD	(410-647-3100)
Silver Spring, MD	(301-989-WILD)
Burke, VA	(703-323-7898)
Herndon, VA	(703-742-0605)
Vienna, VA	(703-938-55788)
Woodbridge, VA	(703-490-5000)

Virginia

Arlington Public Schools Planetarium

1426 North Quincy Street, Arlington, VA 22207 (703-358-6070).
Located between Lee Highway and Washington Boulevard.

- Call the Planetarium office for exact information on programs, dates and times.
- Adults, $2; senior citizens and children 12 and under, $1.
- Parking available.
- Metrorail, Orange line (Ballston).
- Wheelchair access.
- Strollers permitted.

Used primarily for school programs during the day, this modern planetarium offers varied programs for the general public on the weekends. Programs are changed frequently and include seasonal shows on the constellations.

Frying Pan Park, Kidwell Farm

2709 West Ox Road, Herndon, VA 22071 (703-437-9101). Take Beltway (Route 495) to Route 66 west; exit at Route 50 west; turn right on Fairfax County Parkway; left on West Ox Road; park is on right.

- Open daily, 8 A.M.–6 P.M. Closed Christmas.
- Parking available.
- Wheelchair access.
- Strollers permitted.
- Picnic areas.
- School tours can be arranged in advance.

This model farm of the 1920s offers the urban child a rich experience in rural living. Take a picnic lunch and spend some time looking at this subsistence farm with its blacksmith shop, historic schoolhouse, numerous farm animals, fields, farm buildings, and horse arena. The arena is generally booked on the weekends.

Special activities include the Draft Horse and Spring Farming Days, which takes place in early May. During this event the Mid-Atlantic National Draft Horse Show goes on in the activity center, country music bands provide live entertainment, and visitors can take rides in a hay wagon. The Fairfax County 4-H Fair takes place here in August.

Green Spring Gardens Park

4601 Green Spring Road, Alexandria, VA 22312 (703-642-5173). Take the Beltway (Route 495) to Little River Turnpike (Route 236) towards Annandale; turn left on Green Spring Road. Or, from Route 395, take Duke Street west about one mile; turn right on Green Spring Road.

- Grounds open daily, dawn to dusk. Visitor center open March–December, Monday and Wednesday–Friday, 9 A.M.–5 P.M.; Saturday 8:30 A.M.–5 P.M.; Sunday, noon–5 P.M.; closed Tuesday. Manor house open, Monday and Wednesday–Sunday, 1–4 P.M.

Park and buildings closed Thanksgiving and Christmas; on other holidays open noon–5 P.M. January–February, buildings open weekends only.
- Parking available.
- Wheelchair access to greenhouse only.
- Strollers permitted.
- Guided tours available by appointment.
- Picnicking is allowed on the grounds.
- Call for information on gardening programs for children.

This park features formal demonstration gardens and an extensively renovated 18th century house that is now the home of the Fairfax County Council of the Arts. The house includes an art gallery and crafts shop. The grounds include formal rose, herb, and vegetable gardens, a fruit orchard, and an iris bed. Smaller children especially will enjoy the woods and two ponds with ducks and geese. The park includes a greenhouse where gardening classes and horticultural demonstrations are held. Call 703-642-5173 for information on these classes.

Gulf Branch Nature Center

3608 North Military Road, Arlington, VA 22207 (703-358-3403). Near the intersection of North Military Road and Chain Bridge.

- Open Tuesday–Saturday, 10 A.M.–5 P.M.; Sunday, 1–5 P.M. Closed Monday and Federal holidays.
- Parking available on site and on surrounding streets.
- No wheelchair access.
- Strollers permitted.
- Picnics allowed in adjoining Old Glebe Park.

This nature center, located in a 53-acre wooded stream valley, features interpretive displays on Arlington and Virginia plants, animals, and natural history. Attractions include a Native American display with a dugout canoe, a hands-on discovery corner, a moderately strenuous ¾ mile trail to the Potomac River, and an observation bee hive. The Special Events Calendar for Arlington County Nature Centers, published quarterly, advertises special programs for preschoolers through adults. A Junior Naturalist program for Arlington children in grades 1–8 operates during the summer.

Hidden Oaks Nature Center

Annandale Community Park, 4020 Hummer Road, Annandale, VA 22003 (703-941-1065). Take the Beltway (Route 495) to Little River Turnpike east (Route 236); turn left at first traffic light onto Hummer Road. Proceed ½ mile, then left into Annandale Community Park; follow signs to Nature Center.

- Open weekdays, 9 A.M.–5 P.M.; Saturday and Sunday, noon–5 P.M. January–February, open weekends only. Closed Tuesday, and Thanksgiving, Christmas, and New Year's Day.
- Parking available.
- Wheelchair access.
- Strollers permitted.
- Reservations are necessary for special programs.
- Picnic area and tot lot in the park.
- Group tours for schools and other youth organizations.
- "Stepping-Out" for children ages 3–5 on Monday; reservations required.

The Nature Center focuses on the discovery of evidence of landscape changes caused by the forces of nature and man. There are seasonal displays and small live animals such as turtles and snakes. Many of the exhibits provide "hands-on" options. The surroundings, including an oak forest, woodland stream, and traces of a Civil War railroad as well as timbering and farming lands, make for an interesting visit. There are discovery programs, story-telling sessions, and many other special events.

Hidden Pond Nature Center

Hidden Pond Park, 8511 Greeley Boulevard, West Springfield, VA, 22152 (703-451-9588). Take Route 95 south to Springfield exit; bear right on Keene Mill Road; continue about 5 miles to Greeley Boulevard; turn left. Or, take the Beltway (Route 495) to Route 95 south; quickly exit at Springfield; bear right to Keene Mill Road and continue as above.

- Open weekdays, 9 A.M.–5 P.M.; Saturday and Sunday, noon–5 P.M. January–February, open weekends only. Closed Tuesday, and Thanksgiving, Christmas, and New Year's Day.
- Parking available.
- Wheelchair access.
- Strollers permitted.
- Wide variety of programs for all ages. Group tours by reservation.
- Picnic area and tot lot.

The nature center, overlooking Hidden Pond, prepares the visitor for investigating and experiencing the ecology of the pond and stream. Exhibits include an island display on "the food chain" (with live animals), a touch-table, a children's corner, and aquatic displays of all kinds. The building also boasts a lab/all-purpose meeting room with a microprojector which allows the contents of a specimen slide to be magnified and projected onto a screen. Outside there are self-guided trails, some leading to the stream valley. If "treasure" hunting is more your thing, the naturalists will gladly loan you nets and buckets so you can go on your own to search in and around Hidden Pond. (Treasures must be returned to the pond before leaving.) Seasonal calendars of special events are available at the center.

Huntley Meadows Park

3701 Lockheed Boulevard (at Harrison Lane in Hybla Valley), Alexandria, VA 22306 (703-768-2525). Take the Beltway (Route 495) to Exit 1 (Richmond Highway, Route 1) south 3½ miles; turn right at Lockheed Boulevard for three blocks to the park entrance on the left at Harrison Lane.

- Park open dawn to dusk. Visitor Center open Monday, Wednesday, Thursday, Friday, 9 A.M.–5 P.M.; Saturday and Sunday, noon–5 P.M. Closed Tuesday, and Thanksgiving, Christmas, and New Year's Day.
- Parking available.
- Wheelchair access to some areas. Plans are to open a new boardwalk which will have wheelchair access.
- Strollers permitted.
- Group tours by reservation.
- Picnic Stoneybrook, or Lee District Park

This 1,261 acre park, tucked away in the midst of suburbia, will introduce your children to several diverse habitats — wetland, forest, and meadow. Dogue, Little Hunting, and Barnyard Run Creeks flow through the park on their way to the Potomac River. There are hundreds of plant species and many varieties of birds. Be sure to bring your bird books and binoculars. Climb to the top of the wetlands observation tower and you might see some of the 70 nesting species and 130 different migratory birds that have been sighted here, including yellow-crowned night herons, blue herons, cuckoos, and ovenbirds — which nest on the ground. A ⅔ mile wetland boardwalk trail takes you into the marsh where you can look for some of the other residents of this park, including raccoons, beavers, gray fox, and crayfish.

The Visitor Center includes several interactive exhibits depicting the cultural and natural history of the park and the natural habitats that are found here. Children especially enjoy the wetlands diorama and photo murals. Special programs are presented in the auditorium. For more information on park programs see the latest issues of *ParkTakes*, a quarterly publication of the Fairfax County Park Authority or call the Visitor Center at the number listed above.

Long Branch Nature Center

625 South Carlin Springs Road, Arlington, VA 22204 (703-358-6535). Take Route 50 west to South Carlin Springs Road exit. Turn left on South Carlin Springs Road, then look for the Long Branch Nature Center on the left side of the road.

- Open Tuesday–Saturday, 10 A.M.–5 P.M.; Sunday, 1–5 P.M. Closed Monday and holidays.
- Park at the nature center or in adjoining Glencarlyn Park.
- Wheelchair access.
- Strollers permitted.
- Picnic in nearby Glencarlyn Park.

This nature center is situated in a hardwood forest with hiking and biking trails, swamp, meadow, and streams. The Washington and Old Dominion (W & OD) Bike Path (see Chapter 6, Parks and Recreation) passes through the area. The Nature Center offers many things for children and adults to explore, including displays of live reptiles and amphibians, an indoor turtle/fish pond, seasonal displays, and a discovery corner for young naturalists. The Special Events Calendar for Arlington County Nature Centers, published quarterly, advertises special programs for preschoolers through adults. Although most programs are free, reservations are required and can be made by calling the Nature Center. See Glen Carlyn Park in Chapter 6, Parks and Recreation.

Claude Moore Colonial Farm at Turkey Run

6310 Georgetown Pike, McLean, VA 22101 (703-442-7557). Take the Beltway (Route 495) to Georgetown Pike (Route 193) east 2½ miles; go left onto access road; farm is ½ mile on left. Or, take George Washington Memorial Parkway to Route 123 south; after one mile turn left on Route 193, then right onto access road; farm is ½ mile on the left.

- Open April–December, Wednesday–Sunday, 10 A.M.–4:30 P.M. Closed January–March, holidays, and rainy days.
- Adults, $2; children, 3–12, $1; members free.
- Parking available.
- Wheelchair access. Please call ahead to make arrangements.
- Strollers permitted.
- Group visits must be scheduled in advance.

Step back to 1771 and observe a lower-income farm family dressed in period clothing going about their daily chores of planting, gardening, harvesting, cooking, and tending the animals, using period tools and technology. Dirt paths lead past the tobacco barn, crop fields, the one-room house, orchard, and pastures.

Special activities include seven special events, such as an 18th century Market Fair in July and seasonal harvests. Call for a calendar of special events and a list of educational programs.

Potomac Vegetable Farms

9627 Leesburg Pike (Route 7), Vienna, VA 22182 (703-759-2119). Take the Beltway (Route 495) to Route 7 west; continue for 4½ miles to entrance on left.

- Open daily; call for hours.
- Parking available.
- Wheelchair access limited as there are no sidewalks.
- Call in advance for school or community groups. $3 per child for guided farm tours.
- Picnicking allowed.

This certified organic farm specializes in lettuce and greens, tomatoes, beans, squash, peppers, cut-your-own flowers, and fresh eggs. Potomac Vegetable Farms also grows pumpkins and berries for pick-it-yourselfers. The proprietors encourage informal visits to their fields, animals, and ongoing operations. They are also happy to recycle your used (and in good condition) egg cartons and plastic and paper bags.

River Farm Garden Park

The American Horticultural Society, East Boulevard Drive, Alexandria, VA 22308 (703-768-5700) Located between Old Town and Mount Vernon. Take the George Washington Parkway through Old Town and beyond. Turn left on East Boulevard Drive and follow the signs to River Farm Garden Park.

- Grounds are open year round, Monday–Friday, 8:30 A.M.–5 P.M.; May–October, also open Saturday, 10 A.M.–4 P.M. Please phone ahead to verify Saturday openings.
- Parking available.
- Wheelchair access to grounds and to house with assistance.
- Strollers permitted.
- Guided tours for 6 to 12 children can be arranged by calling in advance.
- Cottage gift shop in the house.

River Farm was one of the original five farms comprising George Washington's Mt. Vernon estate. Be sure to show your children the great walnut tree between the farm house and terrace wall that is said to have been one of Washington's favorites. Two Kentucky coffee bean trees also are survivors from Washington's time — he introduced this variety of tree to the area.

Visitors are welcome to tour the house and the farm. A self-guided tour helps you identify the many flowers, plants, and trees that are cultivated at River Farm. In the fall, as you wander through the wildflower meadow, goldfish pool water garden, and rose gardens you may see migrating water fowl.

Special activities include an annual Spring Festival, usually held in May, featuring demonstrations and talks on gardening topics, and sale of plants, books, food, and seeds.

Scotts Run Nature Preserve

7400 Georgetown Pike, at the intersection with Swink's Mill Road, Great Falls, VA. No phone on site. Take the Beltway (Route 495) to Virginia, Route 193 west; proceed on Route 193 less than a mile to Scotts Run Nature Preserve parking lot on the right. Mailing address: Fairfax County Park Authority, 3701 Pender Drive, Fairfax, VA 22030 (703-246-5700).

- Open daily, dawn until dusk.
- Parking available.
- Picnicking permitted.

Fairfax County naturalists refer to Scotts Run as the "Hot Spot for Wild Flowers." The surroundings also offer hiking, bird-watching, and spectacular scenery. The 3-mile trail follows a "stepping-stone stream" to a small waterfall and an awe-inspiring view of the Potomac. It is said that many of the huge trees are more than 100 years old. Below lies an abundance of dogwood and papaw as well as wildflowers in the spring. The trail gets more challenging as it approaches the river.

Theodore Roosevelt Island

George Washington Memorial Parkway, Arlington, VA (703-285-2601). Take Theodore Roosevelt Bridge to George Washington Memorial Parkway north, on the Virginia side of the Potomac River; follow signs to parking area for Roosevelt Island. Not accessible from the southbound lanes. Mailing address: Turkey Run Park, George Washington Memorial Parkway, McLean, VA 22101.

- Open daily, 7 A.M. to dusk.
- Parking available.
- Wheelchair access, with assistance.
- Strollers permitted.
- Call for information on guided tours and lectures.
- Picnicking allowed.

From the parking lot cross over a footbridge to enter this 88-acre wildlife refuge, preserved in its natural state as a tribute to conservationist President Theodore Roosevelt. The deeply wooded island includes a clearing where a 23-foot bronze statue of Roosevelt rises from a plaza that incorporates small shallow pools. It is a pleasant place to rest or have a picnic lunch. The park boasts a vast variety of plants, beasts, birds, and bugs in the swamps and forests. Sturdy, low-heeled shoes are a must for exploring the 2½ miles of foot trails that wander through the varied habitats. Insect repellant is recommended, especially in the summer.

6   Parks and Recreation

The Washington area both inside and outside the Beltway boasts an impressive array of parks. Parks provide a natural backdrop for outdoor activities of all kinds for all ages and interests, including hiking, picnicking, studying nature, and playing sports such as tennis, golf, biking, ice skating, and horseback riding. For those who prefer to be near or on the water during Washington's sweltering summer months, there are parks such as Montgomery County's Lake Needwood, where families can ride on the Needwood Queen, a replica of a Mississippi sternwheeler. Also, at the area's water-oriented parks, visitors can rent rowboats, pedal boats, or canoes to pilot their own voyages. Community parks often feature recreation centers offering a variety of summer programs for children. Nature centers in area parks enhance appreciation for the natural environment through their talks and exhibits on park wildlife and history. (See Chapter 5, Nature, for descriptions of local nature centers.) Then, there are the simple, unstructured pleasures of a challenging playground, a carousel or miniature train ride, or a leisurely picnic in some scenic bower.

All of the sights listed in this chapter have parking, wheelchair access, and rest rooms, unless otherwise noted. Most parks charge nominal fees for their activities and services — swimming, golf, boat launching, carousel rides, and so on.

State, Local, and National Parks and Recreation Departments

For information about the area's parks, programs, and facilities call or write to the following state and local park and recreation departments.

Maryland

Maryland National Capital Park and Planning Commission, Montgomery County Department of Parks

9500 Brunette Avenue, Silver Spring, MD 20901 (301-495-2525).

Maryland National Capital Park and Planning Commission, Prince George's County Department of Parks

6600 Kenilworth Avenue, Riverdale, MD 20737 (301-699-2407).

Maryland State Parks

580 Taylor Avenue, Tawes Office Building, E-3, Annapolis, MD 21401 (410-974-3771).

Montgomery County Department of Recreation

12210 Bushey Drive, Silver Spring, MD 20902 (301-217-6860).

Virginia

City of Alexandria, Department of Parks and Cultural Activities

1108 Jefferson Street, Alexandria, VA 22314 (703-838-4343).

Arlington County, Department of Parks, Recreation, and Community Resources

Courthouse Plaza #1, Suite 414, 2100 Clarendon Boulevard, Arlington, VA 22201 (703-358-3323).

City of Fairfax, Department of Parks and Recreation

3730 Old Lee Highway, Fairfax, VA 22030 (703-385-7858).

Fairfax County, Department of Recreation and Community Services

12011 Government Center Parkway, Suite 1050, Fairfax, VA 22035 (703-324-5570).

Fairfax County Park Authority

3701 Pender Drive, Fairfax, VA 22030 (703-246-5700).

Northern Virginia Regional Park Authority

5400 Ox Road, Fairfax Station, VA 22039 (703-352-5900).

Washington, DC

District of Columbia, Department of Recreation and Parks

3149 16th Street, NW, Washington, DC 20010 (202-673-7660).

National Park Service, National Capitol Parks, East

1900 Anacostia Drive, SE, Washington, DC 20020 (202-690-5185).

National Park Service, National Capital Region

1100 Ohio Drive, SW, Washington, DC 20242 (202-619-7222).

Daily recording of park events on Dial-A-Park: 202-619-PARK. To receive free monthly calendar of events call 202-619-7222.

For a general map showing the national parks, or a map of and information on a particular national park, write: Department of the Interior, National Park Service, P.O. Box 37127, Washington, DC 20013.

Washington, DC

Anacostia Park

1900 Anacostia Drive, SE, Washington, DC 20020 (202-690-0862). Along the Anacostia River between South Capitol Street and Benning Road, SE. The Anacostia Freeway parallels the park boundary.

- Open daily dawn to dusk.
- Picnic tables.
- Outdoor swimming pool operated by DC Department of Recreation. For schedule and fees call 202-889-3665.
- Supervised roller skating May–September. For information on times and fees call 202-472-3873.

This large area along the east bank of the Anacostia River has playing fields for football and baseball, picnic spots, playgrounds, basketball courts, a swimming pool, and an outdoor pavilion for roller skating and community gatherings. One section of the park has been designated as a bird sanctuary where you might see a variety of marshland birds such as herons, egrets, ducks, and geese. For a close-up view of plants and wildlife, bring your own canoe and paddle along the banks of the river and its inlets.

Kenilworth Aquatic Gardens are located in this park. See Chapter 5, Nature, for more information.

Battery-Kemble Park

On Chain Bridge Road, NW, below Loughboro Road, Washington, DC. The park is bounded by Chain Bridge Road, MacArthur Boulevard, 49th Street, and Nebraska Avenue. Mailing address: Rock Creek Park, 5000 Glover Road, NW, Washington, DC 20015 (202-426-6833).

- Open daily dawn to dusk.
- Limited parking on site during the summer. In winter, park on nearby streets.
- No rest rooms.
- Picnicking permitted.
- Cross-country skiing and sledding.

Without leaving the city you can enjoy an afternoon picnic in this fine, hilly, woodsy park. Before or after eating you might want to take a nature walk. In the winter, Battery-Kemble is one of the better area locations for sledding and cross-country skiing. There also are baseball, soccer, and football playing fields. The park is ideal for kite flying.

East Potomac Park

Turn off Maine Avenue, SW near the 14th Street Bridge and follow signs, or follow Ohio Drive from the Lincoln Memorial. Mailing address: National Park Service, 1100 Ohio Drive, SW,
Washington, DC 20242 (202-619-7222).

- Open daily dawn to dusk.
- Picnic tables.
- Outdoor tennis courts. Reservations and fees call 202-554-
  5962.
- Outdoor swimming pool. Schedule and fees call 202-863-
  1309.
- Golf and miniature golf. Schedule and fees call 202-863-9007.

East Potomac Park is a 1½-mile-long finger of land between the
Washington channel and the Potomac River. The path along the
sea wall is fine for strolling, biking, and fishing. Kids will enjoy an
unusual hands-on statue, "The Awakening," by J. Seward John-
son, which resembles a giant about to arise from the ground.
Other attractions include an outdoor swimming pool, tennis,
miniature golf, a driving range, and two 18-hole golf courses.
Hains Point, at the southern edge of the park, is a pleasant place
to stay cool on a hot summer day. No matter how steamy the rest
of the city is, there is always a breeze at Hains Point.

Fort Stevens Park

Located at Piney Branch Road and Quakenbos Street, NW,
Washington, DC. Mailing address: Rock Creek Park, 5000
Glover Road, NW, Washington, DC 20015 (202-426-6833).

- Open daily dawn to dusk.
- No rest rooms.
- Picnicking permitted.

"Get down, you fool!" shouted Lt. Col. Oliver Wendell Holmes at
President Lincoln, whose tall figure towered over the ramparts of

Fort Stevens. The year was 1864 and Confederate troops were advancing down Georgia Avenue toward the Capitol. Although rebel bullets whiz by no more, children can climb on the restored earthworks and gun emplacements that remain in this small park, or have a picnic under the trees. The historian at Rock Creek Park gives tours of the park and reenactments of the battle of Fort Stevens are performed. For information on the forts that guarded the Capitol, call 202-426-6829.

Montrose Park

Located on R Street at Avon Place, NW, Washington, DC. Take Wisconsin Avenue north from Georgetown to right turn on R Street. Park is on the left. Mailing address: Rock Creek Park, 5000 Glover Road, NW, Washington, DC 20015 (202-426-6833).

- Open daily dawn to dusk.
- On-street parking.
- Picnic tables.
- Outdoor tennis courts, no reservations needed.

Open space provides room for games at this popular city park, which features tennis courts, a boxwood maze, a playground, and picnic tables. This is a nice place to visit after a trip to nearby Dumbarton Oaks (see Chapter 2, Main Sights and Museums in Washington, DC, and Chapter 5, Nature).

Rock Creek Park

5000 Glover Road, NW, Washington, DC 20015 (202-426-6833). The park includes areas on both sides of Rock Creek Parkway, NW and connects with other parkland throughout the city.

- Open daily dawn to dusk.
- To reserve picnic areas call DC Department of Recreation, 202-673-7646.

- Tennis courts at 16th and Kennedy Streets and Beach and Tilden Streets (Pierce Mill) open from April–mid November by reservation only; call Guest Services, 202-723-2669. The rest of the year courts are free on a first-come, first-served basis.
- Tennis courts at Park Road, NW, east of Pierce Mill, open May–September by reservation only. Reserve and pay fees through Washington Area Tennis Patrons at the courts.
- The 18-hole golf course at 16th and Rittenhouse Streets, NW, 202-723-9832, is open daily dawn to dusk. Closed Christmas. Clubs and carts can be rented.
- Rock Creek Park Horse Center, Inc., Military and Glover Roads, NW, 202-362-0117, is the only riding facility in Washington, DC. The Center offers barn tours, a summer camp, lessons for all ages, trail rides, and more.
- Hiking, biking, equestrian, and cross-country skiing trails, and sledding.
- Rent bikes, canoes, and rowboats at Thompson's Boat House, 202-333-4861, opposite the entrance to Rock Creek Parkway at Virginia Avenue (near the Watergate).

Rock Creek is a woodsy 1,754-acre park, about 4 miles long and 1 mile wide, that runs through northwest Washington from the Potomac River into Montgomery County. Picnic groves with tables, fireplaces, and shelters are abundant. A 1½ mile exercise course begins near Calvert Street and Connecticut Avenue, NW and another begins at 16th and Kennedy Streets. The park's many resources include: the National Zoo (see Chapter 2, Main Sights and Museums in Washington, DC), Rock Creek Nature Center and Planetarium (see Chapter 5, Nature), Pierce Mill, where millstones are still used to grind corn and wheat into flour, and the Art Barn, site of children's activities and art exhibits. Call 202-244-2482 for information on Art Barn programs.

Bikers and walkers should note that Beach Drive, between Military and Broad Branch Roads, is closed to cars on weekends and holidays. A marked bike trail, much of which is paved, runs from the Lincoln Memorial to Maryland and from the Memorial Bridge to the Mount Vernon Trail in Virginia.

Hiking trails are maintained by the Potomac Appalachian Trail Club. Check at the Nature Center (202-426-6829) for information on hiking trails.

Montgomery County, Maryland

Black Hill Regional Park

20930 Lake Ridge Drive, Boyds, MD 20841 (301-972-9396; 302-972-3476, Visitor Center). Take the Beltway (Route 495) to Route 270 north; exit at Boyds-Clarksburg (Route 121); turn left on Clarksburg Road; continue for 2½ miles then take a sharp left on Old Baltimore Road; continue for 1 mile to park entrance on right.

- Open March–October, 6 A.M.–sunset; November–February, 7 A.M.–sunset. Closed Thanksgiving, Christmas, and New Year's Day.
- Wheelchair access includes pontoon boat.
- Picnic tables, grills, and shelters. Call to reserve shelters.
- Horseshoe pits, volleyball courts, and playgrounds.
- Groups with advance reservations can tour Little Seneca Lake on the "Osprey," a pontoon boat, during the week. The general public can ride the boat on weekends. Fee $1 per person.
- Boat launching and canoe and rowboat rentals.
- Fishing (with Maryland fishing license) in Little Seneca Lake.
- Hiking, biking, and equestrian trails.

This park is located on 1,854 acres, including Little Seneca Lake with almost 16 miles of shoreline. The two challenging playgrounds are favorites of Green Acres' younger classes. There is also a picnic area, a small nature center, a paved hiker/biker trail, and 10 miles of unpaved hiking and equestrian trails. A variety of special events and programs take place throughout the year. For information on the exhibits and programs of the Black Hill Regional Park Visitor Center, see Chapter 5, Nature.

Cabin John Regional Park

7400 Tuckerman Lane, Rockville, MD 20852 (301-299-4555).
Take the Beltway (Route 495) to Old Georgetown Road; go
north to left on Tuckerman Lane; continue to park at corner
of Westlake Drive.

- Open daily dawn to dusk. Closed Thanksgiving, Christmas,
  and New Year's Day.
- Picnic tables, grills, and shelters. To reserve group picnic areas
  call 301-495-2525.
- Indoor and outdoor tennis courts and practice walls. For
  reservations and fees call 301-365-2440.
- Ice skating rink open September–June. For fees, schedule,
  and lessons call 301-365-2246 or 301-365-0585.
- Camping area with 7 primitive, walk-in sites. For permits and
  fees call 301-495-2525.
- Miniature train operates April and September, weekends and
  school holidays; May–August, open daily. For schedule and
  fees call 301-495-2525.
- Snack bar open weekends.
- Athletic field reservations call 301-495-2525.
- Hiking and biking trails.

This park has many attractions for children, including a miniature replica of an 1863 train that offers a brief, pleasant trip
through a wooded portion of the 525-acre park. The playground
features adventure playland, a large play unit designed to encourage creative play on ropes, ladders, and tube slides. In
addition to the ice skating rink, other sports facilities include
lighted indoor and outdoor tennis courts, handball courts, a
volleyball court, a lighted baseball field, and five softball fields
(one lighted). The park also features a hiker/biker trail and the
Locust Grove Nature Center (see Chapter 5, Nature).

Candy Cane City

Beach Drive at East Leland Street, Chevy Chase, MD. Take Connecticut Avenue to East-West Highway; then go east on East-West Highway to Beach Drive; right on Beach Drive to park entrance at Leland Street corner. Mailing address: Maryland National Parks and Planning Commission, 9500 Brunette Avenue, Silver Spring, MD 20901 (301-495-2525).

- Open dawn to dusk year round.
- Picnic tables, grills, and shelter.
- Enclosed building for parties. For reservation and fees call 301-495-2525.

With a variety of equipment to crawl through, slide down, climb on, and swing from, this playground is a real crowd pleaser. The elasticrete underneath helps cushion the feet and protect against injury. The adjacent recreation center, like other Montgomery County park centers, has ball fields, tennis courts, a well-equipped building, covered picnic area, and a year-round activity program.

C&O Canal National Historical Park/ Great Falls, MD

The Park follows the Potomac River from Georgetown to Cumberland, MD. Georgetown canal information center in Foundry Mall between 30th and Thomas Jefferson Streets, NW (202-653-5844). Great Falls canal information center in the Great Falls Tavern, 11710 MacArthur Boulevard, Potomac, MD 20854 (301-299-3613).

- Open daily dawn to dusk.
- Entrance fee at Great Falls, $3 per vehicle; $1 per person not arriving by car.
- Wheelchair access to Great Falls Tavern and boat rides.
- Picnic tables in some areas.

- Rent canoes, boats, and bicycles at Thompson's Boat House, 202-333-9543; Fletcher's Boathouse, 202-244-0462; or Swain's Lock, 301-299-9006.
- The Canal Clipper Barge, a replica of 19th century mule-drawn barges, operates on the Canal from mid-April through mid-October. For information on the trips from Great Falls Tavern, MD call 301-299-2026, and from Georgetown call 202-472-4376. The barge ride lasts about 1½ hours and costs $4 for adults ($3 for seniors) and $2 for children. The barge can be reserved by groups at special rates for a one-hour day trip or a two-hour evening journey.
- Snack bar at Great Falls Visitor Center open April–October.
- **WARNING:** Do not wade in the water or climb on rocks in restricted areas. The current here is exceptionally powerful; many people who did not obey the warning signs have drowned.

The Canal towpath is a pleasant place to walk and bike ride. Canal canoeing is also popular, but you should be prepared to portage around each lock. There are various places to enter and exit the canal and a number of pleasant picnic sites. You will see the locks of the historic C&O Canal, through which the mule-drawn barges used to travel between Cumberland and George-town. Contact either visitor center for an official map and guide.

The three-room Canal Museum, in the Great Falls Tavern, features exhibits such as a lock model and artifacts from the days when the canal was operating, historic photographs, and short films explaining the story of the canal.

The Swain's Lock part of the canal (off Swain's Lock Road) is ideal for boating, fishing, and picnicking. Boat rentals, bait, and snacks are available at the lockkeeper's house.

The Great Falls area of the C & O Canal is one of the most impressive natural sights in this area, with spectacular rock formations. Here the river drops more than 70 feet over nu-merous falls and proceeds downstream through rapids and river islands to its junction with the tidal estuary at Little Falls (Chain

Bridge). The park consists of 900 acres on the Maryland side of the Potomac. Children ages 6 and older will enjoy the Billy Goat Trail, a vigorous, three mile, three hour round trip hike that provides spectacular views of the Potomac River and Mather Gorge. Stop at the Great Falls Visitor Center to get directions for this and other less strenuous hikes.

Little Bennett Regional Park

23701 Frederick Road, Clarksburg, MD 20871 (301-972-6581). Take the Beltway (Route 495) to Route 270 north; exit at Boyds-Clarksburg (Route 121); turn right on Clarksburg Road and continue for 1 mile; turn left on Route 355; continue for ¾ mile to park entrance on right.

- Open daily dawn to dusk.
- Picnic tables and grills.
- Fishing (with Maryland fishing license) at Little Bennett Creek and Little Seneca Lake.
- Family camping (91 sites) April–October; no reservations; fee is charged. Primitive camping areas for groups; call 301-972-9187.
- Camp store at registration office.
- Hiking and equestrian trails.

Take a short ride north of the busy Washington, DC area to a pleasant and secluded camping and hiking area in Little Bennett Regional Park. The family campground features picnic tables and grills, comfort stations (sinks, showers, and toilets), water spigots, horseshoes, volleyball, and a full program of nature activities. This is also an excellent place to go for a day hike. Pack a lunch and set out on one of the park's many trails. The remains of several sites of historic interest are located on these trails — sumac and saw mills, a 19th century schoolhouse, and several houses.

Martin Luther King, Jr. Park

1100 Jackson Road, Silver Spring, MD 20904 (301-622-1193).
Take the Beltway (Route 495) to New Hampshire Avenue
north; turn right on Jackson Road. The park is behind White
Oak Intermediate School.

- Open daily dawn to dusk.
- Playground is designed for use by children with special needs.
- Picnic tables, grills, and shelters.
- Indoor swimming pool. For schedule and fees call 301-622-4191.
- Outdoor tennis courts.
- Athletic fields.

This park has a unique feature: the Martin Luther King, Jr.
Playground for All Children. The playground features attractions
for kids with special needs, including multi-level sandboxes with
wheelchair access and specially designed swings that do not
require leg power to pump. There is a shelter at the playground
(covering the sandbox area) that includes picnic tables and
benches. The park offers tennis and basketball courts, an Olym-
pic-sized indoor swimming pool (with classes for a full range of
ages and abilities) and athletic fields (softball, baseball, and
soccer). There are also a play area set aside for lawn games and
another picnic area with grills.

Montgomery Aquatic Center

5900 Executive Boulevard, Rockville, MD 20852 (301-468-4211). Take Rockville Pike (Route 355) north to left on Nichol-
son Lane; turn right on Executive Boulevard.

- Open weekdays, 11:30 A.M.–2:30 P.M., 3:30–5 P.M., 7–8:20 P.M.;
  Friday, 7–9 P.M.; Saturday, 2–4 P.M., 5–7 P.M.; Sunday 2–5 P.M.
  Call first to confirm hours.
- Metrorail Red Line (White Flint).
- Montgomery County residents pay $3 per session; nonresi-
  dents pay $5. Family and seasonal passes are also available.

- Lockers (bring your own lock), saunas, hot tubs, and weight room.
- Swimming lessons, swim and diving teams.
- Racquetball court.
- Outdoor playground and field.

The main attraction at this spectacular new facility is a 51-meter, L-shaped indoor swimming pool. For divers there are 1 and 3-meter springboards and an 18-foot diving well with 5, 7½, and 10-foot platforms. For an exciting thrill children and parents will enjoy the 233 foot water slide. For younger children there is a shallow pool featuring a waterfall.

Rock Creek Regional Park, Lake Needwood

6700 Needwood Road, Derwood, MD 20855 (301-948-5053). Take the Beltway (Route 495) to Georgia Avenue north; turn left on Norbeck Road. Turn right on Muncaster Mill Road, continue to left turn on Needwood Road. Follow signs to Visitor Center.

- Open daily dawn to dusk.
- Picnic tables, grills, and shelters.
- Two golf courses, 18-hole and 9-hole. For schedule and fees call 301-948-1075.
- Groups with advance reservations can ride the "Needwood Queen" during the week. The general public can ride on weekends. For schedule and fees call 301-762-9500.
- Canoe, rowboat, and paddleboat rentals. For schedule and fees call 301-762-9500.
- Fishing (with Maryland fishing license) in Lake Needwood. Licenses available at boat shop.
- Snack bar.

Lake Needwood is a man-made lake, well-used for boating and fishing. You can take a trip on this 74-acre lake aboard the "Needwood Queen," replica of a Mississippi sternwheeler, or rent a pedal boat, rowboat, sailboat, or canoe. Needwood is a good place to go fishing. You can purchase bait at the boathouse. There are also play areas, picnic groves, and hiking trails. The Meadowside Nature Center is located here (see Chapter 5, Nature).

Seneca on the C&O Canal

Rileys Road, Seneca, MD. Take the Beltway (Route 495) to River Road north; at dead end turn left on Route 112; go less than one mile to left on Rileys Road. Mailing address: Great Falls Tavern, 11710 MacArthur Boulevard, Potomac, MD 20854 (301-299-2026 or 301-299-3613).

- Open daily dawn to dusk.
- No wheelchair access to lock house.
- Boat ramp.
- Picnic tables and grills.
- Snack bar.

At this spot, Riley's Lock, the Seneca Creek flows under the C&O Canal's Seneca Aqueduct into the Potomac. There are good picnic spots along the canal and fishing in the creek and river. Girl Scouts give tours of the lock house weekend afternoons during spring, summer, and fall.

Seneca Creek State Park

11950 Clopper Road, Gaithersburg, MD 20878 (301-924-2127). Take the Beltway (Route 495) to Route 270 north; exit at National Bureau of Standards, Darnestown; turn right at the second light on Clopper Road; continue 1½ miles to park headquarters on the left.

- Open May–September, 8 A.M.–sunset; October–April, 10 A.M.–sunset.
- Car entry fee, May–September, Maryland, $3; out-of-state, $4. Wednesday is half price day. October–April, weekdays, free; weekends and holidays, 50¢. Walkers or bikers, $1, though you may not be charged if you do not plan to picnic.
- Wheelchair access includes boats and visitor center.

- Picnic tables, grills, and shelters.
- Canoe, paddleboat, sailboat, and rowboat rentals and pontoon boat rides. For schedule and fees for individuals and groups call 301-924-2127.
- Fishing.
- Cross country skiing, sledding, and ice skating.
- Biking, hiking, equestrian, and cross-country skiing trails.
- Snack bar.

This stream valley park begins at Route 355 north of Gaithersburg and covers both sides of Seneca Creek for 13 miles, all the way to the Potomac River. Some 500 acres are developed for public use, and a number of self-guided tours meander through this area. Follow the signs or stop by the Clopper Road office for free trail guide booklets. There are several historic sights within the park — old mills, stone quarries, an old schoolhouse, and Indian grounds. No pets, including horses, are permitted in the developed area of the park, but riding is permitted in the 4,000 undeveloped acres.

Sligo Creek Park

Parallels Sligo Creek Parkway from University Boulevard in Montgomery County to New Hampshire Avenue in Prince George's County. Mailing address: Maryland National Parks and Planning Commission, 9500 Brunette Avenue, Silver Spring, MD 20901 (301-495-2525).

- Open daily dawn to dusk.
- Picnic tables and grills.
- Outdoor tennis courts.
- Golf course. For schedule and fees call 301-585-6006.
- Athletic fields. For fees and reservations call 301-495-2525.

This peaceful park, which runs through Silver Spring and Takoma Park, is a pleasant place to bike, walk, or have an old-fashioned family picnic. Remarkably, deer have been sighted recently in this urban park. There are picnic tables, drinking fountains, playground equipment, a hiking/exercise course, athletic fields, tennis courts, and basketball courts. A flat (perfect for families) bike trail parallels the creek for 8 miles. Begin at Piney Branch Road and Sligo Creek Parkway, continue until you cross University Boulevard. A spur will take you to the Kemp Mill Shopping Center. From there you can continue to nearby Wheaton Regional Park. Community buildings are located at the Dennis Avenue and Wayne Avenue intersections.

Wheaton Regional Park

2000 Shorefield Road, Wheaton, MD 20902 (301-622-0056). Take the Beltway (Route 495) to Georgia Avenue north; right on Shorefield Road to park entrance.

- Open 9 A.M. to sunset.
- Picnic tables, grills, and shelters.
- Indoor and outdoor tennis courts. For fees and reservations call 301-649-4049.
- Fishing in a 5-acre stocked lake.
- Riding at Wheaton Park Stables, 301-622-3311.
- Covered ice skating rink operates from November–March. Call for fees and lessons, 301-649-2250.
- Volleyball, basketball, and handball courts and athletic fields. For information on use of the 4 softball fields and 2 baseball fields (one lighted) call 301-495-2525.
- Carousel and train rides, April and September, weekends and school holidays; May–August, open daily. For schedule and fees call the train station, 301-946-6615 or carousel, 301-946-6396.
- Snack bar open, weekends and holidays from late spring–Labor Day.
- Hiking and biking trails.

This 500-acre park in the heart of Montgomery County is a great favorite with area residents, and for good reason: there is something for every age group. The park boasts many child-pleasing features including a 10-minute, two-mile miniature train ride. The Herschell-Spillman Carousel, built at the turn of the century, is enjoyed by children and adults of all ages. The park offers a 2-mile paved bicycle trail, 7 miles of hiking trails, and horseback riding stables. There are lighted basketball, handball, and tennis courts. An all-weather bubble encloses six of the tennis courts. There is also Pine Lake, a 5-acre lake stocked with several species of fish. For information on the Brookside Nature Center and the Brookside Gardens located in the park see Chapter 5, Nature.

White's Ferry

24801 White's Ferry Road, Dickerson, MD 20842 (301-349-5200). Take the Beltway (Route 495) to Route 270 north; exit at Route 28 west towards Dawsonville; take Route 107 west until it becomes White's Ferry Road.

- Ferry operates daily, 5 A.M.–11 P.M.
- Fees per car, $4 round trip; $2.25 one way. No charge for large groups of children on foot, for example, scout troops.
- Rowboat, canoe, and bicycle rentals.
- Store open mid-April through October, weekdays 6 A.M.–7 P.M.; weekends, 6 A.M.–8 P.M. Usually closed from mid-December through mid-April.

The General Jubal A. Early, a 15-car ferry, crosses the Potomac River, not very wide here, to connect with Route 15 two miles from Leesburg on the Virginia side. The store, equipped with a grill, sells hot and cold food and live bait. The fishing is reputedly good in the area because a Pepco plant upstream in Dickerson warms the river. For a minimum of four people, you (and canoe) get a ride up river to Point-of-Rocks, about 10 miles upstream. Depending on weather conditions, the trip downstream will take about 6 hours, during which you can fish, float, or socialize. You might also plan a hike on the C & O Canal, which crosses White's Ferry Road near the ferry landing.

Woodside Urban Park

Georgia Avenue and Spring Street, Silver Spring, MD. Take 16th Street north to Georgia Avenue, or take the Beltway (Route 495) to Georgia Avenue exit and go south about ½ mile to the park. Mailing address: Maryland National Parks and Planning Commission, 9500 Brunette Avenue, Silver Spring, MD 20901 (301-495-2525).

- Open daily dawn to dusk.
- Picnic tables.
- Paddle tennis courts.
- Horseshoes and shuffleboard court.
- Gymnasium. For fees and reservations call 301-495-2525.

This 2+ acre area next to the Silver Spring central business district is an exceptionally challenging playground for children of all ages. Equipment includes timber-form climbing structures with cargo nets, tires, firehouse poles, and slides. There are checkers tables, benches, two horseshoe pits, a shuffleboard court, two paddle tennis courts, picnic tables, and a gazebo.

Prince George's County, Maryland

Cosca Regional Park

11000 Thrift Road, Clinton, MD 20735 (301-868-1397). Take the Beltway (Route 495) to Branch Avenue south; right on Woodyard to left on Brandywine Road; turn right on Thrift Road to the park.

- Open daily, 7:30 A.M.–dusk, except athletic areas.
- Picnic tables and grills.
- Indoor and outdoor tennis courts. For schedule and fees for indoor courts call 301-868-6462.

- Paddle and rowboat rentals.
- Fishing (with Maryland fishing license).
- Family camping (no reservations).
- Hiking and equestrian trails.
- Snack bar.

The 15-acre lake is the big attraction at this large park. The park also features equestrian and hiking trails, lighted athletic fields, indoor and outdoor tennis courts, picnic grounds and play areas. Campers have access to bathhouses, toilet facilities, water hook-ups, and electricity. For information on Clearwater Nature Center see Chapter 5, Nature.

Fort Washington Park

Fort Washington Road, Fort Washington, MD (301-763-4600). Take the Beltway (Route 495) to Indian Head Highway south; continue for 4½ miles to right on Fort Washington Road; go 3 miles to park entrance. Mailing address: National Capitol Parks-East, 1900 Anacostia Drive, SE, Washington, DC 20020.

- Open daily 8 A.M.–dark.
- Entrance fee, March–November, $3 per vehicle.
- Picnic tables and grills.
- Call ahead to learn about tours of the fort.

Fort Washington, completed in 1824, is an outstanding example of early 19th century coastal defense works. Its ramparts stand 140 feet above the Potomac and are entered by a drawbridge over a dry moat. After touring the fort you can enjoy a picnic lunch on the grounds.

Greenbelt Park

6565 Greenbelt Road, Greenbelt, MD 20770 (301-344-3948). Take the Beltway (Route 495) to Kenilworth Avenue south; turn left on Route 193 to park entrance.

- Open daily dawn to dusk; 24-hour access to the campground.
- Three developed picnic areas with rest rooms, water, tables, and charcoal fireplaces. Call for reservations.
- Family camping (no reservations, nominal fees).
- Hiking trails.

This nearby park (12 miles from downtown Washington), is operated by the National Park Service. The park has 174 woodland campsites for tents, recreation vehicles, and trailers up to 30 feet long. Rest rooms, picnic tables, fireplaces, and water are available, but there are no showers or utility hook-ups. There are several hiking trails and one large field for playing ball. The 1,100-acre woods has picnic areas and three nature trails. The 1-mile fitness trail has 20 exercise stations suitable for family or individual competition. Each station has suggested exercises for different levels of ability.

Piscataway National Park

3400 Bryan Point Road, Accokeek, MD 20607 (301-763-4600). Take the Beltway (Route 495) or the Route 295 bypass to Indian Head Highway south (Route 210). To reach the National Colonial Farm area continue on Indian Head Highway for 10 miles to a right turn on Bryan Point Road; follow to end of the road. To reach the Marshall Hall area continue on Indian Head Highway for 4 more miles to right turn on Marshall Hall Road (Route 227); follow for 3 miles to park entrance.

- Open daily dawn to dusk.
- Limited wheelchair access.
- Picnic areas.
- Boat launching.
- Hiking trails.

Several sections of this park are open to visitors. The Marshall Hall area was once a thriving plantation (only the walls remain) and in later years an amusement park visited by excursion boats from Washington, DC. Today visitors can launch boats, picnic, or take a hike on a wetland trail. The Hard Bargain Farm Environmental Center offers educational programs for groups of school children. Students can study the wildlife found along the river including beavers and great blue herons. The park's visitor center and a fishing dock are located in the National Colonial Farm area. See Chapter 5, Nature, for more information on activities at the farm.

Watkins Regional Park

301 Watkins Park Drive, Upper Marlboro, MD 20772 (301-249-9220). Take the Beltway (Route 495) to Central Avenue (Route 214); follow Route 214 through Largo; right on Enterprise Road to park.

- Open daily 7:30 A.M.–dusk.
- Nonresidents (other than Prince George's and Montgomery Counties) pay nominal entrance fee Memorial Day weekend–Labor Day.
- Picnic tables, grills, and group areas. For fees and reservations call 301-699-2415.
- Indoor and outdoor tennis courts and hitting wall. Free lighting for evening outdoor play. For fees and reservations (indoor courts, early October–early May) call 301-249-9325.
- Miniature golf course. For schedule and fees call in summer 301-390-9224 and in winter 301-249-9325.
- Athletic fields. For league play reservations call 301-699-2415.
- Camping area with 34 campsites and comfort stations and showers. Camp store open weekends in summer. For fees and reservations call 301-249-6900.
- Miniature train ride and carousel open late April–Labor Day. Snack bar in train station. For schedule and fees call in summer 301-390-9224 and in winter 301-249-9325.
- Hiking and biking trails.

This 437-acre park offers a wide variety of activities with something to please every family member. There are athletic fields, tennis and basketball courts, picnic tables and grills, campsites, and hiking and biking trails. A scenic miniature train ride on a replica of an 1863 C. P. Huntington locomotive winds through the park. In addition, visitors can ride a turn-of-the-century carousel, once housed at Chesapeake Beach and now restored to its original splendor. Children will also enjoy a trip to the nature center and farm. (See Chapter 5, Nature, for information on the nature center and Old Maryland Farm.)

Other Parks In Maryland

Catoctin Mountain Park

6602 Foxville Road, Thurmont, MD 21788 (301-663-9330). Take Route 270 west to Frederick; then Route 15 north to second Thurmont exit (Route 77 west); continue for 3 miles to park entrance on right.

- Open daily dawn to dusk.
- Wheelchair access to some areas. Call for specific information.
- Picnic tables and grills.
- Family camping; $6 per night; no reservations.
- Hiking and cross-country skiing trails.

The park has campsites, trails, and fishing streams. In winter, when there may be up to 12 inches of snow, families can go cross-country skiing, snowshoeing, and sledding. A variety of special events for children and adults, including campfire programs and nature walks, make this a park a memorable retreat for the whole family. Some cabins are available for rent, usually for groups.

Cedarville State Forest

Route 4, Box 106A, Brandywine, MD (301-888-1622). Take the Beltway (Route 495) to Route 5 south; then go south on Route 301 to Cedarville exit; continue east for 3 miles to right turn on Cedarville Road to park.

- Park open 8 A.M.–sunset year round. Closed Christmas and Thanksgiving.
- Picnic tables, grills, and shelters.
- Fishing.
- Family and group camping, April–December. There are 130 family campsites (reservations accepted) and 6 youth group campsites (reservations required) for up to 25 persons.
- Nature, hiking, and equestrian trails.

This area was once the winter home of southern Maryland's Piscataway Indians, who lived near Zekiah Swamp, where wildlife was abundant and the weather was mild. There are plenty of picnic tables and charcoal grills (no wood fires permitted). The park features trails for hiking and horseback riding, a pond for fishing, nature walks, and campfire programs. Campers have access to fireplaces, picnic tables, water, showers, a playground, and a dump station. In summer the visitor center at Maryland's only warm water fish hatchery is open to the public.

Cunningham Falls State Park

14039 Catoctin Hollow Road, Thurmont, MD 21788 (301-271-7574). There are two areas to the park; the Manor Area and the William Houck area. Take Route 270 west to Frederick; then Route 15, north from Frederick to entrance to Manor Area on Route 15, adjacent to Catoctin Mountain National Park. To reach the William Houck Area continue north on Route 15 to second Thurmont exit (Route 77 west); continue to park entrance on Catoctin Hollow Road.

- Admission fee per car on weekends and holidays, May–September; and daily, Memorial Day weekend–Labor Day, $4 resident, $5 nonresident. Non-holiday Wednesdays, admission is half price.
- Wheelchair access includes picnic areas and self-guided nature trail.
- Picnic tables, grills, and shelters.
- Swimming in large lake.
- Boat launching.
- Canoe rentals Memorial Day–Labor Day; $4 an hour with $10 deposit.
- Family camping (179 sites), April–mid-October (reservations accepted not more than 10 days in advance), and a camp store.
- Hiking trails including the Appalachian Trail.
- Cross-country skiing and sledding.

Named for the splendid 78-foot waterfall which cascades in a rocky gorge, this 4,446-acre park offers boat launching, canoe rental, fishing, nature walks, campfire programs, picnicking, and playgrounds. The 43-acre lake offers swimming, boating, and fishing. There are family campsites in both areas of the park — Manor Area and William Houck Area.

Patapsco Valley State Park

8020 Baltimore National Pike, Ellicott City, MD 21043 (301-461-5005). On the Patapsco River between Elkridge and Sykesville, MD. Take the Beltway (Route 495) to Route 29 north to Ellicott City and follow signs.

- Admission fee per car, March–October, weekends and holidays, $3 residents, $4 out of state.No charge for cars with senior citizens (62 years and over) .
- Picnic tables, grills, and shelters.
- Canoeing.
- Fishing.
- Family camping (84 sites), April 1–October 1, $10. Group camping (5 sites for up to 25 persons each) by reservation.
- Nature, hiking, equestrian, and cross-country skiing trails.

In 1608 Captain John Smith discovered the river that runs through this historic park. Battles of the Revolutionary War, War of 1812, and Civil War were fought here. Look for the old stone viaduct, the country's first train depot, and the dam that was the world's first underwater hydroelectric power plant. Patapsco offers nature walks, campfire programs, picnicking, playgrounds, hiking and horseback riding trails, and playing fields. Fishing is good in the river and pond. Campers have access to fireplaces, picnic tables, water, toilets, and showers.

Alexandria, Virginia

Cameron Run Regional Park

4001 Eisenhower Avenue, Alexandria, VA 22304 (703-960-0767). From the Beltway (Route 495) exit at Telegraph Road north where you will see signs for the park; bear right immediately onto Pershing Avenue; at stop sign turn left onto Stovall; go one block to Mill Road and follow Mill as it curves under Telegraph Road and feeds onto Eisenhower Avenue.

- Open daily, Memorial Day weekend–Labor Day, 10 A.M.–8 P.M.
- Wave pool admission, ages 12–59, $7; children 2–11 and senior citizens 60 and over, $6; children under 2, free. Discounts on weekdays after 5:30 P.M. Season passes and discount tickets good for 15 admissions are available.
- Wheelchair access including pool and miniature golf course.
- Picnic area.
- Practice batting cage, 25 balls for $1.
- Miniature golf.
- Snack bar.

This water-oriented park is tremendous fun for both children and adults. Cameron Run features the only wave pool in Northern Virginia and a three-flume, 40-foot high water slide. The wave pool is most appropriate for strong swimmers. Children under 13 must be accompanied by a person age 16 or older. Younger children will enjoy the creative play pool featuring giant water creatures — turtle, alligator, snake — rain jets, and a shallow body flume. There is also a very shallow wading pool for the youngest children. Cameron Run recently opened a miniature golf course, with rolling hills and a garden motif, that has full wheelchair access. Baseball enthusiasts will enjoy the practice batting cage.

Chinquapin Center and Park

3210 King Street, Alexandria, VA 22302 (703-931-1127). From Route 395, take King Street east exit, and go down King Street about 3 miles, past T.C. Williams High School to park and center on right.

- Open weekdays, 6 A.M.–10 P.M.; weekends, 8 A.M.–8 P.M. Call for holiday hours.
- General admission fee covers use of pool, sauna, and fitness room, $5 for nonresidents. Fees for city residents, adults, 16–59, $3; children, 2–15, $2.50; senior citizens, 60 and over, $2. Discount passes available.
- Picnic tables and fireplaces.
- Lighted outdoor tennis courts.
- Indoor swimming pool with diving well.
- Fitness room, sauna, and locker rooms.
- Handball/racquetball/wallyball courts. For information on fees and reservations call 703-931-6333.
- Outdoor fitness and nature trail.
- Garden plot rental.
- Snack bar.

Chinquapin Park is a 45-acre park in the heart of Alexandria. It has a nature area and trail, picnic tables, and fireplaces. The center boasts a 25-meter pool with separate diving well, four racquetball courts, a fitness room, saunas, snack bar, and activity rooms. The center offers a birthday party package suitable for children ages 6–12. Included are swimming, lunch or dinner, balloons, and a gift certificate for the birthday child. The center also offers fitness, racquetball, athletic, and aquatics classes for children and adults.

Fort Ward Park

4301 West Braddock Road, Alexandria, VA 22302 (703-838-4843). Take Route 395 to Seminary Road east; after about 1 mile turn left on North Howard Street; then right on West Braddock to entrance.

- Open daily 9 A.M.–sunset.
- Picnic areas. Organizations can reserve the park for group picnics; call 703-838-4831.
- Outdoor tennis courts.
- Athletic fields.

Fort Ward was the fifth largest of 68 Union Forts built to defend Washington during the Civil War. Learn more about it at the park museum or enjoy the azalea and flower displays in the garden area of this 40-acre park. The amphitheater in the park offers free twilight concerts in the summer; for information call the above number. See also Fort Ward Museum in Chapter 3, Main Sights and Museums in Maryland and Virginia.

Arlington County, Virginia

Barcroft Park and Playfield

4100 South Four Mile Run Drive, Arlington, VA 22206 (703-350-3317). Take Route 395 to Shirlington exit; turn left on Four Mile Run Drive; entrance to park is on left.

- Open daily dawn to dusk.
- Picnic tables and grills. To reserve picnic pavilions call 703-358-4747.
- Lighted outdoor tennis courts.
- Nature and biking trails.

In addition to outdoor lights for tennis, soccer, softball, baseball, and basketball, the park's facilities include bicycle trails, nature trails, playground equipment, athletic fields, and picnic area. Tennis courts are lighted until midnight Memorial Day through Labor Day.

Bluemont Park

601 North Manchester Street, Arlington, VA 22205 (703-358-3317). From Rosslyn take Wilson Boulevard to North Manchester Street and park entrance.

- Open daily dawn to dusk.
- Picnic tables, grills, and shelter. For fees and reservations call 703-358-4747.
- Lighted outdoor tennis courts. For fees and reservations call 703-358-4747.
- Frisbee golf.

This park's facilities include basketball courts, baseball diamonds, athletic fields, lighted tennis courts, and a soccer and softball area. There are also picnic areas, playground equipment and bicycle trails. The park connects to Four Mile Run bike trail. Bluemont features the first 9-hole Frisbee golf course in the area.

Bon Air Park

850 North Lexington Street, Arlington, VA 22205 (703-358-3317). Just across Wilson Boulevard from Bluemont Park (see directions to Bluemont Park).

- Open dawn to dusk year round.
- Picnic tables, grills, and shelter. For fees and reservations call 703-358-4747.

This attractive park boasts a flower garden with 3,500 plants and 120 different varieties of roses. In spring the azalea garden is quite spectacular. There is a picnic area near the garden and an open air shelter.

Glencarlyn Park and Playground

301 South Harrison Street, Arlington, VA 22204 (703-358-3317). Take Route 50 west to Carlyn Springs Road; go south on Carlyn Springs Road, then left on South Harrison Street.

- Open daily dawn to dusk.
- Wheelchair access includes a picnic pavilion designed for use by groups.
- Picnic tables, grills, and pavilion. For fees and reservations call 703-358-4747.

Long Branch Nature Center is located in this 90-acre park (see Chapter 5, Nature). The park also offers bike trails, playground equipment, and an open-air shelter.

Lubber Run Park and Recreation Center

North Columbus and Second Street North, Arlington, VA 27203 (703-358-3317; 703-358-4722, recreation center). Take Route 50 west to the North Columbus Street exit; continue to park entrance on Second Street North.

- Open daily dawn to dusk.
- Picnic tables, grills, and shelter. For fees and reservations call 703-358-4747.
- Hiking and biking trails.

This park boasts an amphitheater used for a variety of music and theater programs during the summer months. The park also has an open-air shelter, picnic areas, playground equipment, and hiking and biking trails. The Lubber Run Recreation Center is adjacent to the park.

Potomac Overlook Regional Park

Located in Arlington, VA (703-528-5406). Take George Washington Parkway to Spout Run exit; go right on Lorcom Lane; right on Nellie Custis (becomes Military Road); right on Marcey Road to park entrance. Mailing address: Northern Virginia Regional Park Authority, 5400 Ox Road, Fairfax Station, VA 22039.

- Open daily dawn to dusk.
- Picnic tables.

- Hiking trails.
- Friday evening concert series in the summer.

Here is a welcome open area in the heart of urban Arlington. In the fall and winter an overlook from one of the trails offers a view of the Washington Monument, five miles downstream. An Indian spring provided a source of water for the Necostin Indians who once inhabited these slopes. Visitors can enjoy a variety of exhibits and programs at the park's recently remodeled nature center.

Tuckahoe Park and Playfield

Lee Highway and North Sycamore Street, Arlington, VA 22207 (703-358-3317, 703-358-4747, for reservations). From Rosslyn take Route 29-211 (Lee Highway) until you reach North Sycamore Street; turn right to park.

- Open daily dawn to dusk.
- No rest rooms.
- Picnic tables.
- Lighted outdoor tennis courts.

A unique creative playground with fortress-like climbing equipment is a main attraction at Tuckahoe. The challenging equipment includes a stone tunnel recommended for youngsters who are at least 12 years old. The park also features athletic and softball fields, a soccer area, and tennis courts which are lighted at night from Memorial Day through Labor Day.

Upton Hill Regional Park

6060 Wilson Boulevard, Arlington, VA (703-534-3437). Take Wilson Boulevard to park entrance at Patrick Henry Drive. Mailing address: Northern Virginia Regional Park Authority, 5400 Ox Road, Fairfax Station, VA 22039.

- Open daily dawn to dusk.
- Wheelchair access includes the swimming pool, batting cage, and the first eight holes of miniature golf.

- Picnic tables.
- Outdoor swimming pool open Memorial Day weekend–Labor Day, daily 10 A.M.–8 P.M. For schedule and fees call 703-534-3437.
- Miniature golf. For schedule and fees call 703-237-4953.
- Practice batting cage (25 balls for $1), shuffleboard, horseshoe pits.
- Hiking trails.

This park offers visitors a woodland oasis in the heart of the most populated area of Northern Virginia. Upton Hill offers a large swimming pool complex, woodland nature trails, shuffleboard courts, and horseshoe pits. The popular miniature golf course features the longest miniature golf hole in the world. Other attractions include a gazebo and a scenic pond with waterfall.

Fairfax County, Virginia

Bull Run Marina

13200 Yates Ford Road, Clifton, VA 22024 (703-631-0549). Take the Beltway (Route 495) to Route 66 west; exit at Route 123 south; continue on Route 123 to right turn on Clifton Road; turn left on Henderson to Old Yates Ford Road.

- Open April–Labor Day, Friday through Sunday, dawn to dusk.
- Picnic tables and grills.
- Boat launching and fishing.
- Canoe and boat rentals.
- Hiking trails.
- Snack bar.

This heavily wooded park on Lake Occoquan is an ideal spot for teaching children the art and lore of fishing. Picnic tables and grills are scattered under the trees overlooking the water. There are hiking trails and a playground. Boat launching and rentals are available. Bait and tackle for fishing are sold in the park.

Bull Run Regional Park

Located in Centreville, VA (703-631-0550). Take the Beltway (Route 495) to Route 66 west; exit on Route 29 west (Centreville); continue 3 miles to park signs. Mailing address: Northern Virginia Regional Park Authority, 5400 Ox Road, Fairfax Station, VA 22039.

- Open dawn to dusk, mid-March through Thanksgiving. Skeet and trap shooting and archery open all year.
- Picnic shelters, tables, and grills.
- Outdoor swimming pool open daily, Memorial Day weekend–Labor Day. For schedule and fees call 703-631-0552.

- Miniature and Frisbee golf.
- Family and group campsites. Reservations accepted.
- Hiking and equestrian trails.

This park, deep in Civil War battlefield country, has 1,000 untouched acres of woods, fields, and streams. A half-acre swimming pool is one of its chief attractions. The park offers playgrounds, Frisbee golf, miniature golf, tent and tent-trailer camping sites, picnic areas with grills, a 14-mile nature trail, and some 18 miles of bridle paths. The "Blue Bell Walk" is a treat in spring when many wild flowers are in bloom. A skeet and trap shooting gallery and indoor archery range help make this a park rich in activities to please virtually all interests. Bull Run is a sanctuary for small animals and a wide variety of birds. Each spring the nation's largest all-breed dog show is held here. Call for exact date.

Burke Lake Park

7315 Ox Road, Fairfax Station, VA 22039 (703-323-6600). Take the Beltway (Route 495) to Braddock Road west; continue to left on Burke Lake Road. Park entrance is on left.

- Open daily dawn to dusk.
- Picnic tables and grills.
- Golf course, club and pull cart rentals. For schedule and fees call 703-323-1641.
- Boat launching, rentals, and fishing. Marina open early spring–late November.
- Family campsites and store open spring–fall, no reservations. Groups can reserve a wilderness camping area.
- Miniature train and carousel rides.
- Biking and hiking trails.
- Snack bar and ice cream parlor.

Rent a rowboat, fish, or follow the trails around this 894-acre park. The marina rents boats and sells bait for fishing in the 218-acre lake. There is a 5-mile walking trail, nature trail, 163 wooded campsites, and a camp store. For younger children the park offers a miniature train, old-fashioned carousel, and playground. Picnic areas are plentiful in wooded spots. There is also an 18-hole golf course. Bikes can be rented for use on the blue chip stone bike path.

Fountainhead Regional Park

On Lake Occoquan in Lorton, VA (703-250-9124). About 25 miles south of Washington, DC. Take Route I-95 south; exit at Lorton; right on Lorton Road to Furnace Road; right onto Ox Road; left onto Hampton Road and park entrance. Mailing address: Northern Virginia Regional Park Authority, 5400 Ox Road, Fairfax Station, VA 22039.

- Open March–November, dawn to dusk.
- Wheelchair access includes fishing pier.
- Picnic tables, grills, and shelters.
- Miniature golf.
- Boat launching and boat rentals.
- Fishing pier (licenses are sold at the park).
- Observation deck overlooking lake.
- Hiking and equestrian trails.
- Visitors Center sells snacks, tackle, and bait.

This scenic park on Lake Occoquan is a conservation area that shelters a profusion of birds, geese, ducks, raccoons, deer, and other forest creatures. Picnic tables and grills overlook the water, and nature trails wind over hills and ravines to views of the lake and low marshlands. It is an ideal spot to teach children to fish.

Great Falls Park

9200 Old Dominion Drive, Great Falls, VA 22066 (703-285-2966). Take the Beltway (Route 495) to Georgetown Pike (Route 193); go north 4 miles to right on Old Dominion Drive (Route 738); continue one mile to park entrance. Mailing address: P.O. Box 66, Great Falls, VA 22066.

- Open daily 9 A.M. to dusk; Visitor Center, 10 A.M.–5 P.M. Closed Christmas.
- Entrance fee, $3 per vehicle.
- Parking for handicapped persons near Visitor Center. The Patowmack Canal Interpretive Trail is accessible by wheelchair as far as Lock 1.
- Picnic tables.
- Visitor Center staffed by park rangers. Special tours and walks held all year.
- Hiking and equestrian trails.
- Snack bar.
- **WARNING:** Do not wade in the water or climb on rocks in restricted areas. Stay away from the river's edge and watch children closely at all times. The current here is exceptionally powerful; many people who did not obey the warning signs have drowned.

Great Falls is an 800-acre park that overlooks the magnificent Great Falls of the Potomac. Families come here to explore the remains of the 18th century Patowmack Canal, built to bypass the falls, or to fish in the river. The park Visitor Center features a bookstore, snack bar, and museum. Call for information on weekly programs.

Jefferson District Park

7900 Lee Highway, Falls Church, VA 22042 (703-573-0444). Take the Beltway (Route 495) to Route 50 west; turn right on Gallows Road; then right on Route 29-211 (Lee Highway) to park entrance on left at Hyson Lane.

- Open daily dawn to dusk.
- Picnic tables.
- Lighted outdoor tennis courts. Courts can be reserved for a fee.
- Golf and miniature golf courses open mid-April through October 15. For schedule and fees call 703-573-0443.
- All facilities except golf are lighted until 11 P.M.

This 60-acre park features a 9-hole executive golf course and 18-hole miniature golf course. It also offers lighted tennis courts and horseshoe pits.

Lake Accotink Park

5660 Heming Avenue, Springfield, VA 22152 (703-569-0285). Take the Beltway (Route 495) to Braddock Road east; continue for ½ mile to right turn on Heming Avenue; go 1½ miles to park entrance.

- Open daily, dawn to dusk.
- Picnic tables, grills, and shelter (by reservation).
- Miniature golf.
- Boat launching and fishing.
- Canoe, pedal boat, and rowboat rentals and pontoon rides.
- Carousel.
- Hiking and biking trails.

The 77-acre lake is popular with fishing and boating enthusiasts. On land, children and adults enjoy miniature golf, nature walks, and biking trails. The park also features a carousel, playground, lovely picnic areas, a baseball field, and a basketball court.

Lake Fairfax Park

1400 Lake Fairfax Drive, Reston, VA 22090 (703-471-5414). Take the Beltway (Route 495) to Route 7 west; continue about 6½ miles; turn left on Route 606 and left again on Lake Fairfax Drive to park entrance.

- Open daily dawn to dusk.
- Admission fee weekends and holidays. No fee for Fairfax County and Fairfax City residents.
- Picnic tables and grills.
- Outdoor swimming pool.
- Miniature golf.
- Boating and fishing, pedal boat rentals, and excursion pontoon boat ride.

- Family camping, March–November, no reservations. Group camping area must be reserved.
- Miniature train and carousel.

Formerly a private lake, this 479-acre park offers a 15-acre lake for boating as well as an Olympic-size pool and wading pool. Landlubbers can play miniature golf, ride the train and carousel, or enjoy a picnic in the park. The family camping area has 200 sites, bathrooms and showers, picnic tables and grills, and a camp store.

Lee District Park and Robert E. Lee Recreation Center

6601 Telegraph Road, Alexandria, VA 22310 (703-922-9841). Take the Beltway (Route 495) to Telegraph Road south; go 3 miles to park entrance on left.

- Open daily dawn to dusk.
- Picnicking permitted.
- Racquetball/handball courts.
- Indoor swimming pool.
- Gymnasium and racquetball/handball courts.
- Miniature train and carousel.
- Hiking trails.

The recreation center boasts a 50-meter swimming pool, gymnasium, 6 racquetball/handball courts, saunas, and meeting rooms. In addition to the train and carousel, the park features playing fields, tennis courts, play equipment, an amphitheater, and hiking trails.

Mason District Park

6621 Columbia Pike, Annandale, VA 22003 (703-941-1730). Take the Beltway (Route 495) to Little River Turnpike east; continue for 2 miles to left at John Marr Drive; right on Columbia Pike to park entrance on the right, just before Sleepy Hollow Road.

- Open daily dawn to dusk.
- Picnic tables.
- Outdoor tennis and basketball courts.
- Hiking trails.

Mason District Park boasts 121 acres in the heart of Fairfax County. The park features tennis and basketball courts, ball fields, and jogging trails. Visitors can enjoy a wildlife pond, take a hike or follow self-guided nature trails. There are picnic and open play areas as well as a tot lot. An amphitheater offers a full and varied schedule of day and evening programs in the summer.

Mount Vernon District Park and Recreation Center

2017 Belleview Boulevard, Mount Vernon, VA 22307 (703-768-3224). Take the Beltway (Route 495) to Richmond Highway, Route 1 south; bear right onto Fort Hunt Road; go 1½ miles to Belleview Boulevard; right on Belleview, park entrance on left.

- Park open dawn to dusk.
- No picnic area.
- Indoor swimming pool. Call for operating hours.
- Ice rink open year round. Call for operating hours.
- Snack bar.

The Mount Vernon Trail (see listing below) passes through this park. Other key features include an indoor ice rink, swimming pool, saunas, and whirlpool facilities.

Mount Vernon Trail

Parallels the Potomac River and the George Washington National Parkway from Theodore Roosevelt Island to Mount Vernon (703-285-2590). Mailing address: George Washington Memorial Parkway, Turkey Run Park, McLean, VA 22101.

- Open daily dawn to dusk.
- Parking available at Theodore Roosevelt Island, LBJ Memorial Grove, Gravelley Point, Daingerfield Island, Jones Point Lighthouse, Belle Haven, Fort Hunt Park, Riverside Park, and Mount Vernon.
- Rest rooms at Theodore Roosevelt Island, LBJ Memorial Grove, Daingerfield Island, Belle Haven, Fort Hunt Park, and Mount Vernon.
- Picnicking at Daingerfield Island, Jones Point Lighthouse, Belle Haven, Fort Hunt Park, and Riverside Park.
- Connects to the Arlington County trail system and the Washington and Old Dominion bike trail at Theodore Roosevelt Island. Cross Memorial Bridge and connect to the bike trail to the C & O Canal.

This 18½ mile trail is shared by joggers, bikers, and walkers. Families with older children can ride the whole way, others can park along the way and bike a portion of the trail. Wherever you start, there are numerous interesting places to stop for a picnic lunch or to take a rest. At Roosevelt Island you can walk the trails, LBJ Grove provides a clear view of the Washington skyline, Gravelly Point is a favorite place to watch planes take off and land, Daingerfield Island has water sports and a restaurant, Dyke Marsh is a 240-acre wetland where you might spot some rare species of birds, and Mount Vernon was George Washington's home.

Nottoway Park

9601 Courthouse Road, Vienna, VA (703-938-7532). Take the Beltway (Route 495) to Route 66 west; exit at Route 243 (Nutley); left on Courthouse Road to park entrance on left.

- Open daily, fall, winter, and spring, dawn to dusk; summer, dawn to 11 P.M.
- Picnic tables and grills.
- Outdoor tennis and basketball courts.

The restored Hunter House and former winery sits on 84 acres with basketball and tennis courts, ball fields, picnic area, and playgrounds. Hunter House is available for rent for private parties, though there are no tours or general access. Garden plots are available in the park.

Occoquan Regional Park

Across the water from the Town of Occoquan, VA, on the Fairfax County shore (703-690-2121). Take Route I-95 south to Route 123 north; follow for 1½ miles to park entrance on right. Mailing address: Northern Virginia Regional Park Authority, 5400 Ox Road, Fairfax Station, VA 22039.

- Open mid-March through Thanksgiving, dawn to dusk.
- Picnic shelters, gazebos, and grills for rent; call 703-352-5906.
- Boat launching.
- Batting cage (25 balls for $1) and ballfields.
- Hiking and biking trails.
- Visitors center/snack bar.

This 400-acre park boasts a beautiful parkland setting overlooking the Occoquan River. Refreshments are available at a park facility that features three levels of deck on a scenic overlook. In addition to the launching ramps and boat storage, the park offers picnic shelters and grills for rent and athletic fields.

Pohick Bay Regional Park

Located on the Mason Neck peninsula in Fairfax County, VA (703-339-6100). Take Route I-95 south to Lorton exit; then follow Gunston Hall and camping signs to park. Mailing address: Northern Virginia Regional Park Authority, 5400 Ox Road, Fairfax Station, VA 22039.

- Open dawn to dusk all year.
- Nonresident admission fee. No fee for 6 participating jurisdictions in Northern Virginia.
- Picnic shelters, tables, and grills. Call for rental fees.

- Outdoor swimming pool open Memorial Day weekend to Labor Day. For schedule and fees call 703-339-6102.
- Miniature and Frisbee golf.
- Golf course and driving range. For schedule and fees call 703-339-8585.
- Boat launching.
- Sailboat and pedal boat rentals.
- Family campsites (no reservations) and camp store. For information call 703-339-6104.

"Pohick," the Algonquin Indian word for "the water place," is an apt description of this waterside park. Visitors can swim, boat, and fish. Other activities include family camping (hot showers available), flying kites, and picnicking. Golfers should find the 18-hole, par 72 course a challenge. The park also features a 4-mile bridle path, hiking trails, and an observation deck that overlooks the Potomac River. Most of the area around the park is maintained as a wildlife refuge, and the recreation areas are planned to minimize the disturbance to the animals.

Providence Park and Recreation Center

7525 Marc Drive, Falls Church, VA 22042 (703-698-1351). Take the Beltway (Route 495) to Route 50 east; right on Jaguar Trail; right on Marc Drive to park.

- Open daily dawn to dusk.
- Fees for use of facilities. Reduced fees for Fairfax County residents.
- Wheelchair access includes racquetball/handball courts.
- No picnic area.
- Indoor swimming pool.
- Racquetball/handball courts.
- Snack bar.

This recreation center in a park setting offers an indoor swimming pool with teaching area and poolside spa. The facility also boasts a snack bar, dance room, sauna, and weight room.

Riverbend Park

8700 Potomac Hills Street, Great Falls, VA 22066 (703-759-9018). Take the Beltway (Route 495) to Route 193 west; turn right on Riverbend Road; go 3 miles to right on Jeffery Road; continue 1½ miles to park.

- Open daily dawn to dusk.
- Wheelchair access includes an interpretive nature trail.
- Picnic tables and grills.
- Boat launch and rowboat rentals. For information call the boating marina at 703-759-9018.
- Snack bar.

Riverbend Park encompasses 409 acres of Potomac shoreline and has a service and information center with a wooden deck overlooking the Potomac River. The park features picnic areas, walking trails, fishing, boat launch for small boats, and rowboat rentals. The Riverbend Nature Center, 703-759-3211, has a naturalist staff, environmental exhibits, and many special programs.

Wakefield District Park and Recreation Center

8100 Braddock Road, Annandale, VA 22003 (703-321-7080). Take the Beltway (Route 495) to Braddock Road west; continue to park entrance on right.

- Open daily dawn to dusk.
- Fees for most facilities and classes. Lower fees for Fairfax County residents.
- Picnicking permitted.
- Lighted outdoor tennis courts.
- Indoor swimming pool.
- Handball, squash, and racquetball courts.

Wakefield Recreation Center is the first indoor recreational facility of its kind in Fairfax County. Its 290 acres encompass both indoor and outdoor recreational facilities, including 11 lighted tennis courts, a lighted practice court, and shuffleboard. The indoor facility features a 50-meter pool, sauna and showers, weight room, lockers, gymnasium, dance and exercise rooms, game room (pool, ping pong, etc.), and courts for handball, squash, and racquetball. Visitors also can enjoy the arts and crafts rooms as well as pottery and photography labs. In addition, Wakefield has a preschool program and a wide range of instructional classes.

Nearby is Wakefield Chapel, which was built in 1899 as an affiliate of the Methodist church. The chapel can be rented for appropriate community activities. Call 703-321-7081 for information.

Other Parks In Virginia

Algonkian Regional Park

Located at Loudoun-Fairfax County Line (703-450-4655). Take the Beltway (Route 495) to Route 7 west; continue about 16 miles to Cascades Parkway exit; go north on Parkway to park. Mailing address: Northern Virginia Regional Park Authority, 5400 Ox Road, Fairfax Station, VA 22039.

- Open daily dawn to dusk.
- Picnic tables, grills, and shelters.
- Outdoor swimming pool open daily, Memorial Day weekend–Labor Day. For schedule and fees call 703-430-7683.
- Golf and miniature golf courses and a driving range. Power pull carts and club rentals.
- Boat launching and fishing.
- Hiking trails.
- Snack bar.

Located on the Potomac shore, this park features a boat-launching ramp that provides public access to the wide Seneca Lake section of the Potomac River and includes a large swimming pool among its 500 acres. Picnic tables are scattered under trees along the shoreline, and covered shelters may be reserved for group picnics. Twelve riverfront cottages are available for rent, as is a Meeting Center/Clubhouse. Visitors can enjoy fishing on the Potomac or playing miniature golf. There is an 18-hole, par 72 golf course.

Prince William Forest National Park

Located in Prince William County, VA. Take Route I-95 south from Washington, DC about 35 miles; exit at route 619 (near Quantico) then follow signs to park. Mailing address: P.O. Box 208, Triangle, VA 22172 (703-221-7181).

- Open daily dawn to dusk.
- Visitor Center open daily, 8:30 A.M.–5 P.M. Closed Christmas and New Year's Day.
- Entrance fee, $3 per vehicle.
- Picnic tables, grills, and shelter.
- Family camp sites, $7; group camp sites, $15.
- Hiking, biking, and cross-country skiing trails.

There are several campgrounds in this park offering a variety of camping experiences: Oak Ridge, with over 86 sites for tents and trailers (no reservations); Chopawamsic, offering primitive camping not accessible by car (permits required, reservations suggested); and Turkey Run Ridge, for group tent campsites for 25–30 people (reservations required). The Turkey Run Education Center can be rented for group activities.

Washington and Old Dominion (W & OD) Railroad Regional Park

Mailing address: Northern Virginia Regional Park Authority, 5400 Ox Road, Fairfax Station, VA 22039 (703-352-5900, 703-729-0596).

- Open daily dawn to dusk.
- A wheelchair race of champions is held here in early October.
- Rest rooms at several community centers along the way.
- Picnicking permitted.
- Refreshment concession at Smith switch in Ashbourn (Loudoun County), VA.
- Call for information on bike rentals.

This 45-mile strip of park follows the roadbed of the old W&OD Railroad. It is the most heavily used park in Northern Virginia. The paved path, which connects with numerous other trails and parks, serves bikers, hikers, joggers, and skate boarders from Alexandria to Purcellville. The park boasts a dual bridal path west of Vienna. There are several parcourse fitness stations along the trail. The trail begins in Arlington, near the intersection of Shirlington Drive and Four Mile Run Drive, and there are several access points near Metro stations. A 54-page informational Trail Guide on the W & OD Railroad Regional Park, which notes where bathrooms are located, is for sale at all Northern Virginia Regional Parks.

7 Arts and Entertainment

Whether a visitor to Washington or a resident, be sure to take advantage of the city's many opportunities to introduce your children to the performing arts. Most special events for children are scheduled on weekends or during school vacations. Check the entertainment sections of the newspapers to keep up to date on performances (see Starting Out, Chapter 1) and call to confirm hours. Half-price tickets to many Washington events can be purchased on the day of the performance at TICKETplace, located on the F Street Plaza between 13th and 14th Streets, NW (Metrorail Red, Orange, and Blue lines, Metro Center). Call 202-TICKETS for information on what is available on a particular day. Both Arena Stage and the Kennedy Center also have half-price ticket programs.

This chapter begins with descriptions of several theaters and groups that offer a variety of programs for children in the performing arts. Film, music, and theater offerings are then discussed in individual sections.

Programs in the Performing Arts

District of Columbia Jewish Community Center Goes Live for Kids

Tifereth Israel Congregation, 7701 16th Street, NW, Washington, DC 20009 (202-775-1765).

- Performances are held at Tifereth Israel.
- Admission $6 per show, or $16 for a series of three.
- On-street parking is available.
- No wheelchair access.

Offers varied entertainment — folk music, puppet shows, and magic — at Sunday matinees. Call for the schedule as there is one performance in the fall, one in January, and one in February.

Jewish Community Center (JCC) of Greater Washington

6125 Montrose Road, Rockville, MD 20852 (301-881-0100 and TDD 301-881-0012).

- Performance times vary.
- Ticket prices vary.
- Parking available on site.
- Wheelchair access.

A resident symphony orchestra and a school of performing and visual arts encompassing music, dance, and drama make the JCC a busy arts center. The orchestra performs all year, and special concerts for very young children as well as frequent recitals by local and nationally known artists are given. The free monthly newsletter lists the performance schedule and admission fees. Call to become a subscriber.

John F. Kennedy Center for the Performing Arts

2700 F Street, NW, Washington, DC 20566 (202-467-4600, touch tone recording for general information, Concert Hall, Opera House, ticket information, and Instant Charge).

- Tickets to all performances may be purchased at the box office or with a major credit card by calling Instant Charge, 202-467-4600.
- Children 18 and under can qualify for half-price tickets for most events. Check at the Friends of the Kennedy Center desk, then purchase tickets at the box office.
- Parking is available under the building and in nearby lots.

- The Kennedy Center sets aside certain boxes and seats for handicapped persons and has wheelchair access.
- Call the Education Office at 202-416-8820 or 8830 and ask to be put on the mailing list for children's programs and for brochures on specific events.

The splendid halls of the Kennedy Center are the scene of many musical happenings throughout the year (see Chapter 2, Main Sights and Museums in Washington, DC). In addition to seasons of the resident companies, the National Symphony Orchestra, the Washington Opera Society, and the American Ballet Theater, guest artists from all over the world provide entertainment experiences from rock to opera. Individual programs are described below. The American Film Institute is also housed at the Kennedy Center. See the listing below under "Film" for further information.

The National Symphony (202-416-8820, information and free schedule) presents *Young People's Concerts,* scheduled in the spring and in the fall, for the Washington area school community. There are free concerts for school groups in the spring by finalists of the NSO Young Soloists' Competition. There is also a *Family Concert Series* for area families.

The Imagination Celebration is a 2-week National Children's Arts Festival presented in April. This family-oriented festival features entertainment and participatory events.

Kennedy Center Terrace Theater for Young People (202-416-8830, to be added to their mailing list and for schedule) includes classics as well as commissioned works performed in the Theater Lab by groups from all over the United States. Programs are usually scheduled throughout the school year on Friday evenings and Saturday and Sunday matinees. It is best to order tickets ahead (through Instant Charge or the box office) although there are times when tickets are available the day of the performance. Tickets are $8.50 per person. Group sales available with discount.

Theater for Young Children (202-416-8830, information and free schedule) presents outstanding productions in both spring and fall series of Programs for Children and Youth that provide culture-can-be-fun entertainment for Washington area youngsters and for any adults lucky enough to accompany them. All productions — plays, musicals, mime, puppetry, and dances from around the world — are performed by topnotch local, national, and international talent. Performances are held on selected Fridays at 7:30 P.M., Saturdays at 10:30 A.M. and 12:30 P.M., and Sundays at 1 P.M. Tickets can be obtained through the mail or on a first-come, first-admitted basis. Whether you have tickets or not, you must report to the Roof Terrace level at least ½ hour before the performance to be assured of a seat.

Kennedy Center Terrace National Symphony Concerts for Families (202-416-8820, for information) are scheduled in December and in the spring on Saturday or Sunday. The December concerts usually have a holiday theme. Prior to each concert there is a hands-on activity in the grand foyer. One of the most popular of these hands-on activities is the instrument "petting zoo" before the spring concert. Wonderful family entertainment for children three and older. Admission ranges from $3–$12.50.

Prince George's Publick Playhouse for the Performing Arts

5445 Landover Road, Hyattsville, MD (301-277-1710).

- Reservations are required and should be made early as many performances sell out.
- Free car and bus parking to the rear and east of the Playhouse.
- Wheelchair access; some performances are signed for the hearing impaired.

This performing arts center advertises "affordable family entertainment," which is certainly an understatement. The Playhouse, once an abandoned movie theater, seats almost 500 and is home to community theater groups, actors, dancers, musicians, and more. The lobby gallery features the work of local artists. The Playhouse's performance series are described below.

Community Arts at the Publick Playhouse features a wide variety of drama, music, comedy, and dance performances from an Annual Seniors' Revue to Broadway Tunes to familiar productions such as *Peter Pan* and *The Snow Queen.* There are evening and matinee performances. Ticket prices range from $1.50 to $8, with lower prices for senior citizens and children.

Dance Etc. features a wide variety of dance from cultures around the world. Weekend evening performances are offered. Ticket prices range from $8 to $13, depending on the performance.

Midweek Matinees feature dance, music, drama, and improvisation, often by performers from the Playhouse's evening productions. Performances at 10 A.M. are recommended for elementary school children and those at noon for 7th grade and up. Tickets are $2 per child or adult.

Saturday's Finest is a series of 45–60 minute dramatic productions for families. Performances are at 11 A.M. Tickets are $2 per child or adult.

Saturday Morning at The National

National Theater, Helen Hayes Gallery, 1321 E Street, NW, Washington, DC 20006 (202-783-3372).

- Performances throughout the school year, Saturday at 9:30 and 11 A.M.; Monday at 7 and 8:30 P.M.
- Free admission, on a first-come, first-seated basis.
- Parking in nearby commercial lots.
- Wheelchair access.

These dynamic one-hour shows abound with audience participation and are irresistible to kids of elementary school age. Magicians, dancers, mimes, and puppets are some of the colorful potpourri offered by top performers of local and national renown.

Smithsonian Institution Young Associate Program

Ripley Center, 1100 Jefferson Drive, SW, Washington, DC 20560 (202-357-3244, general information and 202-357-3030, information about classes).

- Event times and admissions vary; reduced prices for associate members.
- Metrorail Yellow, Blue, and Orange lines (Smithsonian, Mall exit).
- Parking is very limited.
- Wheelchair access.

The Smithsonian Young Associate Program sponsors performing arts events, concerts, dance, and theater. In the fall, winter and spring terms there are a variety of classes to choose from, including science, cooking, language, and art. Films are offered for members only. They also sponsor a Summer Camp program and host the weekly Discovery Theater performances (see the listing in this chapter under "Theater.")

Strathmore Hall Arts Center

10701 Rockville Pike, Bethesda, MD (301-530-0540).

- Indoor and outdoor performances for children.
- Admission $3–$4 per person.
- Parking lot.
- Wheelchair access.

On six Thursdays during the summer, two performances per day are presented on Strathmore's outdoor stage. One-hour performances begin at 9:30 and 11:30 A.M. Special rates are available for groups. Strathmore's indoor concerts for children are presented on four Saturdays in February at 11 A.M. and 1 P.M. In February you can also view the Youth Art Exhibition, which displays elementary school children's creations.

Sylvan Theater

Located between 15th and 17th Streets, off Constitution Avenue, NW, on the Washington Monument grounds (202-426-6843). Mailing address: National Park Service Mall Operations, 900 Ohio Drive, SW, Washington, DC 20242.

- Spring and summer performances, weather permitting. Call for information about specific events.
- Free big band concerts at 8:00 P.M. Wednesday.
- Metrorail Yellow, Blue, and Orange lines (Smithsonian, Mall exit).
- Parking very limited.
- Wheelchair access. Handicapped parking available off Independence Avenue at the rear of the theater.

Shakespearean plays, ballets, musicals, military concerts, and puppet shows under the stars are some of the attractions offered at Washington's downtown outdoor theater. There is something to please the taste of every age and inclination throughout the season. Bring cushions, blankets, and insect repellent. An impressive Torchlight Tattoo is presented by the U.S. Army Band and The Old Guard on Wednesdays at 8:30 P.M. on the Ellipse.

Wolf Trap Farm Park for the Performing Arts and the Barns at Wolf Trap

1624 Trap Road, Vienna, VA 22181 (703-255-1868, box office; 703-255-1900, general information and to get on the mailing list; 703-255-1916, the Barns at Wolf Trap). Take the Beltway (Route 495) to Dulles Airport limited access highway; go to Wolf Trap exit (open for performances only). Or take Route 7 west 5 miles past Tysons Corner to Wolf Trap sign and left turn on Towlston Road.

- Admission $6 and up; even infants pay.
- Call 703-255-1827 for information on children's programs, including Theater in the Woods in the summer.
- Parking lot with plenty of space.
- Wheelchair access.
- For a season brochure write to the Wolf Trap Foundation at above address.

Wolf Trap is America's only National Park for the Performing Arts. The Filene Center combines under-the-roof and under-the-stars seating. It is surrounded by 100 acres of rolling hills, woods, and streams. Resident professional companies as well as world-renowned artists perform during the summer. Workshops in the various performing arts are held. The International Children's Festival, featuring songs, dances, costumes, and crafts from around the world, is held at the end of the summer (see Chapter 11, Annual Events for Children and Families). Participatory theater and puppet and dance programs for children take place in the summer.

During the fall and winter, children's performances are scheduled in the Barns of Wolf Trap. A wide variety of programs from folk singing to puppetry are offered. Call 703-255-1916 for more information.

Dance

The African Heritage Dance Center

4018 Minnesota Avenue, NE, Washington, DC 20019 (202-399-5252). Located near RFK Stadium, at Minnesota and Benning Avenues, NE.

- Weekend performances.
- Admission varies.
- Metrorail Orange line (Minnesota Avenue, South).

- Free parking available.
- Wheelchair access.
- Group rates and bookings on request.

The center is a combination dance studio and art gallery, where classes and performances in African dance and music are held. The African Heritage Dancers and Drummers, one of the first African-American dance companies in the Washington area, specializes in the traditional dances of West Africa. Harvest dances, mask dances, stick dances, many performed in colorful robes, are all fascinating to watch. The center also offers workshops in West African dance, drumming, and instrument making.

American Youth Ballet Company

10111 Colesville Road, Silver Spring, MD 20901
(301-593-5060).

- Performances at various high schools and theaters in the metropolitan area on Saturday and Sunday afternoons.
- Admission ranges from $4–$6, depending on the performance. Group rates are available.
- Parking available.
- Wheelchair access.

This touring company's repertoire consists of original productions of children's stories, such as "Alice in Wonderland" and "Hansel and Gretel."

Arlington Center for Dance

3808 Wilson Boulevard, Arlington, VA 22209 (703-522-2414).

- Performances held at Thomas Jefferson Community Theatre (Route 50 at South Glebe Road, Arlington).
- Adults, $10; children, $6.
- Parking available on site.
- Wheelchair access.

The Arlington Center for Dance is both a dance school and performance company. Classes in ballet, modern, jazz, and tap are offered for children and adults. Performances are scheduled three times per year, in the spring, summer, and winter. In addition, the company brings its programs to schools in Arlington and Alexandria. A participatory dance production provides a historical celebration of America's ethnic diversity.

Classical Ballet Theatre

1430 Spring Hill Road, Suite 200, McLean, VA 22102
(703-506-8911).

- Performances year-round, throughout the Washington, DC area.
- Adults, $12–$15; senior citizens and children, $10. Discount for military personnel and groups of 5 or more.
- Wheelchair access and parking vary according to location of performance.

This professional-level ballet company features several award-winning dancers. Productions include *The Nutcracker, Cinderella,* and *Sleeping Beauty.* They also offer ballet classes for boys and girls.

Jones-Haywood Youth Dancers

1200 Delafield Place, NW, Washington, DC. 20011
(202-882-4039).

- Performances at Montgomery Blair High School in Silver Spring, the Post Office Pavilion, and the Terrace Theater, Kennedy Center. Call for performance information and schedule.
- Admission varies; sometimes performances are free.
- Parking and wheelchair access vary according to location of performance.

Sponsored by the Capitol Ballet Guild, these accomplished young dancers, ages 9–17, from the Jones-Haywood School of Ballet, focus on contemporary as well as classical ballet. World-renowned dancers sometimes appear as guest artists in the company's performances during the school year. Call the number listed above for performance information and a schedule.

Manassas Dance Company

9004 Mathis Avenue, Manassas, VA 22110 (703-368-6621).

- Performances twice per year, in December and in Spring, at schools in Prince William County.
- Adults, $8–$10; children, $3–$5.
- Parking available.
- Wheelchair access.

Enchanting performances of *The Nutcracker* and *Coppelia* in December and *Les Sylphides* in the spring. The company can also be booked for performances at other sites. Other productions include the *Four Temperaments* and *Pas de Trois Variation from Swan Lake*, and there are plans to add *Sleeping Beauty* to the company's repertoire.

Washington Ballet

3515 Wisconsin Avenue, NW, Washington, DC 20016 (202-362-3606).

- Christmas season performances of *The Nutcracker* at Lisner Auditorium, George Washington University, 21st and H Streets, NW (call 202-432-0200 for reservations) and a concert series offered at the Kennedy Center. Call for more information on other performances.
- Admission $20 for *The Nutcracker*; $25–$30 for concerts. Everyone needs a ticket including infants.
- Group bookings available.

The Washington Ballet is synonymous with *The Nutcracker*, which is performed during the Christmas holiday season, but this is only part of its contribution to the ballet scene. The professional company offers colorful performances in its fall, winter and spring dance series. The Young Dancers, the apprentice company of The Washington Ballet, presents performances and lecture-demonstrations at schools, community centers, and churches.

Film

American Film Institute

John F. Kennedy Center for the Performing Arts, 2700 F St. N.W.,Washington, DC 20566 (202-828-409, for schedule or 785-4600, for recorded message).

- Admission $5 for AFI members; non-AFI, $6; senior citizens, students, and children, $5. Season membership $15; includes invitations to premiers and other benefits.
- Daily at approximately 6 and 8 P.M., Saturday afternoon matinees offered. Call to verify times of films.
- Parking at Kennedy Center and nearby commercial lots.

Special programs for children occasionally are offered throughout the year, but many of the AFI regular film series— classics old and new, foreign, and domestic — are enjoyed by children who are junior high age and up.

Hirshhorn Museum and Sculpture Garden

7th Street and Independence Avenue, SW, Washington, DC 20560 (202-357-3235).

- Performances September–June, Saturday at 11 A.M. Call for a schedule.
- Metrorail Yellow, Blue, and Orange lines (L'Enfant Plaza, Maryland Avenue exit).
- Parking in commercial lots.
- Wheelchair access.

The 70-minute programs offer collections of short animated films, some experimental and some vintage animation. All films are intended to entertain the elementary-age audience with selections not seen on early morning TV. See also Chapter 2, Main Sights and Museums in Washington, DC, for more information about the Hirshhorn Museum.

Music

Capitol Concerts

West Lawn of the Capitol. For more information call the National Park Service (202-224-2985). Mailing address: 119 D Street, NE, Washington, DC 20510.

- Summer performances Monday, Tuesday, Wednesday, and Friday at 8 P.M., weather permitting.
- Free admission.
- Metrorail Orange and Blue lines (Capitol South).
- Parking on Maryland Avenue.
- Wheelchair access.

Bring a picnic and spend a pleasant summer evening on the steps of the Capitol listening to patriotic and pops concerts presented by the Armed Forces bands.

Concerts in the Country, Boyds Negro School

19501 White Grounds Road, Boyds, MD 20841 (301-972-1161). This school is located across the street from the Edward U. Taylor Elementary School.

- Performance days and times vary. Call for information.
- There is a suggested donation at the entrance.
- Parking available.
- No wheelchair access.

Family entertainment emphasizing local cultural and historical heritage is offered by this group. Performances take place in a one-room school house and range from early music festivals to gospel celebrations and contemporary mixed media theater.

Concerts on the Canal

The C&O Canal National Historical Park, between 30th and Thomas Jefferson Streets, NW, Washington, DC 20007 (202-653-5844). Located below M Street in Georgetown.

- Performances June–September, every other Sunday, 1:30 and 4:30 P.M.
- Admission free: a Mobil Corporation public service.
- Parking in Georgetown is difficult.
- Call for information on wheelchair access.

These hand-clapping, toe-tapping Sunday afternoon concerts feature music from the era of the canal builders, and bring the C&O Canal alive with the sound of an exciting array of music, dance, and song. Plan a family picnic, and let the whole gang listen, watch, and participate. There is something for everyone's taste: classical, jazz, bluegrass, gospel, Scottish country dance, and flamenco. Even the toddlers feel the beat and improvise their own dances in this relaxed, informal atmosphere. There is water in this portion of the canal, so supervision of small children is necessary.

The District of Columbia Youth Chorale Program

Duke Ellington School of the Arts, 35th and R Streets, NW, Washington, DC 20007 (202-282-0096).

- Performance times and places vary. Performances are at places such as the Kennedy Center, Constitution Hall, the Foundry Mall, and in DC schools, churches, hotels, and community centers.
- Admission, parking, and wheelchair access vary.

Founded in 1961, the DC Youth Chorale is the official city-wide chorus of the District of Columbia Public Schools. There are 2 performing groups. The Elementary and Junior Division (60 voices, grades 3–8) is the prep group for the Senior Division (40 voices, grades 9–12). An alumni division of 35–40 voices has been added in recent years. Most selections are classical, although the Junior singers also perform folk, semi-classical, and some popular numbers. Beethoven's *Ninth Symphony* has been performed by the seniors in conjunction with the DC Youth Orchestra. The performance rivals that of many college groups. Open auditions are held annually, and any school child in the metropolitan area may try out.

The District of Columbia Youth Orchestra Program

P. O. Box 56198, Brightwood Station, NW, Washington, DC 20011 (202-723-1612).

- There are 6 performances per year featuring the 4 major and 2 auxiliary orchestras.
- Performances are at Coolidge High School Auditorium, 5th and Sheridan Streets, NW, Washington, DC.
- Adults, $2.50; children pay less.
- Parking available.
- Wheelchair access.

The DC Youth Orchestra Program teaches children ages 5 and up to play orchestra instruments (no pianos, saxophones, or guitars). Lessons, which take place on Tuesday and Thursday evenings and Saturdays, are free for Washington, DC residents and $75 per semester for others. The performances feature classical music. This is an inexpensive way to introduce young children to classical music.

Fairfax Symphony Orchestra

c/o Fairfax County Park Authority, 3701 Pender Drive, Fairfax, VA 22030 (703-642-7200).

- Performances from June–September in the late morning, early afternoon, and early evening.
- Admission free to most concerts. Occasionally there is a fee to enter the park or historic site where the concert is held.
- Wheelchair access varies by site.

Each summer the Fairfax Symphony performs 30 concerts in area parks and historic sites. You can pack a picnic and have a relaxing meal while you listen to the music in a beautiful outdoor setting. Several concerts, called Overture to Orchestra, are designed to introduce children to the different instrument sections in an orchestra — percussion, string, brass, woodwind. Other concerts feature instrumental soloists or a particular style of music such as a Dixieland or German band. Call for more information about the summer's offerings.

The Overture to Orchestra program is also used to introduce the instruments of the orchestra to elementary school children. Each of the four musical ensembles, string quartet, woodwind quintet, brass quintet and percussion duo, has a program designed to develop recognition and understanding of the instruments and to make music fun to hear. Call for more information.

Friday Night in the Park Concerts

Potomac Overlook Regional Park, 2845 Marcey Road, Arlington, VA 22207 (703-528-5406).

- Performances summer through early fall, every other Friday evening at 7 P.M.
- Free admission, although donations to cover the costs of performers are appreciated.

This concert series features a mix of folk, bluegrass, contemporary, and classical music. Call for more information on which musical groups will be featured during the summer.

Marine Barracks Evening Parade

Marine Barracks, 8th and I Streets, SE, Washington, DC 20003 (202-433-6060).

- Performances mid-May through mid-September, Friday, 8 P.M. Tickets are free, but reservations are necessary. Call precisely 3 weeks in advance for the Friday you would like to attend; phone lines open at 8 A.M. (Call early and be persistent because they "sell" out quickly and the phones are very busy.)
- Write at least 2 months in advance for group reservations.
- Parking is very limited. It is best to park at the Navy Yard, N and 11th Streets, SE, and take the free shuttle bus to parade grounds.
- Call for information on wheelchair access.

With glorious pomp and precision the Marine Band performs a concert followed by an hour-long drill and marching show. Marines in full dress escort each group to their seats. It is an impressive spectacle and a wonderful way to spend a summer evening.

Merriweather Post Pavilion

Columbia, MD 21044 (301-982-1800). Take the Beltway (Route 495) to Route 29 north; go 18 miles to sign "Symphony Woods," and follow signs to pavilion.

- Performances late May–early September. Performance times vary.
- Admission varies. No refunds.
- Parking available.
- Wheelchair access.

■ Bring a blanket and picnic on the grassy area before you turn in your admission ticket. No beverages allowed in this area. You can also purchase snacks and beverages once you are inside the pavilion complex.

Located in 40 acres of woods, the pavilion presents a summer season of evening concerts, variety shows, and children's performances. You can purchase tickets to sit on the lawn or under cover for some lively entertainment. This is a great way for adults to share their favorite performers with their children, and vice versa.

Netherlands Carillon Concerts

Marshall Drive and Meade Street, Arlington, VA 22101 (703-285-2598). Off Route 110, near Iwo Jima Memorial and Arlington Memorial Cemetery.

■ Performances April–September, Saturdays, 2–4 P.M.; June–August, 6:30–8:30 P.M.
■ Special performances on Federal holidays, July 4, and Easter Sunday.

Come sit on the grass to hear the free carillon concerts of popular, classical, and religious music. A gift from the people of the Netherlands, the 49-bell carillon, housed in its open steel-structure tower, is an impressive auditory and visual experience. Visitors may go up into the tower to watch the carillonneur perform and to view the city of Washington.

Sunset Serenades at the National Zoo

National Zoological Park, Washington, DC 20008 (202-673-4717). Rock Creek Park entrances at Adams Mill Road, Beach Drive, and 3000 block of Connecticut Avenue, NW.

■ Summer performances on Thursday evenings, 6:30–8 P.M., at the Lion/Tiger Hill Stage.

- Admission free.
- Parking available in the Zoo's many lots.
- Wheelchair access.
- Call 202-673-4978 a day ahead to reserve a picnic basket, or bring your own dinner.

This summer concert series features a diverse mix of ethnic and contemporary music. A recent season included a mariachi band, classic rock and roll from the 50s and 60s, progressive reggae, and traditional Andean folk songs.

Theater

Adventure Theatre

Glen Echo Park, 7300 MacArthur Boulevard at Goldsboro Road, Glen Echo, MD 20816 (301-320-5331).

- Performances Saturday and Sunday, 1:30 and 3:30 P.M.
- Admission $4.50.
- Group rates for 10 or more, $4.
- Parking lot with plenty of spaces.
- Reservations recommended.

Housed in the old penny arcade building of the now-historic amusement park, this children's theater adds vitality to Glen Echo Park every weekend. Major productions year-round provide good professional entertainment. After the matinees children can collect autographs from the performers and then run off for a ride on the carousel. See Chapter 3, Main Sights and Museums in Maryland and Virginia, for more information on Glen Echo Park.

Bethesda Academy of Performing Arts (BAPA)

7300 Whittier Boulevard, Bethesda 20817 (301-320-2550, TDD 301-229-3739).

- Performances two weekends per month.
- Admission $5 per person.
- Parking on site.
- Wheelchair access; many performances are signed for the hearing impaired.

In addition to offering a wide range of children's classes in the performing arts, BAPA offers a full season of entertainment for children and families from September to May at the Academy's theater. Productions include dramas, musicals, reviews, and showcases. Summer programs include three day camps. Call for information on community activities such as the annual Halloween Spooktacular.

Blue Sky Puppet Theatre

4301 Van Buren Street, University Park, MD, 20782 (301-927-5599).

- Performances in schools, churches, civic organizations, and theaters in the metropolitan area. Also private party performances (homes, picnics, etc.).
- Admission, parking, and wheelchair access vary.
- Since there is no resident theater please call to request performance booking.

A pre-show musical warmup with audience participation sets the stage for these large, humorous, fast-paced, and socially aware puppet shows. This touring group offers clever original scripts with themes that range from brotherhood, unselfishness, and individuality to a whimsical folk tale with a "how-it-all-began" plot. Family appeal is a special emphasis of these performances. Parents will appreciate the sensitive treatment of subjects such as alcohol abuse, television addiction, and child abuse.

Bob Brown Puppet Productions

1415 South Queen Street, Arlington, VA 22204 (703-920-1040).

- Performance times and places vary. Please call for information on the next scheduled performance. Many performances at the Smithsonian's Discovery Theater and at Wolf Trap; regular performances in Washington area theaters, schools, and community centers.
- Admission, parking, and wheelchair access vary.

With the house lights on, the puppeteers warm up the audience, help get rid of the wiggles, and explain proper theater etiquette. They then assume their puppet personalities and proceed to entertain for about 45 minutes as preschool and elementary school children sit spellbound by the action. Parents, too, are amused by the sophisticated humor and enlightened by the multi-level messages the shows bring. Many performances are given Bunraku-style. Puppeteers, wearing hoods and gloves, work in front of a black curtain. The humans virtually disappear as they manipulate the puppets.

Children's Theater of Arlington

2700 South Lang Street, Arlington, VA 22206 (703-548-1154).

- Spring, fall, and winter productions at Gunston Arts Center; summer productions at Lubber Run Amphitheater. All performances on weekends.
- Admission at Gunston Arts Center, $5; all seats reserved; you can exchange tickets. Summer productions free (donations accepted).
- Parking available on site.
- Wheelchair access at both sites.

Fully staged and beautifully costumed musicals and dramas for children. Some are original, some are traditional, but all are well done and performed by talented young actors. Open auditions for ages 9–14 are held for each production.

Clarion Shadow Theatre

12415 Chalford Lane, Bowie, MD 20715 (301-262-7406).

- Performances of touring productions in schools, churches, and organizations. Larger productions and residencies available for theaters and universities.
- Admission, parking, and wheelchair access vary.

The most ancient of entertainments blends with the most sophisticated technology in the productions of the Clarion Shadow
Theatre. Updating the exotic art of shadow puppetry with modern
projection equipment and cinematic storytelling techniques, this
touring company produces superb "shadow plays" to the music
of Stravinsky, Mussorgsky, Grieg and other composers.

Columbia School of Theatrical Arts, Inc.

9650 Basket Ring Road, Columbia, MD 21045 (410-992-4315 or
410-992-7853).

- Performances in Columbia high school auditoriums.
- Admission and times vary.

Although primarily a school for the theatrical arts, this group
usually presents one production a year with large casts of accomplished young actors, ages 5–18. The shows are usually
musicals such as *Peter Pan* and *The Wiz* which can be enjoyed by
the entire family. They also offer after school and weekend classes
in acting, musical theater, and dance for children in grades K–12.
This organization also produces and presents quality children's
shows throughout the Washington, DC area.

Dinner Theaters

A number of dinner theaters in the Washington area offer special
theater programs for children. In addition, some offer matinee
performances and family-oriented productions, often with reduced prices for children. Admission, parking, and wheelchair
access vary. Some examples follow:

Burn Brae Dinner Theater

3811 Blackburn Lane, Burtonsville, MD 20866 (301-384-5800).

A Children's Theater, often featuring children's classics, takes
place on Saturdays. Live musicals with adult players are
presented three Saturdays per month and a magic show is

scheduled for the fourth. Come early for cookies and juice before the show. Doors open at 1 P.M. for the 1:30 P.M. performance. Performances last 1½ hours. Reserve tickets at $6.50 per person. Burn Brae also offers discounts for children ages 5–12 for its regular adult dinner theater, Sunday–Friday evening and for Sunday matinee brunch. Reservations are required.

Harlequin Dinner Theater

1330 East Gude Drive, Rockville, MD 20850 (301-340-8515).

This theater always offers half price tickets for children 12 and under at their matinee performances — every Sunday and three Wednesdays and Saturdays per month. All productions are family-oriented. There are occasional special children's programs. Call for information and reservations.

Toby's Dinner Theater

P.O. Box 1123, Columbia, MD 21044 (301-730-8311). Located on South Entrance Road off Route 29, south entrance to Columbia. Look for sign on the second building as the theater has no specific address.

Children's Theater is presented weekday mornings and afternoons, except Wednesday, at 10 A.M. and 12:30 P.M. Audiences are primarily school groups, but some individual tickets are available. For groups of 20 or more, tickets are $6 per person; individual tickets are $7. Reservations are required. Discounts are available for children 12 and under for regular adult performances Tuesday–Friday and Sunday. Matinees are held Sundays and selected Wednesdays. Dinner is served at all adult performances except the Sunday matinee, which features brunch. Special performances are presented during the holidays. Call for information and reservations.

West End Dinner Theater

4615 Duke Street, Alexandria, VA 22304 (703-370-2500).

Children's Theater is presented every Saturday at 1 P.M. (suggested arrival time is 12:30 P.M.). Snacks may be purchased and reservations are required. Tickets are $6 per person; groups of 10 or more pay $5 per person. Regular adult programming includes many performances suitable for children. All adult evening performances and Wednesday and Sunday matinees include a buffet dinner. Two children's discounts are available — for children 12 and under and for children 18 and under. No discounts for Saturday evening performances. Reservations are required.

Fairfax County Children's Theater

Fairfax County Recreation Department, 12011 Government Center Parkway, Fairfax, VA 22035 (703-324-5559).

- Friday evening performances in late November and early May; times vary. Saturday and Sunday performances, 2:30 P.M. at Fairfax County high schools.
- Admission $3.

This is theater for the children and by the children. Open auditions are held for aspiring players. The spring and fall shows are aimed at preschool and elementary school audiences. The excellent productions add to the enjoyment kids get from seeing their peers perform.

Kaydee Puppets

9020 Southwick Street, Fairfax, VA 22031 (703-560-2108 and 703-385-6432).

- Performance times and places vary. Performances are at area preschools, elementary schools, libraries, and recreation centers.

- Admission, parking, and wheelchair access vary.
- Best for children preschool–3rd grade.

These charming and humorous "Muppet-style" mouth puppets present a modern approach to the fantasy world of fairy tales. The shows are clever, colorful, and witty with a lot of warmth and personal involvement. After the show children can ask questions about the scenery, sound effects, and anything they have ever wanted to know about puppets.

Library Theatre

7210 Hidden Creek Road, Bethesda, MD 20817 (301-320-0093).

- Morning performances on school days in Prince George's and Montgomery Counties, Washington, DC, and Northern Virginia.
- Admission $3.50. Individual and group bookings available.
- Appropriate for children in grades K–6.

The Library Theatre's goal is to create a love for literature through musical theater, and it succeeds. For some children Library Theatre's productions are an introduction to books. For those already sold on reading, it's a thrill to see their favorite stories come to life in a one-hour educational, fun-filled musical produc-

tion. You can come to Library Theatre, or Library Theatre can come to you. This group also offers music theater classes for children.

Maryland Children's Theater

11141 Georgia Avenue, Suite 505, Wheaton, MD 20902 (301-933-7999).

- Performances at area schools and churches.
- Admissions and performance times and places vary. Group bookings available.
- Call for information on birthday party performances.
- Saturday youth program provides training for television and stage.

In a television-stage studio, the players introduce both contemporary plays and the classics via adaptations suitable for all ages. They will also lead a round of "Happy Birthday" for a birthday child as a pre-program highlight. Frequently, the performers will complete make-up and costuming on stage and in the audience so that children are introduced to every facet of the theater. At the end of the performance, children get some personal contact with the actors during autograph time. Each child carries away a souvenir autograph/program suitable for coloring. The theater will also provide staff to work with children on location at a school or youth organization.

Olney Theater, Acorn Theater Project

2001 Route 108, Olney, MD 20832 (301-924-4485). Take Georgia Avenue north to Olney. Turn right on Route 108 in the center of town. Theater is ½ mile on left.

- Ticket prices vary according to the show.
- Parking on site.
- Wheelchair access.

The children's theater project plans 4 performances a year, including one during the holiday season. The performances are held on Saturdays. Call for more information.

Playground Touring Puppet Company

Fairfax County Department of Recreation and Community Services, Performing and Fine Arts, 12011 Government Center Parkway, Suite 1050, Fairfax, VA 22035 (703-324-5559).

- Admission is free.
- Wheelchair access depends on the site of the performance.

This puppet company is staffed by college students who write and perform their own original plays based on topics and characters of current interest to children. The 30–40 minute productions take place in playgrounds, libraries, parks, and other recreation sites, and at the Fairfax Hospital. The shows are geared to children in grades K–6.

The Puppet Company Playhouse

Glen Echo Park, 7300 MacArthur Boulevard at Goldsboro Road, Glen Echo, MD 20816 (301-320-6668).

- Performances Wednesday–Thursday, 10 and 11:30 A.M.; Saturday–Sunday, 11 A.M., 1 P.M., 2:30 P.M.
- Productions change each month.
- Parking lot with plenty of spaces.
- Generally appropriate for children age 3 and older.

If you are looking for a theater open all year round, you've found it. Each month there is a different production. Call for specific information about this month's activity.

The Round House Theatre

Montgomery County Recreation Department, 12210 Bushey Drive, Wheaton, MD 20902 (301-468-4234).

- Box office open daily, 11 A.M.–5 P.M.
- Call for information on their lively, professional stage shows for children.
- Round House Theatre School (fall to spring) offers children's theater classes, specialty classes, and a teen touring troupe. In the summer, the theater offers arts day camps and theater day programs.

Round House is Montgomery County's professional resident theater. Since 1973 the theater has offered an outstanding program of teaching, touring in schools, and performing for all ages. All programs are directed by the professional actors and directors of the Round House.

Smithsonian Discovery Theater

Arts and Industries Building, 900 Jefferson Drive, SW, 20560 (202-357-1500).

- Performances October through June, and occasionally in summer. Call for information on shows, dates, times.
- Adults, $3.50; children 12 and under, $3. Ten-admission punch card and discounts for groups available.
- Reservations are strongly recommended.

Thousands of children in the Washington area have had their introduction to theater at these performances. Discovery Theater brings new and diverse programming, including many live performances, as well as outstanding puppet shows by artists of local and national renown.

Vienna Theater Company

c/o Vienna Community Center, 120 Cherry Street, Vienna, VA 22180 (703-255-6360).

- Annual summer production, featuring child actors.
- Admission varies, depending on the play.
- Parking lot on site.

- Wheelchair access.
- Plays are most appropriate for children ages 8–14.

Each summer the Department of Parks and Recreation in Vienna, VA sponsors the production of a full length play for children, and acted by children. Recent performances included: *Snoopy, Really Rosie, How to Eat Like a Kid*, and *Free to Be You and Me*. Throughout the year this production company provides opportunities for children to be involved in their other plays as actors and in "behind the scene" roles such as house managers and setting up props for scenes.

Darrell W. Smith

8 Behind the Scenes

Residents and visitors seeking an unusual experience should find this chapter helpful. It describes several fascinating facilities that are "off the beaten track," yet give insight into the day-to-day operation of a major city. Note that you may have to plan ahead, as many tours are for groups, have age specifications, and must be arranged weeks in advance. Many sites will tailor their tour to your special interests if given enough advance notice.

Agriculture

Beltsville Agricultural Research Center

U.S. Department of Agriculture, Beltsville, MD 20705 (301-504-8483). Take the Beltway (Route 495) to Route I north; after 1½ miles turn right on Powder Mill Road; continue for 2½ miles to Center.

- Open weekdays, 8 A.M.–4:30 P.M. Closed Federal holidays.
- All ages permitted, but most suitable for school-age children.
- Plenty of free parking at the Visitors' Center.
- Wheelchair access.
- Strollers allowed to point of bus departure.
- Tours are given mostly to school and camp groups. Call ahead to make arrangements.

This Center is one of the largest and most diversified research farms in the world. Work done here has led, for example, to the development of America's meaty Thanksgiving turkey and to the production of leaner pork. Visitors may be stimulated by the nature of the research, which demonstrates the impact of agricultural science on our daily lives. After a brief orientation at the Visitors' Center, you go on a bus tour of the facility. As this is a riding tour and not a "touching farm," it may not be suitable for younger children.

Airports

Baltimore-Washington International Airport

BWI Airport, MD 21240-0766 (301-859-7034). Take the Baltimore-Washington Parkway north and follow signs, or travel north on I-95 and follow the exit signs.

- Tours daily, between 10 A.M. and 4:30 P.M. Groups must be a minimum of 15 and a maximum of 25 children. Call the manager of Promotions, Marketing, and Development at least one month in advance to arrange for a group tour.
- Children must be in 3rd grade or older.
- No Metrorail, but the MARC train between Union Station and Baltimore does make a stop here. (See "MARC Trains" in Chapter 1, Starting Out.)
- Ample paid parking available.
- Wheelchair access.
- Strollers permitted.
- Typical airport fast food is available in the terminal.

This one-hour tour of the terminal includes the ticketing area, observation lounge, baggage area, and international section. The terminal's unusual space-frame design, popular in Europe, is uncommon in the United States.

Federal Aviation Administration, Air Traffic Control Center

Leesburg, VA 22075 (703-771-3521 or 703-478-1521). Take the Beltway (Route 495) to Route 7 west (Tysons Corner) to the Control Center on the left just before Leesburg. The Center is about 25 miles from Tysons Corner.

- Tours Tuesday, Wednesday, and Thursday, between 9 A.M. and 3:30 P.M. Tours are for a maximum of 15 people and must be scheduled at least two weeks in advance.
- Children must be at least 14. Younger groups will be considered if properly supervised.
- Ample free parking.
- Wheelchair access.

Using highly sophisticated equipment, this center controls all air traffic for the busy Middle Atlantic area of the United States. The 2-hour-long tours, conducted by air traffic control staff or technicians, are of value to older children interested in electronics or careers in air traffic control.

Washington Dulles International Airport

The airport is located in Chantilly, VA (703-471-7838). Take Route 123 or the Beltway (Route 495) to the Dulles Airport limited access highway. Mailing address: P.O. Box 17045, Washington, DC 20041.

- Tours weekdays at 10 A.M. for a minimum of 5 people. Call the Airport Manager to schedule a tour.
- Children must be at least five years old.
- Ample pay parking is available.
- Wheelchair access.
- Strollers permitted.
- Typical airport fast food is available in the terminal.

The magnificent terminal building is one of the late architect Eero Saarinen's masterpieces. Passengers ride to and from most planes in bus-like mobile lounges. The one-hour tours include a walk through the terminal, a ride on a mobile lounge, and a film. Tours can be tailored to the special interests of the group.

Washington National Airport

Airport is located in Alexandria, VA (703-685-8000 for recorded message, 703-685-8003 for airport manager). Take George Washington Memorial Parkway to airport exit. Mailing address: Washington National Airport, Washington, DC 20001.

- Open daily, 7 A.M.–10 P.M. Tours on Thursday mornings for up to 30 people. Call the Airport Manager to schedule a tour.
- Metrorail Blue line (National Airport). The terminals are a short walk or bus ride away.
- Pay parking. Car traffic gets very heavy and parking can be difficult.
- Wheelchair access.
- Strollers permitted.
- Typical airport fast food is available in the terminals.

Though this busy airport is often very congested, children can still see planes landing, taking off, or just standing on the runway from the large window in the central (old) terminal. There are also good sightseeing spots north and south of the airport in Roaches Run Park (north) and the Washington Sailing Marina (south) where car and bus parking is more readily available. The 2½ hour tours can be tailored to the special interests of the group and usually include visiting a parked airplane. Special arrangements can be made to accommodate larger groups.

Crafts

Torpedo Factory Art Center

105 North Union Street, Alexandria, VA 22314 (703-838-4565). Take George Washington Memorial Parkway (becomes Washington Street) to left turn on King Street. Continue for five blocks, then turn left on North Union Street.

- The building is open daily, 10 A.M.–5 P.M. Tours are offered every Tuesday, Wednesday, and Thursday at 10:30 A.M. Call in advance to arrange a tour for groups of 10 to 15 people.
- Adults, $1; children free.
- Ample pay parking is available.
- Wheelchair access.
- Strollers permitted.

The Friends of the Torpedo Factory offer regularly-scheduled tours of this working craft center at the times mentioned above, though additional tours may be specially arranged on Monday or Friday. For more information on the Torpedo Factory, see Chapter 3, Main Sights and Museums in Maryland and Virginia.

Fire Stations

Putting out fires seems to be a preoccupation of preschoolers, but the technology involved is often intriguing to older children and adults, too. Most fire stations are happy to show visitors their quarters and let them take a close look at the shiny trucks. Each fall during Fire Prevention Week area fire stations hold open houses when, depending on the station, children can climb on the trucks, try on the firefighters' gear, learn about fire safety,

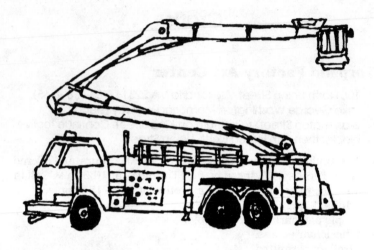

watch an aerial rescue from a roof, watch car rescue demonstrations, and get to know the rescue workers. Local stations are listed by communities in the telephone directory. Fire prevention programs are available for schools. Call in advance.

Food

Fast Food

Some fast-food restaurants are happy to take small groups of children of all ages on informal tours, so call around to see if you can arrange a tour. Call at least a week in advance, and ask to speak with the manager of the individual restaurant. Some tours are scheduled during off-hours, others during business hours. Sometimes the tours include a film; occasionally the children get to make their own sodas or bag their own french fries. Sometimes they assemble their own sandwiches or chat with the cook as he or she prepares food. The enormous refrigerators and freezers and the tall stacks of paper goods are always impressive. Something good to eat is usually given to the children at the end of the visit. Such tours are naturally a big hit!

Ice Cream

Seibel's Restaurant
15540 Old Columbia Pike, Burtonsville, MD 20866
(301-384-5661).

Sutton Place Gourmet/Jeffrey's Ice Cream
3201 New Mexico Avenue, NW, Washington, DC 20016
(202-364-1000).

Venezia's-Sully Plaza
   14154 E. Willard Road, Chantilly, VA 22021 (703-378-4900).

White Mountain Creamery (3 locations)
   □ 806 Muddy Branch Road, Gaithersburg, MD 20878 (301-670-0220).
   □ The Village, 9812 Falls Road, Potomac, MD 20854 (301-469-4846).
   □ Metro Pike Shopping Center, 11530 D Rockville Pike, Rockville, MD 20852 9301-468-68100.

What food tour could be more popular than a visit to an ice cream store or factory? Several local restaurants and shops offer informative tours replete with free samples of their excellent products. Call the establishments listed above for more information on their hours and age requirements.

Giant Food Stores

   Headquarters, 6300 Sheriff Road, Landover, MD 20785 (301-341-4100).

- Tours Tuesday and Wednesday morning at local stores. To arrange a tour for up to 25 people, call the Public Affairs Office at least one week in advance.
- Tours are for children in Kindergarten through 3rd grade only.
- Wheelchair access at all stores.

Tours can be arranged at your closest Giant Store and are directed by the store manager. The basic tour covers nutrition. If there is another special interest it should be mentioned when calling the Public Affairs Office.

Safeway Distribution Center

   1501 Cabin Branch Road, Landover, MD. 20785 (301-386-6571). Take the Beltway (Route 495) to Exit 17 B, Route 202, Landover Road. Turn left at light on Sheriff Road. Go five lights to Cabin Branch Road. Center is on right.

- Tours Tuesday, Wednesday, and Thursday at 10 A.M. Groups of up to 20 people are welcome. Call in advance to make arrangements.
- Suggested age for group tours is at least 12.
- Wheelchair access.

Tours of the warehouse include the grocery, produce, and meat areas. Visitors are especially intrigued by the gigantic freezer, the banana storage room, and the computer-operated high-rise storage area. Here the computer does everything from scheduling deliveries of non-perishable items to dispatching the robots ("robos") to pick up boxes for storage on 90-foot-high shelves.

Health Services

Dentists

Some dentists are glad to share their offices with young visitors. The dentist may begin with a brief discussion of nutrition and oral hygiene. Hands-on experience often follows with the dental chair, lights, mirrors, and other equipment. Call your own dentist for such an appointment or to obtain referrals.

Shady Grove Adventist Hospital

9901 Medical Center Drive, Rockville, MD 20850 (301-279-6099). Take Route 270 north to Route 28 west; continue one mile to the intersection with Shady Grove Road. Turn right, then make first left into medical center.

- Tours Monday–Thursday, 10 A.M.–4:30 P.M.; and Friday, 10 a.m–2 P.M. Tours for a maximum of 30 people per group are scheduled through the Public Relations Department. Preschool children have a shorter tour.
- Free parking in the lots surrounding the hospital.
- Wheelchair access.

- Strollers permitted.
- Cafeteria is available.

This tour is designed to introduce children to some of the different hospital departments. Visits are made to physical therapy and radiology, depending on conditions in the departments on the scheduled day and time of your tour. Visitors will see an actual patient room, the playroom in the pediatrics unit, and the babies in the newborn nursery. This is a nice way for anyone unfamiliar with a hospital to become acquainted with one.

Military

The Pentagon

OASD(PA), Directorate for Community Relations, The Pentagon, Washington, DC 20301 (703-695-1776). In Virginia, just across the 14th Street Bridge off Route I-395. The tour office is at the top of the escalators on the Shopping Mall Concourse.

- Tours weekdays, 9:30 A.M.–3:30 P.M., leaving every 30 minutes. Closed Federal holidays. Special group tours are available for a minimum of 20 persons. Call at least 10 days in advance to schedule a tour.
- Metrorail Blue and Yellow lines (Pentagon).
- Limited pay parking.
- Wheelchair access.
- Strollers permitted.

Be sure to wear your walking shoes for this tour. It lasts about 1½ hours and covers 1½ miles of the 17 miles of corridors that make up the Pentagon. The building was first opened to the public in 1976 as part of Washington's bicentennial celebration and has remained open because of its popularity. Though all ages are welcome, the emphasis on art work and museum-type displays, including model airplanes and ships, makes this tour most interesting to older children with an appetite for military history. The tour begins with a 13-minute film describing the history and construction of the building itself and the work of the people who use it. Some areas not open to the public are shown in the film. After the movie, visitors begin their long walk through corridors lined with offices, flags, portraits of the Presidents, the Time-Life Army Art Collection, halls dedicated to women in the military, medal of honor recipients, the Bicentennial, and much, much more.

U.S. Naval Observatory

Massachusetts Avenue at 34th Street, NW, Washington, DC 20392 (202-653-1507).

- Tours Monday evening in the spring, summer, and fall, at 8:30 P.M. No tours on Federal holidays. Tours accommodate up to 90 persons on a first come, first served basis.
- These tours are most appropriate for children over age 12.
- Group tours are available for 20 or more visitors. Call 202-653-1541 to make a reservation.
- Parking is available just outside the gate.
- Wheelchair access.
- Strollers permitted, but very young children are likely to be bored.

The work of the National Observatory consists primarily of determining the precise time through measurements of star positions. On this 1½ hour tour children watch a short movie on the determination of time, view the highly accurate electronic clocks and other exhibits, and receive an explanation of the workings of the large 26-inch telescope. On clear nights the tours include a look through the telescope.

Newspapers

Journal Newspapers, Inc.

6885 Commercial Drive, Springfield, VA 22159 (703-750-8700). Take the Beltway (Route 495) to Braddock Road east exit. Follow for 2 miles to right turn on Backlick Road. Go 2 miles to left turn on Industrial Road. Then take first left onto Commercial Drive.

- Tours Monday, Wednesday, Thursday, and Friday, 9:30 A.M.– 2:30 P.M. Tours are for a maximum of 20–23 people. Call at least one week in advance.
- Children must be in at least 4th grade.
- Wheelchair access.

The one-hour tour of this modern plant shows how a newspaper is put together. Visitors see the editorial staff, the computers that set the type, the paste-up of the copy, the photography section where negatives and plates of the paste-up are made, the presses (which may or may not be running), and the mailing room.

U.S.A. Today

1000 Wilson Boulevard, Arlington, VA 22229 (703-276-3400).

- Tours Tuesday, Wednesday, and Thursday by appointment for a maximum group of 20. Call the Public Affairs office to schedule a tour, at least three months in advance.
- Tours are for high school students and up with a special interest in journalism or communications.
- Metrorail Blue and Orange lines (Rosslyn).
- Wheelchair access.

U.S.A. Today is a nationally syndicated newspaper which is composed and then transmitted by telecommunication systems and satellite to 32 different printing locations throughout the United States and to two locations abroad. During a 45-minute tour, visitors will see the activities in the newsroom, sports room, and the production area, plus the telecommunication system.

The Washington Post

1150 15th Street, NW, Washington, DC 20071 (202-334-7969).

- Tours Monday, 10 A.M.–3 P.M. Individuals or groups can sign up for tours. Up to 40 people per tour can be accommodated. Call the Public Relations office at least one to two months in advance.
- Children must be 11 or older, or in the 5th grade.
- Metrorail Orange and Blue lines (McPherson Square) and Red line (Farragut North).
- Parking garages are available, but expensive.
- Wheelchair access.
- There are many restaurants nearby.

This comprehensive 45-minute tour of Washington's largest newspaper begins with a brief history of the paper and an explanation of the assets of the Washington Post Company. It includes a stop at the new museum where visitors get a demonstration of pre-computer methods of printing. Visitors are shown the giant presses. (They will not be operating, since *The Washington Post* is a morning paper. The presses run from 10:30 P.M. to 3:30 A.M.) The tour takes you to the vast newsroom where the reporters work, to the composing room where the paper is put together photoelectronically, to the engraving department, where plates are made, and finally to the mailroom, where the newspapers are picked up by distributors for delivery to subscribers and newsstands.

Photo Finishing

The photo finishing process has been revolutionized in the last few years and now many companies offer one-hour automated processing. Prints are produced "while you watch" at several facilities. Check the Yellow Pages for an automatic photo finishing center near you. Call to check on the hours when the process can be observed.

Police Stations

District of Columbia Metropolitan Police

300 Indiana Avenue, NW, Washington, DC 20001 (202-727-4283).

- Tours weekdays, 10 A.M.–2:00 P.M. Tours accommodate a maximum of 30 people. Call one week in advance to schedule a tour.
- Tours are for children in 5th grade and up.
- Metrorail Red line (Judiciary Square, exit through the 4th Street tunnel).
- Parking in commercial lots.
- Wheelchair access.

Tours of the District police headquarters are subject to the political climate and general safety considerations prevailing. When tours are available, one can see the communications center, the line-up room with its two-way mirrors and videotape equipment, and the firearms identification unit with its thousands of confiscated guns. Arrangements can be made in advance to see other District police facilities, such as the fire boats.

Suburban Stations

Most suburban stations, listed by county in the telephone directory, take groups around their facilities. Visitors could see the
holding cells and finger-printing operation, as well as get a
close-up view of a police car. Some stations have programs in
which officers come to the schools with cars and motorcycles to
show the tools of their trade to younger children and tell them
what police officers do.

U.S. Park Police Canine Demonstration

Anacostia Substation, Anacostia Drive, SE, Washington, DC
(202-690-5099). Located between South Capitol Street
Bridge/11th Street and Howard Road. Mailing address: 1100
Ohio Drive, SW, Washington, DC 20242.

- The 11 A.M. show is held on selected Wednesdays in April, May,
  June, September, and October. A maximum of 50 people is
  allowed. Advance reservations are required for individuals or
  groups. Write to the Special Forces Branch, Special Events
  Office, U.S. Park Police, at the mailing address above at least
  four weeks in advance.
- Metrorail Green line (Anacostia Station).
- Ample free parking.
- Wheelchair access.
- Strollers permitted.
- Inclement weather or unscheduled police events/emergencies
  may cause cancellation.

Park Police dogs demonstrate their obedience and agility to
enthralled audiences. The dogs go up ladders, over barricades,
and through hoops. Helicopters and fire hoses are included, too!
It's an excellent show for younger children.

Post Offices

Local Post Offices

Many neighborhood post offices or local substations welcome visitors. Their advantage is that children can view less-mechanized offices and see how mail is sorted and readied for delivery. Check the telephone directory under U.S. Government, Postal Service. Be sure to call well in advance.

Washington, DC General Mail Facility

900 Brentwood Road, NE, Washington, DC 20066 (202-636-1207). Take New York Avenue to Brentwood Road exit and follow signs, or Rhode Island Avenue to right turn on 12th Street to Brentwood Road.

- Tours Tuesday–Friday, 10:30 A.M.–3 P.M. Some evening tours available by special arrangement.Tours accommodate a maximum group of 30. Call the Communications Division one to two weeks in advance to make arrangements for a tour.
- Children must be at least 9 years old.
- Metrorail Red line (Rhode Island Avenue). If special arrangements are made when tour is scheduled you can take a path directly from the station into the building.
- Ample free parking.
- Wheelchair access.

This one-to-two-hour tour displays the people and the machines that sort, cancel, and distribute letters.

Railroads

For children who have never been on a train, or parents who need a rainy day activity, even a short ride can be exciting. The MARC trains offers this opportunity. Children can ride from several Maryland suburbs to Union Station on a commuter train. Another idea is to hop on Washington's efficient Metro system, which goes to National Airport, the Pentagon, and the Mall area as well as suburban neighborhoods. Check the Transportation section in Chapter 1, Starting Out, for details on MARC and Metrorail.

Television and Radio

National Public Radio

2025 M Street, NW, Washington, DC 20036 (202-822-2000).

- Tours Thursday, 11 A.M. Tours are for 8 people maximum, so be sure to call ahead to confirm availability.
- Tours are recommended for those 15 years and older.
- Metrorail Red line (Dupont Circle).
- Pay parking is available, but can be expensive.
- Wheelchair access.
- A variety of eating establishments are available in this central downtown location.

Here visitors can see the studio where *Morning Edition* and *All Things Considered* are produced. Because of the technical nature of broadcast production, these 45-minute tours are recommended for individuals who are familiar with NPR programming and/ or have a strong interest in radio. Visitors may also see the satellite operations and some production facilities.

Voice of America

330 Independence Avenue, SW, Washington, DC 20547 (202-619-3919). Entrance is on the C Street side of the building, between 3rd and 4th Streets, SW.

- Tours weekdays at 8:40, 9:40, and 10:40 A.M. and 1:40 and 2:40 P.M. Closed on Federal holidays.
- School groups must be 8th grade and older; younger children accompanied by their parents are welcome. Call to schedule a tour.
- Metrorail Blue and Orange lines (Federal Center).
- Parking in commercial lots.
- Wheelchair access.

During the 45-minute tour, visitors may watch broadcasts in progress and learn about the U.S. government's international broadcast network. VOA transmits approximately 1200 hours per week in 45 languages to an estimated worldwide audience of 130 million regular listeners!

WETA TV, Channel 26

3620 27th Street South, Arlington, VA (703-998-2697). Take Route I-395 south to Exit 7 (Shirlington/Glebe Road). Follow signs for Shirlington, then turn right at first light on Shirlington Road, then an immediate left on South 27th Street. WETA's studio is the first building on the left.

- Tours weekdays when volunteers and studios are available. Tours should be arranged two to four weeks in advance by calling the number above or writing to Volunteer Coordinator, Box 2626, Washington, DC 20013
- Children must be age 10 or older.
- Street parking is available.
- Wheelchair access.
- Maximum tour group size is 15.

The tour of this Public Broadcasting System facility includes a look at the studios and control rooms, where such programs as *McNeil/Lehrer News Hour* are produced, and an explanation of the technical equipment.

WRC TV, Channel 4

4001 Nebraska Avenue, NW, Washington, DC 20016 (202-885-4037).

- Tours weekdays, though the hours may change. Usually one tour is offered in the morning and one in the afternoon. Tour groups of 5–18 people can be accommodated. Call ahead for specific information on your desired day.
- Minimum age for tours is 6.
- Metrorail Red line (Tenleytown)
- Some street parking is available.
- Wheelchair access.

This 45-minute tour includes the newsroom, control room, editing facility, some studios, and a brief stop in the weather center.

WUSA TV, Channel 9

4001 Brandywine Street, NW, Washington, DC 20016 (202-364-3900 or 202-364-3977).

- Tours Wednesday, 11:40 A.M.–12:40 P.M. Tours for a maximum of 25 people. Call the Promotions Department to arrange a tour.
- Metrorail Red line (Tenleytown).
- Ample street parking.
- Wheelchair access.

WUSA offers one tour during the lunch hour to watch the noon news in progress. Special arrangements can be made to see the newsroom also.

Theater

Arena Stage

1101 6th Street, SW, Washington, DC 20024 (202-554-9066).
Take I-395 over the 14th Street bridge to Maine Avenue exit.
Continue straight from stop sign, then left at light on Maine
Avenue. Theater is 3 blocks further on the left.

- Tours Tuesday–Thursday, 10 A.M.–3 P.M. Tours for a maximum of 15 people. Call ahead to make arrangements.
- Children should be 11 and older.
- Metrorail Yellow, Orange, and Blue lines (L'Enfant Plaza).
- Metered parking on the street and several pay lots within easy walking distance.
- Wheelchair access.

The Arena Stage complex houses three theaters: one in-the-round, one standard proscenium stage, and a cabaret-style room. On the one-hour tour visitors see the costume shop, scene shop, and prop shop in addition to the backstage area, and take a walk underneath the theater stage.

Utilities

Chesapeake and Potomac (C & P) Telephone

Washington Headquarters, 1710 H Street, NW, Washington,
DC 20006 (202-392-4580, Washington DC; 202-515-2168,
Maryland; 804-772-1428, Virginia).

- Tours weekdays, 9 A.M.–5 P.M. Call at least three weeks in advance to schedule a tour. You should call the number listed above for the area where you are located (Washington, DC, Maryland, or Virginia).

- Tours are most appropriate for children ages 10 and up who have a special interest in telecommunications. Upon request, special arrangements can be made for younger groups.
- Metrorail accessibility and parking availability vary according to the tour location you are visiting. Call for more information.
- Wheelchair access.

C & P can link you up to a variety of facilities according to your group's interests. You might splice a cable, observe a switching control center, and/or watch an operator juggling calls.

International Telecommunication Satellite Organization (INTELSAT)

3400 International Drive, NW, Washington, DC 20008 (202-944-7841). At Connecticut Avenue and Van Ness Street.

- Tours by appointment only, Tuesday at 10 A.M. and Thursday at 3 P.M. Tours are for a maximum group of 35. Schedule your tour at least two weeks in advance by calling the Public and External Relations Department.
- Children must be 10 years and older.
- Metrorail Red line (Van Ness).
- Limited street parking available.
- Wheelchair access.

These regular Visitors' Center tours last 45 minutes and include a 12-minute video presentation about INTELSAT, the overlook areas for the Satellite Control Center, and exhibits in the Operations Center and the Ceremonial Lobby.

Potomac Electric Power Company

1900 Pennsylvania Avenue, NW, Washington, DC 20068 (202-872-3571).

- Tours of power plants are available for school groups of up to 35. Three weeks advance reservation is suggested.

- Tours for children in 5th grade and above.
- Parking available.
- No wheelchair access.
- A variety of other programs are available for school groups. Call at least two weeks in advance to schedule a program.

Pepco has an educational services program for elementary through secondary school students. Hour-long tours show children how electricity is produced. Visitors see boilers, turbines, and generators, plus the coal yard and control center. For elementary schools, Pepco provides a "visiting truck" program, complete with lineman and literature. Teachers can arrange for classroom presentations. Pepco also offers professional puppet productions for school assembly programs. The Blue Sky Puppet Theatre's *Lights Out on the Bunny Brothers* deals with conservation around the home. *Hot Wires* focuses on typical safety measures in and around the home. *Phaseshifters* addresses the issues of drug and alcohol awareness. For Pepco's catalog, *Educational Services Programs*, write to the Educational Services Department at the address above.

Washington Aqueduct Dalecarlia Water Treatment Plant

5900 MacArthur Boulevard, NW, Washington, DC 20316 (202-282-2701). From Virginia, cross Key Bridge to left turn on M Street, which will become Canal Road. Follow for about 1 mile to left turn on MacArthur Boulevard. From Maryland, take the Beltway (Route 495) to exit 40 south (Glen Echo). At first stop sign, turn right onto MacArthur Boulevard. Follow for 3 to 4 miles to plant.

- Tours weekdays, 8 A.M.–1:30 P.M. Minimum group size is five, maximum 25 individuals. Schedule tours three to five days in advance.
- Tours are for children ages 12 and up.
- Ample free parking.
- Wheelchair access.

See how water from the Potomac is transformed into drinking water for residents of the District of Columbia, Arlington, and Falls Church, Virginia. The one-hour tour includes a look at the filtration, purification, and chemical treatment processes and lab facilities.

Washington Gas Light Company

6801 Industrial Road, Springfield, VA 22552 (202-624-6758, Washington, DC; 301-595-8046, Maryland; 703-750-5524, Virginia).

- Tours weekdays between 8:00 A.M. and 4:30 P.M. Call the Washington Gas Light office in your jurisdiction (Washington, DC, Maryland, or Virginia) to make arrangements.
- Tours are for children in grades 6, 7, and 8.
- Parking available.
- Wheelchair access.

The Washington Gas Light Company is organized in 3 divisions — DC, Virginia, and Maryland. Their tour for middle school students takes place at the Springfield, Virginia operation. It includes viewing the total energy plant, distribution facility, phone service section, transmission and distribution, welding shop (featuring a pipe fusion demonstration), research department, and transportation area.

Weather

National Weather Service

RD 1, Box 107, Sterling, VA 22170 (703-260-0107, long distance from the metropolitan area). From Route I-66, take Route 28 north to Route 606 west. Follow for 3 miles.

- Tours weekdays, 9 A.M.–5 P.M. Tours are for groups of two to 20 people, by appointment only.
- Children should be in 3rd grade and up.
- Ample free parking.
- Wheelchair access.

Tours last from 20 to 40 minutes, depending on the ages and interests of the group. Visitors can see the entire operation of forecasting here, including the computers, radar, radio studio, and NEXRAD communication system.

9 Shopping

Washington has a full complement of fine shops which market toys, books, crafts, imports, and other specialty items for all ages. This chapter provides a description of several major shopping malls — most are accessible by Metrorail — that feature some unusual shops and some branches of the chain stores visitors may be familiar with from their own locales. We have also featured some of our area's "unique" book and toy shops that we feel provide excellent selections in creative and friendly environments. Parents can use our list as a guide to places with a wide range of merchandise for their offspring. Children can visit these stores to build collections, develop hobbies, or buy a nice souvenir or gift. Of course, shopping is most fun for children when they are making their own choices.

Shopping Centers

All of the shopping centers described below have wheelchair access and permit strollers. Some have ample parking, others do not. See each listing for more specific information.

Georgetown Park

3222 M St., NW, Washington, DC 20007 (202-342-8190).

- Open weekdays, 10 A.M.–9 P.M.; Saturday, 10 A.M.–7 P.M.; Sunday, noon–6 P.M. Restaurant hours may vary.
- Parking under the building.
- Several restaurants, but no food court.

Located in the heart of Georgetown, this 4-story shopping center includes a branch of the famous New York toy store, FAO Schwartz, the Georgetown Park Zoo (stuffed animals only), and numerous other clothing, book, and gift shops. You might also visit the Old Stone House (see Chapter 2, Main Sights and Museums in Washington, DC) and the unique shops and restaurants of Georgetown.

The Pavilion at the Old Post Office

1100 Pennsylvania Avenue, NW, Washington, DC 20004 (202-289-4224).

- Open Monday–Saturday, 10 A.M.–9:30 P.M.; Sunday, noon–6 P.M. Restaurant and food court hours may vary.
- Metrorail Orange and Blue lines (Federal Triangle).
- Parking is limited, although there is free parking for tour buses.
- Food court and several restaurants.

After a visit to the Old Post Office Tower (see Chapter 2, Main Sights and Museums in Washington, DC) you and your family might want to grab a bite to eat and take a look at the shops located on the lower floors of the same building. Shops in this mall tend to feature unique gifts. Pushcarts filled with interesting mementos are scattered throughout. Each day at noon the grand atrium is the sight of free performances featuring dancers, musicians, clowns, and others. Call 202-389-4224 for a monthly calendar of Pavilion performances and seasonal events. This shopping center is located two blocks from the Smithsonian museums, midway between the White House and the Capitol.

The Shops at National Place

1331 Pennsylvania Avenue, NW, Washington, DC 20004 (202-783-9090).

- Open Monday–Saturday, 10 A.M.–7 P.M.; Thursday and Friday, 10 A.M.–8 P.M.; Sunday 11 A.M.–5 P.M. Restaurant and food court hours may vary.

- Metrorail Red, Orange, and Blue lines (Metro Center).
- Parking in nearby commercial lots.
- Food court on Level 3; restaurants and cafes on lower levels.

Attached to the J.W. Marriott Hotel and the National Theater, this 4-floor mall has a food court, several restaurants, and a wide variety of shops including clothing, records, crafts, toys, books, and T-shirts. Nearby sights include Ford's Theater, the FBI Building, and the Washington Monument.

Union Station

50 Massachusetts Avenue, NE, Washington, DC 20002
(202-371-9441).

- Open Monday–Saturday, 10 A.M.–9 P.M.; Sunday, noon–6 P.M. Restaurant, food court, and movie theater hours may vary.
- Metrorail Red line (Union Station).
- Parking garage with plenty of spaces.
- Tourmobile® stop.
- Food court and restaurants.
- Movie theaters.

Completed in 1908, Union Station is considered one of the finest examples of Beaux Arts architecture. It is a busy train terminal and a stylish place to grab a quick meal, do some shopping, see a movie, or enjoy a seasonal exhibit or entertainment. The lower level food court offers hungry visitors a wide variety of traditional American and inviting ethnic foods. Several restaurants are located on the upper floors in what used to be the Presidential Suite, passenger lounges, and baggage claim areas. Shopping ranges from single-focus stores such as The Great Train Store, which features every imaginable kind of railroad memorabilia, to branches of familiar stores, to the East Hall's collection of specialty booths and shops. The whole family will enjoy a stop at this historic building, which is located near Capitol Hill.

Children's Books

Aladdin's Lamp

126 West Broad Street (Route 7), Falls Church City, VA 22046
(703-241-8281).

- Open Monday, Wednesday, Friday, and Saturday, 10 A.M.–6
  P.M.; Tuesday, 11 A.M.–8 P.M.; Thursday, 10 A.M.–8 P.M.; Sunday,
  noon–5 P.M.
- Ample parking behind the store.
- Wheelchair access.
- Strollers permitted.

The founder and owner of this store, a former children's librarian,
is eager to help parents and teachers ensure that their children
develop an appreciation for literature. Discounts are offered to
teachers and there are children's story hours and visits from
authors. In addition to a wide selection of books (from chewable
infant books to folklore, Judaica, children's classics, and fantasy), the store carries tapes, puppets, educational toys, rubber
stamps, greeting cards, posters, puzzles, and other items. There
is also a large selection of parenting books.

Audubon Naturalist Society Book Shop

8940 Jones Mill Road, Chevy Chase, MD 20815 (301-652-3606).

- Open weekdays, 10 A.M.–5 P.M., Thursday, until 8 P.M.; Satur-
  day, 9 A.M.–5 P.M. Closed Sunday.
- Parking lot.
- Wheelchair access.
- Strollers can be parked on the porch.

Located at Woodend, the Society's headquarters, this shop stocks
an extensive selection of books about birds, animals, and plants
as well as storybooks and fiction. Some puppets, puzzles, and

card games are also offered. An environmental resource catalog is available. You might want to schedule your visit to coincide with the beginners' bird walk held every Saturday from 8–9 A.M. No registration is required. See Chapter 5, Nature, for more information about the Audubon Naturalist Society.

The Book Nook

10312 Main Street, Fairfax, VA 22030 (703-591-6545).

- Open Monday–Saturday, 10 A.M.–6 P.M.; Thursday, until 8 P.M. In the fall only, open Sunday, 1–5 P.M.
- Plenty of parking.
- Wheelchair access.
- Strollers permitted.

This full service children's bookstore carries T-shirts, puppets, posters, and stamps, in addition to maintaining large foreign language and parenting sections. A teachers' nook has professional educational materials. Every other Saturday morning is story time. Arts and crafts classes are held in the store during the summer months. Call to be placed on the newsletter mailing list.

Borders Book Shop for Kids

11520 A Rockville Pike, Rockville, MD 20852 (301-816-1067).

- Open Monday–Saturday, 9 A.M.–9 P.M.; Sunday, 11 A.M.–8 P.M.
- Metrorail Red line (White Flint).
- Parking lot with plenty of spaces.
- Wheelchair access.
- Strollers permitted.

At any point in time, Borders Book Shop for Kids has in stock 15–18,000 titles for infants through young adults, and parenting and child care books for their parents. In addition to the classics and Caldecott and Newbury award winners, the store has a strong non-fiction section, a large foreign language section (Korean, Spanish, German, and French) and a selection of children's

Judaica. Children will enjoy special programs such as story-tellers, musicians, and more presented in the store's amphitheater. Hardcover bestsellers (as listed in the New York Times and the Washington Post) are 30% off the retail price. Most other hardcover titles are reduced by 10%. Staff must pass a test on children's books before being hired.

Cheshire Cat Children's Book Store

5512 Connecticut Avenue, NW, Washington, DC 20015 (202-244-3956).

- Open Monday–Saturday, 9:30 A.M.–5:30 P.M.; Thursday, until 8 P.M.
- On-street parking available.
- Wheelchair access.
- Strollers permitted.

This long-time children's bookstore, the oldest in the Washington, DC area, was founded by former staff of the Green Acres School. They offer an extensive selection of paperback and hardback books for and about children. In addition, the store carries records and audio and video tapes. Phone, mail, and special orders are accepted. Extremely knowledgeable personnel are helpful and hospitable. Appealing play and reading areas are available, as is a newsletter with book reviews and announcements of author talks, contests, and other special events. In early September, the shop's front window is transformed into a home for caterpillars going through their life stages as they become monarch butterflies. While children and parents patiently stand and watch, butterflies will emerge from their chrysalises. Well worth a trip at any time of the year.

The Children's Book Shop

The Colonnade at Union Mill, 5730 Union Mill Road, Clifton, VA 22024 (703-818-7270). Located between Route 29 and Braddock Road in the Clifton/Centreville area of Fairfax County.

- Open weekdays, 10 A.M.–7 P.M.; Saturday, 10 A.M.–6 P.M.; Sunday, noon–5 P.M.
- Parking lot with plenty of spaces.
- Wheelchair access.
- Strollers permitted.

This spacious, well-stocked children's bookshop has books for children from infancy through high school. Younger children can unwind in a small play area with a sit-in fire engine or enjoy Saturday morning story hours at 11 A.M. (call for reservations). A newsletter lists special events. Teachers can ask to be put on a separate mailing list. Special orders are no problem and school libraries can receive a discount on purchases.

Chuck & Dave's Books, Etc.

7001 Carroll Avenue, Takoma Park, MD 20912 (301-891-2665).

- Open weekdays, 11 A.M.–8 P.M.; Saturday, 10 A.M.–7 P.M.; Sunday, 10 A.M.–5 P.M.
- Metrorail Red line (Takoma).
- On-street parking available.
- Wheelchair access.
- Strollers permitted.

A large selection of children's paper and hardback books can be found in this full-service book store, along with games and wooden and handmade toys. The children's section of the store emphasizes educational books, toys, and games. Trinkets go for under $10, larger toys and games average between $10–20. A rocking boat is a big favorite for young shoppers. Parents can explore the large selection of new age and contemporary literature.

Fairy Godmother

319 7th Street, SE, Washington, DC 20003 (202-547-5474). Located ½ block from Eastern Market.

- Open Monday, noon–6 P.M.; Tuesday–Friday, 11 A.M.–6 P.M. In the fall and spring open Sunday, 10 A.M.–4 P.M.
- Metrorail Orange and Blue lines (Eastern Market).
- On-street, metered parking.
- No wheelchair access.
- Strollers permitted.

This is primarily a children's book store with a large selection of creative toys, music, and book-related videos and stuffed animals. Special orders and gift wrapping are provided.

Imagination Station

4524 Lee Highway (at Lorcum Lane), Arlington, VA 22207 (703-522-2047).

- Open Monday–Saturday, 10 A.M.–6 P.M.; Sunday, 11 A.M.–4 P.M.
- Plenty of parking behind the store.
- Wheelchair access.
- Strollers permitted.

This store carries a large selection of foreign language children's books, including many Tin Tin books (French graphic novels). There is a wide variety of audio and video tapes and a children's play area. Call to get on the mailing list for a newsletter that lists special events.

Francis Scott Key Book Shop

1400 28th Street, NW, Washington, DC 20007 (202-337-4144). Located at corner of O Street.

- Open Monday–Saturday, 9:30 A.M.–6 P.M.
- Parking in two spaces assigned to the store or on the street.

- No wheelchair access.
- Strollers permitted.

Half of the space in this store is devoted to children's books. The juvenile section specializes in classic children's books for both the younger and older child. Mostly hardcover versions are offered. Special orders and worldwide mailing are available. A children's book club features a different title each month. This is a great store for grandparents to find favorite classics to share with their grandchildren.

A Likely Story

1555 King Street, Alexandria, VA 22314 (703-836-2498).

- Open Monday–Saturday, 10 A.M.–6 P.M.; Sunday, 1–5 P.M.
- Metrorail Yellow line (King Street).
- Parking in front of the store.
- Wheelchair access.
- Strollers permitted.

A wide selection of books can be found at this shop, for children from infancy to young adult. The store also carries tapes, puzzles, games, foreign language books, and lots of rubber stamps. They maintain lists to help grandparents keep track of what gifts they've given. Parenting workshops and story hours also are offered, as are author autographing sessions. A pet rabbit resides at the store. Call for information on scheduled events and to get on the newsletter mailing list.

Politics and Prose

5015 Connecticut Avenue, NW, Washington, DC 20814 (202-364-1919).

- Open Monday–Saturday, 10 A.M.–10 P.M.; Sunday, 11 A.M.–6 P.M.
- On-street parking and a lot behind the store.

- Wheelchair access.
- Strollers permitted.

This general bookstore has a selection of hardback and paper-back books for babies through 12-year-olds. They also have posters, puzzles, and T-shirts. Call to be placed on the newsletter mailing list.

Second Story Books

4836 Bethesda Avenue, Bethesda, MD 20814 (301-656-0170).

- Open daily, 10 A.M.–10 P.M.
- Metrorail Red line (Bethesda).
- Limited on-street parking; several public lots nearby.
- Wheelchair access, but aisles are small.
- Strollers permitted.

Second Story Books has five locations (Baltimore, Alexandria, Rockville, Bethesda, and Dupont Circle). The Bethesda branch of this second-hand book store includes the largest selection of children's books, although all stores have some books for children and teens. Records, audio tapes, and video tapes are also available. Stock varies greatly but there are always gems to be found if you don't mind digging through the sometimes disorganized inventory.

Travel Books and Language Center

4931 Cordell Avenue, Bethesda, MD 20814 (301-951-8533).

- Open Monday–Saturday, 10 A.M.–9 P.M.; Sunday, noon–5 P.M.
- Metrorail Red line (Bethesda).
- Limited on-street parking, several public lots nearby.
- Wheelchair access.
- Strollers permitted.

At this store you will find a comprehensive selection of travel and language books for children. They also offer maps and activity books. A great place to visit when you want to get the whole family involved in planning a trip in this country or abroad.

Toys, Games, Hobbies, and Gifts

Backstage, Inc.

2101 P Street, NW, Washington, DC 20037 (202-775-1488).

- Open Monday–Saturday, 10 A.M.–6 P.M.; Thursday, until 8 P.M.
- Metrorail Red line (Dupont Circle, Q Street exit).
- Parking is difficult to find.
- No wheelchair access.
- Strollers permitted.

At this store near Dupont Circle you can find books, make-up, sheet music, costumes, and other items for children and adults interested in the performing arts. This is a fun place to shop for Halloween makeup and accessories, or at any other time of the year.

Beadazzled

1522 Connecticut Avenue, NW, Washington, DC 20036 (202-265-2323).

- Open Monday–Saturday, 11 A.M.–6 P.M.; Sunday, 1–5 P.M.
- Metrorail Red line (Dupont Circle).
- Parking is difficult to find.
- Wheelchair access.
- Strollers permitted.

This treasure chest of a store is filled with all you need to make beaded jewelry and crafts. Children will enjoy choosing from the trays and strands of beads, cord, twine, earring hooks, necklace clasps, and exotic items from India and the Far East. Instruction books, ready-made jewelry, and handcrafted items from other countries also are available.

Capitol Kids

118 King Street, Alexandria, VA 22314 (703-836-1491).

- Open Monday–Thursday, 10 A.M.–10:30 P.M.; Friday–Saturday, 10 A.M.–midnight; Sunday, 11 A.M.–10 P.M. Reduced hours in the winter.
- Metrorail Yellow line (6 blocks from King Street).
- Limited on-street parking.
- Wheelchair access.
- Strollers permitted.

This store specializes in educational and traditional toys and games. There are puzzles and books that focus on the United States and the Washington, DC area. Shopping bags are made to be colored.

Chaselle

9645 Gerwig Lane, Columbia, MD 21046 (301-381-9611).

- Open Monday–Saturday, 9:30 A.M.–5 P.M., Tuesday and Thursday until 8 P.M.
- Plenty of parking in their private lot.
- No wheelchair access.
- Strollers permitted and shopping carts have seat belts for children.

This school supply warehouse is a little difficult to find (call ahead for directions) but the journey is well worth it. Creative youngsters and aspiring young artists will find everything they will ever need to express themselves. Art and other supplies can be purchased in small quantities or in bulk at the store or through one of several catalogs (general, art, early learning, software, multicultural, plus supplements). You will find treasures you never knew you needed in this gem of a store. They also carry sturdy educational toys, posters, books, software, and raw materials (such as sculpture wire). Teachers (with identification) receive a 10% discount.

The Company Mouse

4932 Elm Street, Bethesda, MD 20814 (301-654-1222).

- Open Monday–Saturday, 10 A.M.–5 P.M.; Sunday, noon–4 P.M.
- Private parking lot for store customers.
- Metrorail Red line (Bethesda).
- Wheelchair access.
- Strollers permitted, but the store is very small so it is best to park them.

This small shop is devoted to doll house furniture and materials. You can find a family to live in your doll house, some wallpaper for a decorating project, and a wide variety of miniature accessories. There is also a selection of children's books and collectible dolls.

John Davy Toys

301 Cameron Street, Alexandria, VA 22314 (703-683-0079).

- Open Monday–Saturday, 10 A.M.–5:30 P.M.; Sunday, 11 A.M.–5 P.M.
- Limited on-street parking; parking lots nearby.
- Wheelchair access.
- Strollers permitted.

This 14-year-old store stocks a unique selection of toys from Europe and the United States, including manipulative toys, games, model soldiers, and books. Children love the large Lucite boxes, each filled with a different type of toy, many for $1 or under. Knowledgeable and helpful sales personnel will make your shopping trip a pleasant one.

Definitely Dinosaurs

125 South Fairfax Street, Alexandria, VA 22314 (703-684-0445).

- Open Tuesday–Saturday, 10 A.M.–6 P.M.; January–March closes at 5 P.M.; Sunday noon–5 P.M.
- Limited on street parking; parking lots nearby.
- No wheelchair access.
- Strollers permitted.

Everything in this store has something to do with dinosaurs — from jewelry to backpacks to toys, games, and T-shirts. Call to get on a mailing list for special events for dinosaur lovers.

Imaginarium

- 7101 Democracy Boulevard, # 1098, Montgomery Mall, Bethesda, MD 20817 (301-365-2970).
- 1961 Chain Bridge Road, Tysons Corner, McLean, VA 22101 (703-847-0011)

- Open at Montgomery Mall, Monday–Saturday, 10 A.M.–9:30 P.M.; Sunday, noon–6 P.M.
- Open at Tysons Corner, Monday–Saturday, 10 A.M.–9:30 P.M.; Sunday, noon–5 P.M.
- Parking is plentiful.
- Wheelchair access.
- Strollers permitted.

These stores, which are branches of a national chain, may be best described by the kinds of toys they do not carry — no Barbie dolls, no guns or other violent toys, no toys based on television shows or products, and no Nintendo games! They do carry unique and educational toys and games that encourage children's creativity and thinking. Included are wooden toys, arts and crafts, science, building materials, and learning computers. These are hands-on stores where children can really explore the toys to find out which ones they enjoy most, and parents can avoid purchasing toys that will never be played with. A child-sized doorway and individual name stickers welcome children to a place where they can belong.

Lowen's

- 7201 Wisconsin Avenue, Bethesda, MD 20814 (301-652-1289)
- 11929 Market Street, Reston Town Center, Reston, VA 22090 (703-742-8106).

- Open in Bethesda: Monday–Saturday, 9:30 A.M.–6 P.M., Thursday, until 9 P.M.; Sunday, noon–5 P.M.
- Open in Reston: Monday–Saturday, 10 A.M.–9 P.M.; Sunday, noon–5 P.M.
- Metrorail Red line (Bethesda). No Metrorail in Reston.
- Plenty of parking in nearby lots.
- Wheelchair access to both stores. In-store elevator reaches three floors in the Bethesda store.
- Strollers permitted in both stores.
- Bathrooms designed for children as well as handicapped persons.

Both Lowen's stores stock a wide selection of toys, books, games, stationery, party favors, and arts and crafts supplies. They carry an excellent selection of dolls from around the world and unusual (and cuddly) stuffed animals. An enormous motorized Lego structure is sure to inspire the builders in your family. They have one of the area's largest selection of children's books, study guides, workbooks, educational materials, records, tapes, and videos. Knowledgeable, experienced sales people can guide you in making selections. In the Bethesda store your children can climb in a "1929" roller coaster car and read a book or watch a video. Both stores feature a play room with a giant fish tank. During their annual four-day September sale everything in the store is 20% off. The Bethesda store is quite a bit larger than the Reston branch.

Now and Then

6939 Carroll Avenue, Takoma Park, MD 20912 (301-270-2210).

- Open Monday–Friday, 11 A.M.–7 P.M.; Saturday, 10 A.M.–6 P.M.; Sunday, 11 A.M.–4 P.M.
- On-street parking available and free parking behind the store.
- No wheelchair access.
- Strollers permitted, but this is a small store so it might be best to park them.

This small store is jam-packed with inexpensive toys and games for children of all ages (including fun-loving adults). A great place to find party favors and stocking stuffers — rubber animals and dinosaurs, stickers, small cars and trucks. As displays are at children's level it is easy for them to fully explore the items for sale. The window displays feature tongue-in-cheek seasonal themes that both children and adults will enjoy.

The Red Balloon

1073 Wisconsin Avenue, NW, Washington, DC 20007 (202-965-1200).

- Open Monday–Wednesday, 10 A.M.– 9 P.M.; Thursday until 10 P.M.; Friday and Saturday until 11 P.M.; Sunday, noon–6 P.M.
- Limited on-street parking. Georgetown Park commercial parking lot is across the street.
- No wheelchair access.
- Strollers are permitted, but you will have to carry them up a small flight of steps.

The Red Balloon boasts Washington, DC's largest collection of kaleidoscopes, all of which are handmade. There are always toys for children of all ages to play with in the store. There are over 600 small toys and trinkets that sell for less than $2. This is a good source for party favors, stocking stuffers, and a fun place for children to spend their own allowance.

Re-Use

The Campagna Center, 418 South Washington Street, Alexandria, VA 22314 (703-549-0111).

- Open Tuesday–Friday, 9 A.M.–5 P.M.; Saturday, 9:30–11:30 A.M.
- Parking on the street or in a small lot behind the Center.
- No wheelchair access.
- Strollers permitted, but must be carried up and down two steps.

This arts and crafts recycling center opened in 1991 and is still evolving. They have a remarkable collection of former throwaways that will soon become works of art. Children and adults can fill bags full of fabric pieces, lace and ribbons, buttons, cardboard tubes, wallpaper books and rolls, wood scraps, crayons, foam rubber pieces, berry containers, and more. You can fill a large bag for $4 or a small one for $2. You may need to go to the office first to find someone to let you in.

Smithsonian Museum Shops

- American History, 14th Street and Constitution Avenue, NW, Washington, DC 20560 (202-357-1527).
- Air & Space, 7th Street and Independence Avenue, SW, Washington, DC 20560 (202-357-1387).
- Natural History, 10th Street and Constitution Avenue, NW, Washington, DC 20565 (202-357-1535).

- Open daily, 10 A.M.–5:30 P.M. Closed Christmas. Extended hours in summer.
- Metrorail Blue and Orange lines (Smithsonian).
- Wheelchair access.
- Strollers permitted.

All of the Smithsonian Museums feature gift shops, but the ones listed above are the largest and include the most diverse selections. Books, posters, toys, collectibles, and gifts are related to the specific subject matter of each museum. Special favorites are the personalized dog tags in the Museum of American History, the "space ice cream" in the Air and Space Museum, and the dinosaurs in the Museum of Natural History.

Sullivan's Toy Store

3412 Wisconsin Avenue, NW, Washington, DC 20016 (202-362-1343).

- Open weekdays, 10 A.M.–6 P.M., Thursday, until 8 P.M.; Saturday, 9:30 A.M.–5:30 P.M.; Sunday, noon–4 P.M.
- On-street parking and a lot behind the store.
- Wheelchair access.
- Strollers permitted, but the aisles are quite narrow.

This 38-year-old store packs a lot of toys in a small space. There are toy, book, and art sections as well as party items. There is a Brio train table for children to play with and a professional art store next door for serious young artists. Family owned (by the same family since it was founded), Sullivan's was the first store to carry the first edition of *Going Places*, over 30 years ago.

Toys...Etc.

11325 Seven Locks Road, Potomac, MD 20854 (301-299-8300).

- Open weekdays, 10 A.M.–8 P.M.; Saturday, 10 A.M.–6 P.M.; Sunday, noon–5 P.M.
- Parking lot with plenty of space.
- Wheelchair access.
- Strollers permitted.

A large assortment of toys, both old-fashioned and new, dolls and stuffed animals, art supplies, and a good selection of books can be found at this shop. They specialize in imported toys. Knowledgeable sales personnel are able and willing to make appropriate toy suggestions for any age child. They also carry greeting cards, wrapping paper, and school supplies. Free gift wrap service is available.

Toy Traders

- ◻ 26437 Ridge Road, Damascus, MD 20872 (301-253-0318)
- ◻ Layhill Shopping Center, 14382 Layhill Road, Silver Spring, MD 20906 (301-598-5588).

- Open Monday–Saturday, 10 A.M.–5 P.M.
- Parking lot in front of store.
- Wheelchair access.
- Strollers permitted.

Good quality second-hand toys and games, baby equipment, sporting equipment, and discontinued lines are available, all at about half the normal retail price. Bring in your own used toys to sell (between 10 A.M.–4 P.M.) and, depending on the condition and demand, Toy Traders will pay you by check. You can immediately turn around and buy more toys, or cash it later. They like name brands, but are not too interested in stuffed animals (except for favorites such as Big Bird). They also carry toys for children with disabilities.

Tree Top Toys

Foxhall Square, 3301 New Mexico Avenue, NW, Washington, DC 20016 (202-244-3500).

- Open Monday–Saturday, 9:30 A.M.–5:30 P.M.
- On-street parking and parking lot (first 2 hours are free).
- Wheelchair access.
- Strollers permitted.

Located near American University, this recently expanded store offers well-selected, high-quality toys such as stuffed animals, dolls, trains, puzzles, and a large selection of favorite books and videos. A Brio table is set up for play, along with several other play areas and a reading nook. A catalog is available.

Turtle Park Toys

4115 Wisconsin Avenue, NW, Suite 105, Washington, DC 20016
(202-362-8697).

- Open weekdays, 8:30 A.M.–6 P.M.; Saturday, 9 A.M.–6 P.M.;
  Sunday, 1–5 P.M.
- Limited on-street parking.
- Wheelchair access.
- Strollers permitted.

A wide array of quality toys including a thoughtful selection of
infant toys. Brio, Lego, Playmobil, and wooden toys are featured,
and this is Washington, DC's largest wooden swing dealer. There
is a yearly 20% off sale in September covering most store items
except the outdoor equipment, which goes on sale separately. A
catalog is available.

Whirligigs & Whimsies

Wildwood Shopping Center, 10213 Old Georgetown Road,
Bethesda, MD 20814 (301-897-4940).

- Open Monday–Saturday, 10 A.M.–6 P.M.,Thursday until 7 P.M.;
  Sunday, noon–5 P.M.
- Parking lot with plenty of space.
- Wheelchair access.
- Strollers permitted.

Toy boutique specializing in the unusual. Games, puzzles, books,
dolls, stuffed animals, and craft supplies. Their tape collection is
unusually good. One of the owners can help you select a tape to
meet your child's interests. A Brio table is set up for play and
there is a wall full of small items for stuffing stockings or
delighting party guests. The younger children are amused by a
small train running back and forth along the top of the store.

Why Not Shop

200 King Street, Alexandria, VA 22314 (703-548-4420).

- Open Monday–Saturday, 10 A.M.–5 P.M.; Sunday, noon–5 P.M.
- Limited on-street parking. Parking lots nearby.
- Wheelchair access to first floor only.
- Strollers permitted.

Located in the heart of Old Town Alexandria, this store carries toys for infants to adults. Children can try almost any toy in the store as a "play" sample is usually available. A playpen area on the first floor is full of sample toys. This store stocks an excellent selection of educational toys and charming stuffed animals.

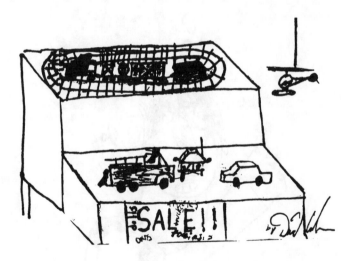

10 Restaurants

Dining out with children can be great fun for the entire family. In the absence of preparation, serving and cleanup, family members can relax, enjoy, and converse with each other. Advance planning often makes the difference between a pleasant experience and one which is far from relaxing for your family. We recommend that you go out early to avoid long delays for a table. Select a restaurant which welcomes children and one where the cuisine served includes the types of food your youngsters usually enjoy. Allowing children to exercise a bit before entering the restaurant is often helpful. When dining with very young children, request, when possible, a table near a window rather than in the middle of the restaurant. Toddlers will find cars and people interesting to watch.

The chapter is divided into two sections. In the first, all dining spots are briefly described and listed alphabetically. In the second section, restaurants are listed alphabetically by geographic location in three separate grids (Maryland, Virginia, and Washington, DC). A fourth grid provides information on cafeterias, buffets, food courts, and restaurants in the Washington, DC sightseeing areas. Each grid summarizes the key information diners might want to know about the restaurant (for example, type of cuisine, availability of high chairs or booster seats, prices). The price categories are estimates only. There is constant change in the restaurant business — chefs, hours, menus, and prices are all subject to change. New ownership can create a whole new restaurant. We suggest you call ahead to verify the information included.

Restaurant Summaries

Washington, DC is a multicultural community. Cuisines from every part of the world are available in and around the city. This chapter includes a few fine restaurants which offer ethnic cuisine. Entire books have been written listing restaurants in the area which serve excellent ethnic fare. The restaurants in this chapter were selected because they welcome children and are comfortable for family dining. Unless otherwise indicated, restaurants are open daily and serve both lunch and dinner.

There are lovely dining spots at or near sightseeing attractions. They offer settings and experiences unlike any other. You can rub elbows with Representatives from the House and with Senators while dining at the Capitol, lunch near a Justice or two in the Supreme Court Cafeteria, have an afternoon snack among fountains and sculptures at the National Portrait Gallery, and take in panoramic views of the beautiful city from many of these dining spots.

Happy dining and bon appetit!

Air and Space Museum, Flight Line

6th Street and Independence Avenue, NW, Washington, DC 20560 (202-357-2700).

Flight Line is a large, airy, and pleasant cafeteria. Floor to ceiling windows offer panoramic views of the Mall and Capitol. Enjoy fresh salads, sandwiches, hot poultry and beef entrees, burgers, pasta, pizza, pastries, and fresh fruit. Open 10 A.M.–5 P.M.

Air and Space Museum, Wright Place

Independence Avenue at 4th Street, SW, Washington, DC 20560 (202-371-8750).

Aviation photographs from the museum's collection decorate the walls of this interesting restaurant. The menu changes and choices vary from sandwiches to grilled fish. An array of freshly baked desserts are offered. Open 11:30 A.M.–3 P.M. for lunch only.

Amalfi

12307 Wilkens Avenue, Rockville, MD 20852 (301-770-7888).

Amalfi is a popular suburban restaurant. The food is good and servings large. White pizza is a specialty. Veal, seafood, and pasta choices are well prepared. Amalfi is often busy and sometimes loud, but continues to be a restaurant to which families return often.

America

Union Station, 50 Massachusetts Avenue, NE, Washington, DC 20002 (202-682-9555).

This is a colorful and upbeat restaurant serving regional specialties from across the United States. The choices range from Santa Fe club sandwiches to shrimp jambalaya and New England roasted turkey. Children enjoy the Vermont apple fritters, macaroni and cheese, sliders (3 ounce hamburgers), pizza, or peanut butter and jelly sandwiches.

The American Cafe

- □ 5252 Wisconsin Avenue, NW, Washington, DC 20016 (202-363-5400).
- □ 1211 Wisconsin Avenue, NW, Washington, DC 20007 (202-944-9464).
- □ 227 Massachusetts Avenue, NE, Washington, DC 20002 (202-547-8500).
- □ 14th and F Streets, NW, Washington, DC 20004 (202-626-0770).
- □ 1200 19th Street, NW, Washington, DC 20036 (202-223-2121).
- □ 1701 Pennsylvania Avenue, NW, Washington, DC 20560 (202-833-3434).
- □ Union Station, 50 Massachusetts Avenue, NE, Washington, DC 20002 (202-682-0937).
- □ 4095 Powder Mill Road, Calverton, MD 20705 (301-937-4755).
- □ 4238 Wilson Boulevard, Arlington, VA 22203 (703-522-2236).

□ 11836 Fair Oaks Mall, Fairfax, VA 22031 (703-352-0368).
□ 1800 Old Meadow Road, McLean, VA 22102 (703-760-7633).
□ 8601 Westwood Center Drive, Vienna, VA 22182 (703-848-9476).

Both the food and setting can be enjoyed here. Large sandwiches on croissants, salads, quiches, and soups are the mainstay of the restaurant. Grilled seafood, poultry dishes, and vegetarian entrees are offered. The children's menu includes favorites such as pizza, peanut butter and jelly sandwiches, and pasta with meatballs.

American City Diner

5532 Connecticut Avenue, NW, Washington, DC 20015 (202-244-1949).

American City Diner is a small and friendly restaurant serving homemade meals and the kinds of foods children enjoy — burgers, shakes, chili, and ice cream desserts. Coke is served in bottles from an old-fashioned vending machine. The entire diner is for non-smokers. It is open 24 hours on Friday and Saturday. You might want to stop here after a visit to The Cheshire Cat bookstore (see Chapter 9, Shopping).

Anchor Inn

2509 University Boulevard West, Wheaton, MD 20902 (301-933-1814)

Fresh seafood, a nautical decor, and cheerful, welcoming service make this a nice choice for families. It is large and busy, but service is attentive. There are several cozy dining rooms which give the feeling that you are in a smaller restaurant. The homemade chowders, imperial crab, stuffed flounder, and crab cakes are house specialties. Fried shrimp are a children's favorite. Originally opened in the 1940s, Anchor Inn has been beautifully renovated.

Anita's

- 9278 Old Keene Mill Road, Burke, VA 22152 (703-455-3466).
- 13921 Lee Jackson Highway, Chantilly, VA 22021 (703-378-1717).
- 10880 Lee Highway, Fairfax, VA 22030 (703-385-2965).
- 701 Elden Street, Herndon, VA 22070 (703-481-1441).
- 521 East Maple Avenue, Vienna, VA 22182 (703-255-1001).
- 147 West Maple Avenue, Vienna, VA 22180 (703-938-0888).

Anita's serves New Mexico-style Mexican food. House specialties include New Mexico green chili. Children also enjoy kiddies' quesadilla and peque — a bean pizza. Tortilla chips sprinkled with cinnamon sugar is an unusual dessert. All six Virginia locations are family-owned and operated.

Bare Bones

617 South Frederick Avenue, Gaithersburg, MD 20878 (301-948-4344).

This is a casual neighborhood restaurant best known for ribs, barbecued chicken, and fried onion loaves. The service is attentive and children are comfortable here.

Bennigan's

- 6002 Greenbelt Road, Greenbelt, MD 20770 (301-982-9780).
- 14180 Baltimore Avenue (Route 1), Laurel, MD 20907 (301-776-4412).
- 12276 Rockville Pike, Rockville, MD 20852 (301-770-2594).
- 2 South Whiting Street, Alexandria, VA 22304 (703-370-7511).
- 11708 Upper Fair Oaks Mall, Fairfax, VA 22031 (703-691-2208).
- 6290 Arlington Boulevard, Falls Church, VA 22044 (703-237-6288).
- 6632 Springfield Mall, Springfield, VA 22152 (703-922-6004).
- 8219 Leesburg Pike, Vienna, VA 22180 (703-556-9417).

Bennigan's is a chain of restaurants offering friendly service and a menu with plenty of appealing selections. Children enjoy corn dogs, mini burgers, popcorn shrimp, fish sticks, grilled cheese, chicken nuggets, and spaghetti. The menu ranges from salads, sandwiches, and quiche to steaks, stir-fry seafood, chicken, and regional entrees. Children receive coloring books and crayons. Different promotions for children under twelve are often in effect.

Bilbo Baggins

208 Queen Street, Alexandria, VA 22314 (703-683-0300).

Bilbo Baggins, named for a character in *The Hobbit*, is an attractive and cozy two-story restaurant in Old Town, Alexandria. The renovated 90-year-old townhouse has a French country decor. The downstairs area has rustic wood floors and wood-paneling. Upstairs there are stained-glass windows and old church pews used for booths. Beautiful plants are placed throughout. The food is fresh and homemade. Bread is baked on the premises. Soups, pasta, salads, quiche, sandwiches, lamb, veal, chicken, and beef can be enjoyed here. The homemade desserts are excellent. The owners have three young children and welcome families. This is a nice place to stop after a day seeing the historic sights of Old Town.

B. J. Pumpernickel's

18169 Town Center Drive, Olney, MD 20832 (301-924-1400).

B.J. Pumpernickel's is fun for children and their parents. The owners, and all who work here, are playful and warm towards children. The walls are covered with caricatures of customers and employees. Each Tuesday from 7 P.M. to closing an artist is available to draw a caricature of any customer; it is displayed for 30 days and then can be picked up at no cost. Each child receives a helium balloon and cookies. There is a treasure chest and live musical performances on the second and fourth Thursday evening of each month. The food is hearty — matzo ball soup is a house specialty. With such a large and diverse menu, there is something to please everyone. The owners often walk around the restaurant with a tray of finger foods (such as potato pancakes or other house specialties) and offer them to the diners. B.J. Pumpernickel's is often busy and can be loud, but the food, selection, service, and extras make it a fine choice for family dining.

Cactus Cantina

3300 Wisconsin Avenue, NW Washington, DC 20016 (202-686-7222).

Families will enjoy this lively and colorful restaurant. It is often busy and loud, but service is friendly and the Tex-Mex cuisine is prepared very well. Grilled entrees such as quail and shrimp are delicious.

Calvert Grille

3106 Mount Vernon Avenue, Alexandria, VA 22305 (703-836-8425).

This family-owned and operated restaurant obviously likes children and offers much to make families feel comfortable. Regulars are greeted by name and the owner often makes special things for children who request their favorites. Children under 12 get free birthday dinners during the month in which their birthday falls. There are toys for toddlers and crayons for older children. House specialties include barbecue baby back ribs, grilled chicken, and crab cakes. Children also enjoy chicken fingers, mini charbroiled burgers, and nightly specials. When Calvert Grille was taken over by its new owners 5 years ago, their family-oriented services began. It is now a thriving neighborhood restaurant where the food is tasty and the atmosphere casual.

The Cheesecake Factory

5345 Wisconsin Avenue, NW Washington, DC 20018 (202-364-0500).

With over 200 items on its varied menu, the Cheesecake Factory is a place where everyone can find something to enjoy. The quality is good and the servings are very large. Choices range from fresh fish, steak, and poultry to California-style Mexican dishes. Children often order pasta or mini burgers. Be sure to save room for dessert — there are 38 types of cheesecake as well as other sweet treats. The restaurant offers unique decor and an upbeat atmosphere, but is very busy. We recommend dining before 6 P.M. on weekdays and before 5 P.M. on weekends to avoid a very long wait for a table.

Chili's

- 11428-A Rockville Pike, Rockville, MD 20852 (301-881-8588).
- 14601 Baltimore Avenue, Laurel, MD 20907 (301-317-6580).
- 4817 A Festival Way, Waldorf, MD 20601 (301-932-9609).
- 5501 Leesburg Pike, Baileys Crossroads, VA 22041 (703-379-2035).
- 2936 Annandale Road, Falls Church, VA 22042 (703-237-8532).
- 11219 Lee Highway, Fairfax, VA 22030 (703-591-7888).
- 10600 Sudley Manor Drive, Manassas, VA 22110 (703-330-0208).
- 11840 Sunrise Valley Drive, Reston, VA 22091 (703-758-9268).
- 6324 Old Keene Mill Road, Springfield, VA 22150 (703-451-0222).
- 14432 Gideon Drive, Woodbridge, VA 22192 (703-490-3118).
- 8051 Leesburg Pike, Vienna, VA 22182 (703-734-9512).

Chili's is a good choice for casual family dining. The primarily Tex-Mex cuisine includes a large variety of salads, ribs, burger combinations, and chicken entrees. Children often enjoy both soft and hard tacos, hot dogs, chicken tenders, chicken drumettes, and grilled cheese sandwiches. Ice cream and frozen yogurt sundaes are favorite desserts at Chili's.

China Inn

631 H Street, NW, Washington, DC 20560 (202-842-0909).

China Inn is Chinatown's oldest restaurant. It enjoys regulars who return year after year. The Cantonese cooking is authentic and food is beautifully presented. After your meal you can stroll through the streets of Chinatown, looking at the unusual items in the food and gift shops.

Chuck E. Cheese

- □ 9404 Main Street, Fairfax, VA 222030 (703-978-5755).
- □ 13807 Outlet Drive, Silver Spring, MD 20904 (301-890-6767).
- □ 516 North Frederick Avenue, Gaithersburg, MD 20878 (301-869-9010).

Chuck E. Cheese is a place for children and their fun-loving parents. Here they find arcade games, skee-ball, rides for toddlers, and singing and dancing characters. Based in Texas, there are 300 Chuck E. Cheese restaurants nationally. Pizza, hot dogs, and a salad bar are offered in a carnival-like setting. Weekends are extremely busy, especially for birthday parties. We recommend trying Chuck E. Cheese on a weekday.

Clyde's

- □ 3236 M Street, NW, Washington, DC 20007 (202-333-9180).
- □ 8332 Leesburg Pike, Vienna, VA 22182 (703-734-1900).
- □ 11905 Market Street, Reston Town Center, Reston, VA 22090 (703-787-6601).

The original Clyde's is a Georgetown tradition, and all locations are extremely popular. There is a wide choice of food, from foot-long hot dogs, burgers, chili, and salads to broiled fish and grilled poultry. All three branches have very interesting and pretty dining areas. When visiting the Georgetown location, try the omelette room with an exhibition kitchen or the patio room — a jungle setting with large papier-mache toucans and parrots.

Crisfield's

- 8012 Georgia Avenue, Silver Spring, MD 20910 (301-589-1306).
- 8606 Colesville Road, Silver Spring, MD 20910 (301-588-1572).

Excellent fish and shellfish are served at both locations of this restaurant, renowned for its preparation of fresh seafood. Oysters, imperial crab, baked shrimp stuffed with crab, and broiled fish are particularly noteworthy. Crisfield's II (Colesville Road location) is more upscale than the plain setting at the original Crisfield's (although when you sit at the counter at the original you can watch the dexterous staff expertly shuck fresh oysters and clams). The original began serving in 1944 and is still in the same location, serving many regular customers who return again and again. Children will be welcome and comfortable at both locations. Dine early to avoid the long lines.

The Dirksen Senate Office Building

1st and C Streets, NE,Washington, DC 20510 (202-224-3121, information).

The Dirksen Senate Office Building has four separate dining choices. All four can be reached via the C Street entrance to the office building. Try the free subway ride from the Capitol building to the Dirksen Office Building.

The Senate Buffet offers a wonderful all-you-can-eat fixed price buffet ($7.15 for adults and $4.89 for children under twelve, plus 15% gratuity). It is open Monday–Friday for lunch only. The buffet choices include roast beef, leg of lamb, vegetables, a full salad and fruit bar, and a make-your-own ice cream sundae bar.

The Dirksen Senate Building Cafeteria and the *Coffee Shop* are open for breakfast and lunch, Monday–Friday, 7:30

A.M.–3:30 P.M. Note, however, that the coffee shop is closed to the public from noon to 1:30 P.M.

The Fast Food Service within the Dirksen Senate Office Building is open Monday–Friday, 7:30 A.M.–7 P.M. and Saturday, 7:30 A.M.–3 P.M.

Duangrat's

5878 Leesburg Pike, Baileys Crossroads, VA 22041 (703-820-5775).

Duangrat's is a very attractive restaurant which serves outstanding Thai cuisine. The food is presented beautifully and portions are plentiful. It's hard to go wrong with regular menu offerings or with specials because the food is delicious. Children often enjoy satay — grilled beef or pork served on a stick. Fried wontons are also a favorite for children. The service is gracious. It is best to leave your infants and toddlers at home, and take older children here on a Monday through Thursday evening when reservations are accepted. The restaurant is very busy on weekends and does not accept reservations on Friday and Saturday evenings. Dining here is memorable.

Encore Cafe at the Kennedy Center

New Hampshire Avenue and F Street, NW, Washington, DC
20037 (202-416-8560).

The Encore Cafe is a very attractive cafeteria. Large windows
throughout provide beautiful views of Washington. The food is
made fresh daily and choices include pizza, hot vegetarian and
poultry entrees, sandwiches, and salads. Open daily, 11 A.M.–8 P.M.

Fuddrucker's

- □ 4300 Backlick Road, Annandale, VA 22003 (703-642-0021).
- □ 6201 Arlington Boulevard, Falls Church, VA 22044 (703-536-3833).
- □ 1030 Elden Street, Herndon, VA 22070 (703-318-9438).
- □ 1300 Rockville Pike, Rockville, MD 20852 (301-468-3501).

This restaurant caters to children. The menu and atmosphere
make this a restaurant children want to return to again and
again. Choose from burgers, ribs, chicken, and salad. Children
enjoy the ice cream and cookie counters. A few arcade games
keep children busy before and after the meal. Periodic specials
include free meals for children dining with adults on a weekday
evening.

Generous George's Positive Pizza and Pasta Place

- □ 3006 Duke Street, Alexandria, VA 22343 (703-370-4303).
- □ 6131 Backlick Road, Springfield, VA 22153 (703-451-7111).

This restaurant is fun, lively, and a wonderful choice for a family
night out. Large carousel animals scattered throughout the restaurant add to the decor and to the festivities. Children can climb
giraffes, lions, and elephants. All children receive a free Generous
George T-shirt with their meal (to size 16–18). The pizza is
delicious, with a slightly sweet crust. Toppings range from the
simple to the elaborate. Specialty pizzas include pizza topped

with chicken breast, broccoli, mushrooms, and onions, or pizza topped with onion, tomato chunks, and feta cheese. Their invention called the "positive pasta pie" is pizza crust topped with entrees such as chicken flamingo, fettucini alfredo, and homemade lasagna, with many more to choose from. Large salads and sandwiches are also served. There are always plenty of families at Generous George's.

Geppetto's

- □ 2917 M Street, NW, Washington, DC 20007 (202-333-2602).
- □ 10257 Old Georgetown Road, Bethesda, MD 20814 (301-493-9230).

This charming restaurant, known for terrific pizza, also serves homemade pastas, veal and chicken entrees, sandwiches, and salads. Named for Pinocchio's father, the restaurant is decorated with puppets and cuckoo clocks.

The Ground Round

- □ 6310 Richmond Highway, Alexandria, VA 22306 (703-765-7469).
- □ 9625 Lee Highway, Fairfax, VA 22030 (703-352-8897).
- □ 7913 Sudley Road, Manassas, VA 22110 (703-361-9759).
- □ 13761 Jefferson Davis Highway, Woodbridge, VA 22192 (703-491-4120).

The Ground Round chain of restaurants does much to focus on children. Old movies and cartoons are shown on a large screen in the dining room, and there are several arcade games, mirrors with optical illusions, and balloons. A bowl of popcorn on each table adds to the friendly atmosphere. There are children's contests, including best environmental tip and best essay. Seasonal events for children include breakfast with Santa, countdown party for New Year's, essay contests for Mother's Day and Father's Day, and Halloween festivities. Bingo the Clown interacts with the children on weekends and some evenings. Children enjoy burgers, chicken fingers, pizza, hot dogs, pasta, fish, and grilled cheese. Parents can select from light fare such as salads and sandwiches or hot entrees such as ribs, seafood, and poultry dishes. The Ground Round is the site of many birthday parties on Saturday and Sunday afternoons. We suggest Sunday through Thursday to avoid crowds. The Ground Round is likely to be a favorite of your children.

Hamburger Hamlet

- 3125 M Street, NW, Washington, DC 20007 (202-965-6970).
- 5225 Wisconsin Avenue, NW, Washington, DC 20017 (202-244-2037).
- 10400 Old Georgetown Road, Bethesda, MD 20814 (301-897-5350).
- 9811 Washingtonian Boulevard, Gaithersburg, MD 20878 (301-417-0773).
- 1601 Crystal Square Arcade, Crystal City, VA 22202 (703-521-4022).

Hamburger Hamlet is considered by many to be the best restaurant in the area for juicy burgers. In addition to burgers, children enjoy nachos, hot dogs, grilled cheese, potato skins, and sandwiches. These comfortable restaurants also serve a variety of large salads, soups, and a few hot entrees including rotisserie chicken and crab cakes. Milk shakes, fresh fruit shakes, and ice cream desserts are favorites. They are very busy on weekends, so come early, or come prepared for a wait.

Hard Times Cafe

- 1117 Nelson Street, Rockville, MD 20850 (301-294-9720).
- 1404 King Street, Alexandria, VA 22303 (703-683-5340).
- 3028 Wilson Boulevard, Arlington, VA 22209 (703-528-2233).
- 394 Elden Street, Herndon, VA 22070 (703-318-8941).

Hard Times Cafe is a lively restaurant featuring a variety of chilis, including Texas, Cincinnati, and vegetarian styles. Burgers served with or without chili, hot dogs, corn bread, and onion rings are also enjoyed here. Pictures of the Old West, including famous cowboys, decorate the walls at these upbeat restaurants. Children enjoy playing "cowboy" songs from the selections on the jukebox.

House of Chinese Chicken

12710 Twinbrook Parkway, Rockville, MD 20852 (301-881-4500).

There are many outstanding house specialities at this relaxing family-style restaurant. Children often enjoy Peking chicken and lo mein dishes. Peking chicken is prepared similarly to Peking duck, but it is far less fatty. It is served with pancakes, scallions, and plum sauce. All food is prepared without MSG. Fine vegetarian choices are served here.

House of Representatives Restaurant

Room H118 in Capitol Building, East Capitol and 1st Streets, NW, Washington, DC 20002 (202-225-6300).

The House of Representatives Restaurant serves hot entrees, burgers, and hot sandwiches. It is open from 8 A.M.–3 P.M. If the House remains in session beyond closing time, the restaurant also remains open.

Il Forno

◻ 4926 Cordell Avenue, Bethesda, MD 20814 (301-652-7757).
◻ 8941 North Westland Drive, Gaithersburg, MD 20878 (301-977-5900).

Il Forno serves pizza made with fresh ingredients. Interesting toppings which appeal to both adults and children include olives, artichokes, capers, spinach, homemade sausage, and pepperoni. Some of the toppings include fresh garlic; you can request the garlic be left out.

Kabul West

4871 Cordell Avenue, Bethesda, MD 20814 (301-986-8566).

For a real treat, your family might try Afghan food. The fare in this small but friendly restaurant promises a new culinary experience for children. Appetizers, kabobs, and vegetable dishes are favorites. Fried dough topped with sugar and pistachios is a treat for children.

L & N Seafood

- 12266 Rockville Pike, Rockville, MD 20852 (301-250-1952).
- South Joy and Hayes Street, Arlington, VA 22232 (703-415-2055).
- Route 50 and I-66, Fairfax, VA 22031 (703-591-1096).
- 2001 International Drive, McLean, VA 22033 (703-790-5754).
- 11811 Freedom Drive, Reston, VA 22090 (703-709-7018).

L & N Seafood offers comfortable family dining with friendly and attentive service. There is a large selection of grilled fish and shellfish. Seafood pasta dishes, beef, and poultry choices are also offered. All-you-can-eat homemade biscuits and bottomless salads will accompany your meal.

Library of Congress Cafeteria

James Madison Memorial Building, 101 Independence
Avenue, SE, Washington, DC 20540 (202-707-8300).

This sixth floor cafeteria has large windows, offering panoramic
city views. The food is fresh and homemade. Hot entrees change
daily but may include fish, beef, and poultry choices. There is a
large salad bar. Sandwiches are also available.

Library of Congress Montpelier Room

James Madison Memorial Building, 101 Independence
Avenue, SE, Washington, DC 20540 (202-707-8300).

This sixth-floor restaurant offers a lovely setting with views from
large windows on two sides. The fixed price lunch includes hot
entrees and salad. Desserts are extra. Lunch is served weekdays,
11:30 A.M.–2 P.M.

Listrani's

5100 MacArthur Boulevard, NW, Washington, DC 20016 (202-
363-0620).

Listrani's is a cheerful neighborhood restaurant which serves
gourmet entrees, unusual salads with homemade dressings, and
excellent pizza. Calzones and white pizza are especially good.
Seafood, chicken, and pasta entrees are delicious. If you still have
room try one of their desserts such as a blondie or brownie
sundae. Children will enjoy looking at the restaurant's display of
gnomes.

Louisiana Express Company

4921 Bethesda Avenue, Bethesda, MD 20814 (301-652-6945).

This is a very small and informal restaurant offering Cajun and
Creole dishes. The jambalaya and fine gumbos are authentic, and
the rotisserie chicken is crisp and juicy. Some dishes are avail-

able in two sizes. Adventurous children like the spicy french fries; parents enjoy the excellent coffee. Be sure to try their interesting appetizers and desserts. A plate of beignets (with strawberries if you like) will top off the meal for the whole family.

Misha's Place of Cheese and Cheer

208 7th Street, S.E., Washington, DC 20003 (202-547-5858).

This gem of an eatery is a rare find located across from the Eastern Market. Old-fashioned Russian and Jewish dishes are offered, and the experience is unlike any other place. It is very small (only seven tables) and very informal. The walls have a hand-painted border of characters from the poems and stories of the famous Russian poet, Alexander Pushkin. The food is extraordinary. There are fifteen salads, including eggplant and beet salads and mushroom caviar. In addition to piroshki, you can enjoy different types of knishes, stuffed cabbage, stuffed grape leaves, and many other choices. The Ukrainian bread and dessert items are outstanding — try honey macaroons, poppy seed breakfast rolls, or any of the exceptional baked items. The owner is very warm, inviting, and enthusiastic. The foods may not appeal to younger children. We recommend Cheese and Cheer for older children and their families.

The National Gallery of Art, Cascade Cafe

4th Street and Constitution Avenue, NW, Washington, DC 20565 (202-347-9401).

This pretty restaurant on the bottom floor of the main building overlooks a fascinating indoor waterfall. While waiting for their food, children will be intrigued by this wall of flowing water. The menu is very limited, usually offering about five items daily, and changes throughout the year, but generally includes salads, burgers, and hot entrees. Freshly baked pastries and hot fudge sundaes are offered for dessert. The restaurant is open Monday–Saturday, 11:30–4:30 P.M. and Sunday, 11 A.M.–4:30 P.M.

The National Gallery of Art, Concourse Buffet

On the Mall between 3rd and 7th Streets, NW, Washington, DC 20565 (202-347-9401).

This is a pretty and cheerful cafeteria set between the East and West wings of the National Gallery of Art. Enjoy the salad bar, croissant sandwiches, burgers, hot dogs, and hot entrees. Freshly-baked desserts and frozen yogurt are also available.

The National Gallery of Art, Garden Cafe

4th Street and Constitution Avenue NW, Washington, DC 20565 (202-347-9401).

This charming restaurant in the West Building offers dining under a skylight at tables situated around a fountain. The menu changes and is nearly identical to the cuisine offered in the other cafes within the National Gallery of Art. The restaurant serves Monday–Saturday, 11 A.M.–4:30 P.M. and Sunday, 11 A.M.–6 P.M.

The National Gallery of Art, Terrace Cafe

600 Constitution Avenue, NW, Washington, DC 20565 (202-347-9401).

This pleasant restaurant in the East Building overlooks the Mall and is in full view of the Calder mobile, the skylights, and the Rodin statuary. The menu changes and is nearly identical to the cuisine offered in the other cafes within the National Gallery of Art (see above). The hours of operation are Monday through Saturday, 11 A.M.–4:30 P.M. and Sunday, noon–6 P.M.

The National Portrait Gallery, Patent Pending Cafeteria

8th and F Streets, NW, Washington, DC 20560 (202-357-1571).

Patent Pending is a small cafeteria located in a courtyard linking the National Portrait Gallery with the National Museum of American Art. Decorated with art posters, the decor is charming. Outdoor courtyard tables offer dining among fountains and sculptures. Sandwiches, a fresh salad bar, and homemade soups are offered for lunch. Breakfast items include eggs, bacon croissants, and muffins. Breakfast is served Monday–Friday, 8–10:30 A.M. Lunch is served daily, 11 A.M.–3:30 P.M.

O'Donnell's

8301 Wisconsin Avenue, Bethesda, MD 20814 (301-656-6200).

O'Donnell's offers casual family dining and fresh, well-prepared seafood. You might want to try the crab dishes, broiled fish, or one of the many Norfolk specialties. Families can feel quite comfortable here. Sweet breads and rolls as well as crackers and cheese are brought as soon as you are seated. Children receive crayons and the children's menu has puzzles and games. After dinner, children can choose a toy from the treasure chest. Be sure to make reservations to avoid a long wait for a table.

The Pavilion at the Old Post Office

1110 Pennsylvania Avenue, NW, Washington, DC 20009 (202-289-4224).

The Pavilion is a cheerful and bustling place located between the White House and the Capitol. The eatery and full service restaurants offer a wide variety of ethnic and American food choices. Daily entertainment varies from musical performances to magicians. Open, January 2–March 4, Monday–Saturday, 10 A.M.–8 P.M.; Sunday, noon–6:00 P.M. From March 5th–January 1st, open Monday–Saturday, 10 A.M.–9:30 P.M.; Sunday, noon–8 P.M. Information on the Old Post Office Tower is in Chapter 2, Main Sights and Museums in Washington, DC; information on the shopping center is in Chapter 9, Shopping.

Peking Gourmet Inn

6029 Leesburg Pike, Fails Church, VA 22041 (703-671-8088).

As the name implies, Peking duck is the house specialty of this well-known Chinese restaurant. The outside is plain, but the inside is very nice and the food is excellent. You will see pictures throughout of the owner with famous celebrities who have enjoyed dining here — including President and Mrs. Bush, who have dined here many times. Peking Gourmet Inn offers a party menu along with the standard menu. The party menu has different selections for parties of four, six, or eight persons. Each person in the party can sample from eight to ten gourmet dishes. This would be an enjoyable dining experience for a group of adults or for several families. Children are welcomed here, and this is a wonderful choice for relaxed family dining.

Pines of Italy

- ◻ 237 North Glebe Road, Arlington, VA 22203 (703-524-4969).
- ◻ 556 South 22nd Street, Crystal City, VA 22202 (703-271-0511).

The Pines of Italy has great family appeal — the food is first-rate, the service is warm and friendly, and children are welcomed. It is a very popular restaurant and enjoys a clientele which returns time after time. The tortellini, pizza, and cannolis are favorites. The newest location in Crystal City offers the same menu and prices in a more upscale setting.

Pizzeria Uno

- 50 Massachusetts Avenue, NE, Washington, DC 20002 (202-842-0438). Located at Union Station.
- 3211 M Street, NW, Washington, DC 20007 (202-965-6333).
- 7272 Wisconsin Avenue, Bethesda, MD 20814 (301-986-8667).
- 11948 Market Street, Reston, VA 22090 (703-742-8667).

Pizzeria Uno is a chain of bright and cheerful restaurants offering a wide choice of foods. There are salads, soups, deep dish pizza, thin crust gourmet pizza, pasta dishes, chicken and steak fajitas, burgers, sandwiches, and tasty desserts.

Red, Hot, & Blue

- 1600 Wilson Boulevard, Arlington, VA 22209 (703-276-7427).
- 677 Main Street, Laurel, MD 20707 (301-953-1943).
- 8637 Sudley Road, Manassas, VA 22110 (703-330-4847).

Red, Hot, & Blue specializes in Memphis pit style barbecue dishes. The restaurant's ribs, pulled pig sandwiches, pulled chicken sandwiches, and barbecued beef brisket are superb. The side dishes are memorable. There are two types of ribs (wet and dry), and they are considered by many to be the best in the Washington area. The chicken drumettes, burgers, and grilled cheese will please children who do not wish to try the barbecued dishes. The atmosphere is casual, with the walls decorated with Memphis blues memorabilia, and blues guitar music playing in the background. We recommend that you dine early; waiting one hour for a table during peak dinner hours is not unusual.

Senate Refectory

Located in the Senate north wing of the Capitol building (202-224-4870).

The Refectory serves light fare including burgers, sandwiches, and fresh pies. It is open for breakfast and lunch only. Hours are 8 A.M.–4 P.M. It remains open later when the Senate is in session.

Renato Trattoria

10120 River Road, Potomac, MD 20854 (301-365-1900).

Renato is a small, cozy, neighborhood restaurant. The wonderful aroma, delicious food and warm service make this a busy spot. The owner describes Renato as a trattoria similar to that which one would find in the cities of Italy. The bread and bread sticks are made here, as well as memorable pasta, veal, and fish entrees. The pizza is also excellent. The menu offers much to please; however, the owner describes his menu as only a guide. He welcomes all who visit to tell him what they like and it will be prepared individually. Every item on the menu can be ordered in child-sized portions. Although the atmosphere is informal and young children are welcomed here, we recommend this restaurant for older children because it is small and quiet.

Rio Grande Cafe

- 4919 Fairmont Avenue, Bethesda, MD 20814 (301-656-2981).
- 4301 North Fairfax Drive, Arlington, VA 22203 (703-528-3131).
- Reston Town Center, Reston, VA 22090 (703-938-4500).

Rio Grande Cafe serves fresh and outstanding Tex-Mex food. It's loud, it's festive, it's whimsically decorated, and it's always crowded. Enjoy exceptionally well-prepared chiles rellenos, tamales, fajitas, tacos, Tex-Mex grilled spareribs, grilled shrimp, or more adventurous dishes such as frog legs and quail. Reservations are not accepted and the restaurant fills even during early hours on weekends.

Rocco's

- 1357 Chain Bridge Road, McLean, VA 22101 (703-821-3736).
- 6804 Commerce Street, Springfield, VA 22150 (703-644-2264).

This family-owned and operated restaurant serves Southern Italian cuisine and pizza. The atmosphere is warm and casual and the portions are very large. All-you-can-eat specials and well-prepared food attract many families.

Roof Terrace Restaurant at the Kennedy Center

New Hampshire Avenue and F Street, NW, Washington, DC 20037 (202-416-8555).

This restaurant at the Kennedy Center is an extremely plush and elegant dining spot. The immense windows provide diners with panoramic views of the Potomac. The menu, which changes seasonally, includes beautifully presented and well-prepared fish, beef, and poultry dishes. Desserts are special treats. We recommend this restaurant for older children only. The hours are from 11:30 A.M.–3 P.M. for lunch. Dinner is served from 5:30–9 P.M.

Sholl's Colonial Cafeteria

- 1990 K Street, NW, Washington, DC 20006 (202-296-3065).
- 1750 Pennsylvania Avenue, NW, Washington, DC 20560 (202-737-5259).

Sholl's Colonial Cafeteria is a longtime favorite known for fresh, homemade dishes and unbeatable prices. Everything served here is prepared on the premises. Home style breakfast, lunch, and dinner are offered. Enjoy hot beef, poultry, and fish entrees ranging from old-fashioned chopped steak to chicken a-la-king, beef stew, or baked chicken. A variety of seasonal vegetables are prepared daily. Sholl's serves memorable biscuits, muffins, fruit pies, and puddings. Light fare and fresh fruit are also served. Staff will help children carry their trays to your table.

The Shops at National Place

1313 Pennsylvania Avenue, NW, Washington, DC 20004 (202-783-9090)

This collection of shops and dining spots offers a wide variety of food options. There are full service restaurants as well as quick eateries. The hours for the eateries are Monday–Wednesday, 10 A.M.–7 P.M.; Thursday–Friday, 10 A.M.–8 P.M.; Saturday, 10 A.M.–7 P.M.; Sunday, noon–5 P.M.

Silver Diner

- 11806 Rockville Pike, Rockville, MD 20852 (301-770-0333).
- 14550 Baltimore Avenue (Route 1), Laurel, MD 20907 (301-604-6995).
- 14375 Smoketown Road, Dale City, VA 22193 (703-491-7376).

The Silver Diner serves home-style meals in a setting which reflects the diners of the 1930s and 40s. There is a broad selection of meals ranging from beef and poultry entrees to salads and sandwiches. Breakfast items are served all day. The chocolate chip pancakes are a special treat for children. Be sure to ask about the daily specials. A large selection of pies and cakes are baked on the premises. Children receive crayons and the children's menu has connect-the-dots and word games. Dine early to avoid a long wait for a table.

The Supreme Court Cafeteria

1st Street, NE, between East Capitol Street and Maryland Avenue, Washington, DC 20543 (202-479-3246).

This attractive cafeteria offers breakfast and lunch on weekdays only. Full breakfasts are available. Soup, hot entree specials, sandwiches on croissants, a salad bar, and homemade desserts are offered for lunch. Open for breakfast, 7:30–10:30 A.M. and for lunch, 11:30 A.M.–2 P.M.

TGI Friday's

- 2100 Pennsylvania Avenue, NW, Washington, DC 20036 (202-872-4344).
- 12147 Rockville Pike, Rockville, MD 20852 (301-231-9048).
- 6460 Capital Drive, Greenbelt, MD 20770 (301-345-2503).
- 4650 King Street, Alexandria, VA 22302 (703-931-4100).
- 13071 Worldgate Drive, Herndon, VA 22070 (703-787-9630).
- 270 Chain Bridge Road, Vienna, VA 22182 (703-556-6173).

TGI Friday's is a large chain of restaurants which is attentive to children. Children receive coloring books, crayons, kiddie cups, and balloons. Service is friendly. There are over 300 choices on the menu, including 13 types of milk shakes. Children often order hot dogs, grilled cheese, chicken fingers, burgers, or fajitas. These restaurants are sometimes loud, but enjoyable for families. Hats off to many of the TGIF restaurants which offer baby changing tables in **both** men's and women's rest rooms.

Tugio's

8737 Colesville Road, Silver Spring, MD 20910 (301-495-5930).

This restaurant and carry-out provides a warm and welcoming experience for children and their parents. It is a family-owned and operated Italian restaurant, with excellent food. Many children enjoy Tugio's "Italian boat," bread in the shape of a gondola stuffed with green pepper, sausage, meatballs, sauce, and cheese. Pizza, calzones, pasta, and veal dishes are also enjoyed here.

Union Station

40 Massachusetts Avenue, NE, Washington, DC 20002 (202-289-4224).

Since its renovation in the late 1980s, Union Station has become a popular dining choice for locals and visitors. It is a very pleasant setting and has something for everyone. The Food Court on the lower level offers diners many fast food options with international appeal. Vendors offer wonderful selections in different price ranges. There are seven full service restaurants and several self-serve cafes. (See the listings for America, The American Cafe, and Pizzeria Uno in this chapter.) Several fine restaurants now occupy areas of the station that used to be the former Presidential Suite, lounges, and baggage claim sections. Entertainment is often offered, including art exhibits, jazz concerts, and strolling singers. Many of the dining spots within Union Station are open early to serve commuters, and several of the full service restaurants stay open well into the evening. See Union Station in Chapter 9, Shopping.

344   Going Places with Children

WASHINGTON, DC

Restaurant	Location	Cuisine	Metro Access	High Chair	Booster Seats	Baby Change	Cost
America	NE, DC	American	✓	✓	✓		M
American Cafe	NW, DC	American					
	1211 Wisc. Ave		✓	✓	✓	✓	M
	5252 Wisc. Ave.		✓	✓	✓		M
	14th & F St.		✓	✓	✓		M
	1200 19th St.		✓	✓	✓		M
	1701 Penn. Ave.			✓	✓		M
	NE, DC		✓	✓	✓		M
	227 Mass. Ave. Union Station		✓		✓		M
American City Diner	NW, DC	American		✓	✓		—
Cactus Cantina	NW, DC	Tex-Mex		✓	✓		M
The Cheesecake Factory	NW, DC	American	✓	✓	✓		M
China Inn	NW, DC	Chinese	✓		✓		—
Clyde's	NW, DC	American		✓	✓		M

Restaurant	Location	Cuisine	Metro Access	High Chair	Booster Seats	Baby Change	Cost
Geppetto's	NW, DC	Italian			✓		M
Hamburger Hamlet	M St., NW / 5225 Wisc. Ave., NW	American	✓	✓✓	✓✓		M / M
Listrani's	NW, DC	Italian	✓	✓	✓		M
Misha's Place of Cheese and Cheer	SE, DC	Russian/ Jewish					—
Pizzeria Unc	NW, DC / Union Station	American/ Italian	✓	✓✓	✓✓		— / —
TGI Friday's	NW, DC	American	✓	✓	✓		—
MARYLAND							
Amalfi	Rockville	Italian			✓		
American Cafe	Calverton	American		✓	✓	✓	M
Anchor Inn	Wheaton	Seafood	✓	✓	✓		M
B.J. Pumpernickel's	Olney	Jewish Deli		✓	✓	✓	—

Restaurant	Location	Cuisine	Metro Access	High Chair	Booster Seats	Baby Change	Cost
Bare Bones	Gaithersburg	American		✓	✓		M
Bennigan's	Greenbelt, Laurel, Rockville	American		✓✓✓	✓✓✓	✓✓✓	– – –
Chili's	Laurel, Rockville, Waldorf	American		✓✓✓	✓✓✓		– – –
Chuck E. Cheese	Gaithersburg, Silver Spring	American		✓✓	✓✓	✓✓	– –
Crisfield's (old)	Silver Spring	Seafood		✓	✓		M
Crisfield's (new)	Silver Spring	Seafood	✓	✓	✓		M
Fuddrucker's	Rockville	American		✓	✓		–
Geppetto's	Bethesda	Italian		✓	✓	✓	M
Hamburger Hamlet	Bethesda, Gaithersburg	American		✓✓	✓✓		M M
Hard Times Cafe	Rockville	American		✓	✓		–

Restaurant	Location	Cuisine	Metro Access	High Chair	Booster Seats	Baby Change	Cost
House of Chinese Chicken	Rockville	Chinese	✓	✓	✓		–
Il Forno	Bethesda Gaithersburg	Italian	✓		✓✓		– –
Kabul West	Bethesda	Afghan	✓		✓		M
L & N Seafood	Rockville	Seafood		✓	✓		M
Louisiana Express	Bethesda	Cajun-Creole		✓	✓		–
O'Donnells	Bethesda	Seafood	✓	✓	✓	✓	M
Pizzeria Uno	Bethesda	American/Italian	✓	✓	✓		–
Red Hot & Blue	Laurel	Memphis BBQ		✓	✓		–
Renato Trattoria	Potomac	Italian		✓	✓		M
Rio Grande Cafe	Bethesda	Tex-Mex	✓	✓	✓		M
Silver Diner	Laurel Rockville	American	✓	✓✓	✓✓	✓✓	– –

Restaurant	Location	Cuisine	Metro Access	High Chair	Booster Seats	Baby Change	Cost
TGI Friday's	Greenbelt Rockville	American		✓✓	✓✓	✓	– –
Tugio's	Silver Spring	Italian	✓	✓	✓		–
VIRGINIA							
American Cafe	Arlington Fairfax McLean Vienna	American	✓	✓✓✓✓	✓✓✓✓	✓ ✓	M M M M
Anita's	Burke Chantilly Fairfax Herndon Vienna East Vienna West	Mexican		✓✓✓✓✓✓	✓✓✓✓✓✓		– – – – – –
Bennigan's	Alexandria Fairfax Falls Church Springfield Vienna	American		✓✓✓✓✓	✓✓✓✓✓	✓✓✓ ✓	– – – – –

Restaurant	Location	Cuisine	Metro Access	High Chair	Booster Seats	Baby Change	Cost
Bilbo Baggins	Alexandria	American		✓	✓		M
Calvert Grille	Alexandria	American		✓	✓		M
Chili's	Bailey's Crossroads Falls Church Fairfax Manassas Reston Springfield Vienna Woodbridge	American		✓✓✓✓✓✓✓✓	✓✓✓✓✓✓✓✓		— — — — — — — —
Chuck E. Cheese	Fairfax	American		✓	✓		—
Clyde's	Reston Vienna	American		✓✓	✓✓	✓✓	M M
Duangrat's	Bailey's Crossroads	Thai			✓	✓	M
Fuddrucker's	Annandale Falls Church Herndon	American		✓✓✓	✓✓✓		— — —

Restaurant	Location	Cuisine	Metro Access	High Chair	Booster Seats	Baby Change	Cost
Generous George	Alexandria Springfield	Italian		✓✓	✓✓		– –
Ground Round	Alexandria Fairfax Manassas Woodbridge	American		✓✓✓✓	✓✓✓✓	✓✓	– – – –
Hamburger Hamlet	Crystal City	American	✓	✓	✓		M
Hard Times Cafe	Alexandria Arlington Herndon	American	✓✓	✓✓	✓✓✓		– – –
L & N Seafood	Arlington Fairfax McLean Reston	Seafood	✓	✓✓✓✓	✓✓✓✓	✓	M M M M
Peking Gourmet Inn	Falls Church	Chinese		✓	✓		M
Pines of Italy	Arlington Crystal City	Italian	✓	✓✓	✓✓	✓✓	– –

Restaurant	Location	Cuisine	Metro Access	High Chair	Booster Seats	Baby Change	Cost
Pizzeria Uno	Reston	American/Italian		✓	✓		–
Red Hot & Blue	Arlington Manassas	Memphis BBQ	✓	✓✓	✓✓		– –
Rio Grande Cafe	Arlington Reston	Tex-Mex	✓	✓✓	✓✓		M M
Rocco's	McLean Springfield	Italian		✓✓	✓✓	✓✓	– –
Silver Diner	Dale City	American		✓	✓	✓	–
TGI Friday's	Alexandria Herndon Vienna	American		✓✓✓	✓✓✓	✓✓✓	– – –

Restaurant	Style	Metro Access	High Chair	Booster Seats	Baby Change	Cost
SIGHTSEEING						
Downtown						
Old Post Office Pavilion	Restaurants & Food Court	✓				I/M
Sholl's	Cafeteria	✓				–
Shops at National Place	Restaurants & Food Court	✓		✓	✓	I/M
Supreme Court Cafeteria	Cafeteria	✓				–
Union Station	Restaurants & Food Court	✓			✓	I/M
The Capitol						
House of Representatives	Restaurant	✓	✓	✓		–
The Refectory	Restaurant	✓	✓	✓		–
The Dirksen Senate Office Building						
The Senate Buffet	Buffet	✓	✓	✓		–
The Senate Cafeteria	Cafeteria	✓	✓	✓		–
The Senate Coffee Shop	Restaurant	✓	✓	✓		–
The Senate Fast Food	Fast Food	✓	✓	✓		–

Restaurant	Style	Metro Access	High Chair	Booster Seats	Baby Change	Cost
Kennedy Center						
Encore Cafe	Cafeteria	✓	✓	✓	✓	–
Roof Terrace Restaurant	Restaurant	✓	✓		✓	M
Library of Congress						
Cafeteria	Cafeteria	✓				–
Montpelier Room	Buffet	✓				–
National Air and Space Museum						
Flight Line	Cafeteria	✓	✓	✓		–
Wright Place	Restaurant	✓	✓	✓		M
National Gallery of Art						
Cascade Cafe	Restaurant	✓	✓			M
Concourse Buffet	Cafeteria	✓	✓			–
Garden Cafe	Restaurant	✓	✓			M
Terrace Cafe	Restaurant	✓	✓			M
National Portrait Gallery						
Patent Pending	Cafeteria	✓		✓		–

11 Annual Events for Children and Families

In every season of the year special events take place at sights throughout Washington, DC and the surrounding area. The events listed in this chapter are either specifically geared towards children's interests (such as the children's needlework workshop at Woodlawn Plantation) or are of interest to the whole family (such as the Smithsonian Institution's Festival of American Folklife). Families will find this a fun chapter to use when planning a visit to Washington, DC or when looking for something special to do on the weekend. Events are free unless otherwise noted in the listing. Approximate dates are provided, but it is best to call ahead or check the newspaper for more information.

Spring (March–May)

Cherry Blossom Time March–April
Washington, DC

Every year thousands of tourists time their visits to Washington to coincide with the delicate, pale harbingers of spring, the cherry blossoms. Some 3,000 cherry trees, the first of which were given to the United States by Japan in 1912, bloom around the Tidal Basin and Hains Point.

Spring Flower Show   March–April
U.S. Botanic Gardens   202-225-8333
Washington, DC

Each year the flower displays focus on a different theme. Coming up are Peter Rabbit's Adventure and the Festival of Garden Lore.

Kite Festival   March
Gunston Hall   703-550-9220
Lorton, VA   Admission fee, 16 and older.

Enjoy kite flying in the pasture, puppet performances, and food vendors.

Mad Hatter's Tea Party   March
Marietta   301-464-5291
Glenn Dale, MD   Admission fee.

A tea party and stories for children. Reservations are required.

Shakespeare Festivals   March (elementary) and
Folger Library   May (high school)
Washington, DC   202-544-7077

Elementary and high school Shakespeare festivals including 20-minute dramatizations of selections from Shakespeare's plays. Children 8 years and older will enjoy watching or perhaps participating in this program.

Easter with the Beasts   Easter Sunday
Baltimore Zoo   410-396-7102
Baltimore, MD   Admission fee.

Traditional Easter activities at the zoo.

Easter Egg Roll   Easter Monday
White House Lawn   202-456-2200
Washington, DC

In the early 1800s, Dolley Madison organized this Easter game on the grounds of the Capitol. In the 1870s the event was moved to the White House lawn, where it has since been enjoyed by thousands of local youngsters. In addition to the egg rolling contest, service bands play, clowns cavort, and the Easter rabbit socializes with the crowd. The event is open to children under age 8 and accompanying adults.

Kite Festival   Late March
Washington Monument   202-357-3030
   Grounds
Washington, DC

Sponsored by the Smithsonian Institution Resident Associate Program. Children of all ages (and adults) may bring their homemade kites to compete in the contests or to fly just for fun.

Point-to-Point Races   April
Oatlands Plantation   703-777-3174
Leesburg, VA   Admission fee.

Pack a picnic and watch the point-to-point horse races.

Spring Tours   April
White House & Gardens   202-456-2200
Washington, DC

Tours of the White House and the gardens in bloom with a variety of spring flowers.

Earth Fair   Late April
Audubon Naturalist Society   301-652-9188
Chevy Chase, MD

The nature-oriented fair includes demonstrations by crafts-people who make new items from recycled goods, sales of "green products" for household and consumer use, a raffle for an exciting trip, a show of live raptors and reptiles, and many hands-on activities for children.

George Mason Day   May
Gunston Hall   703-550-9220
Lorton, VA   Admission fee.

Historic reenactment as actors bring to life George Mason's household in work and play.

Festival of Building Arts   May
National Building Museum   202-272-2448
Washington, DC

This annual event features building demonstrations and hands-on activities for all ages.

Sheep Dog Trials   May
Oatlands Plantation   703-777-3174
Leesburg, VA   Admission fee.

Nationally sanctioned dogs herd sheep, cows, and even ducks. Horse demonstrations, craftspeople, music, and food.

Spring Festival   May
Agricultural History   301-924-4141
    Farm Park
Derwood, MD

Spring festival in the farm's historic section. Draft horses, hay rides, sheep shearing, crafts, baby animals, plantings, nursery sales, and music.

Spring Festival   Early May
River Farm   703-768-5700
Alexandria, VA

Special activities include demonstrations and talks on gardening topics, and sale of plants, books, food, and seeds.

Flower Mart   1st Friday & Saturday in May
Washington Cathedral   202-537-6200
Washington, DC

Antique carousel, and excellent herbs and garden plants for sale.

Market Fair
Claude Moore Colonial
   Farm
Lorton, VA

3rd weekend in May
703-442-7557
Admission fee.

At this 18th-century market fair, children can spin wool, watch a puppet show, make candles, paint fans, attempt woodworking, listen to music, and enjoy refreshments.

Victorian Fair
Fort Ward Museum
Alexandria, VA

Late May
703-868-1121

Children's games, vendors in authentic costumes, living history actors, and speeches.

Civil War Life
Sully Historic Site
Chantilly, VA

Late Spring
703-437-1794
Admission fee.

A Civil War reencampment including a variety of demonstrations by "Confederate Troops," music, dancing, vendors, and tours of the home.

Woodlawn Heritage Arts &
   Crafts Festival
Woodlawn Plantation
Mount Vernon, VA

Late Spring
703-780-4000.
Admission fee.

Storytellers, old-fashioned games, and 19th-century craftspeople.

Summer (June–August)

Sunday Polo   Mid-April–mid-October
Washington, DC   202-619-7222

Spectators can watch on Sunday afternoons on the field east of the Lincoln Memorial. Call for exact times.

Military Band Concerts   Memorial Day–Labor Day
Sylvan Theater   202-426-6843
Washington, DC

All concerts begin at 8 P.M. The Marine Band plays on Sunday, the Army Band on Tuesday, and the Air Force Band on Friday.

Military Band Concerts,   Memorial Day–Labor Day —
West Front Steps of the   202-224-2985
 Capitol
Washington, DC

All concerts begin at 8 P.M. The Navy Band plays on Monday, The Air Force Band on Tuesday, the Marine Band on Wednesday, and the Army Band on Friday.

Wild World   Late May–Labor Day
Amusement Park   301-249-1500
Mitchelville, MD   Admission fee.

This large water park boasts water rides and the Wild Wave, with its four-foot waves. Newest addition is the Lazy River, where riders are propelled by a jet stream while riding on an inner tube. Bring your bathing suits and plan to arrive early, as the lines get quite long by mid-afternoon.

Marine Sunset Parades　　May–August
Iwo Jima Memorial　　202-433-4173
Arlington, VA

On Tuesday nights at 7 P.M., the Marine Drum and Bugle Corps and the Marine Corps Silent Drill Platoon put on a 75-minute performance of music and marching. You can park at Arlington Cemetery for $1 and take a free shuttle bus to the parade grounds.

The American Sailor　　Late May–early September
　　Pageant　　202-433-2219
Washington Navy Yard
Washington, DC

A multimedia presentation highlighting the Navy's history and character is held on Wednesday at 9 P.M.

Summer Flower Show　　May–September
U.S. Botanic Gardens　　202-225-8333
Washington, DC

Each year the display features a different theme using summer blooming flowers, herbs, and hanging baskets

Festival of American　　Late June–early July
　　Folklife　　202-357-2700
Washington, DC

The Mall outside the Museum of Natural History and the Museum of American History comes alive with this stimulating annual celebration of America's folk heritage, with a liberal sprinkling of foreign lore for good measure. This two-week festival features cooking, music, dance, song, and craft demonstrations that range from the merely instructive to the fascinating. The crowds are tremendous, and rightfully so. Activities go on during day and evening hours.

Irish Festival
Glen Echo Park
Glen Echo, MD

Memorial Day weekend
301-492-6282

Washington's Irish community celebrates with traditional music, dance, crafts, and more.

Antique Car Show
Sully Historic Site
Chantilly, VA

Early summer
703-437-1794
Admission fee.

Collectors' cars are on display and there is a fashion show featuring clothes from the Civil War to World War II. Visitors can also tour the house.

Children's Day
Carter-Barron
    Amphitheater
Washington, DC

June
202-543-8600

The Capital Children's Museum co-sponsors a day of hands-on activities, entertainment, and music for children.

Celebrations Day
The Textile Museum
Washington, DC

First Saturday in June
202-667-0441

Hands-on activities for children and free favors.

R. E. Lee Wedding Day
Open House
Arlington House
Arlington, VA

June 30
703-557-0613

The parlor is decorated as it was on the day of Lee's wedding, period music plays, and pound cake and cider are served on the lawn.

**Independence Day
Celebration
Colvin Run Mill
Great Falls, VA**

July 4th
703-759-2771
Admission fee.

Typical Independence Day celebration in a community setting around 1900, including entertainment and a children's parade.

Independence Day   July 4th
  on the Mall
Washington, DC

Annual parade begins at 12:30 P.M. on Constitution Avenue
from 7th to 17th Streets. The National Symphony Orchestra
performs a free concert on the steps of the Capitol Building at
8 P.M. Fireworks are set off from the Washington Monument
Grounds beginning at 9:30 P.M.

Old Fashioned July 4th   July 4th
Carroll County   410-848-7775
  Farm Museum   Admission fee,
Westminster, MD   over age 6.

Picnics, crafts, games, entertainment, and fireworks.

Twilight Tattoos   Late July–August
Ellipse across from   202-696-3647
  White House
Washington, DC

On Wednesday evening at 7 P.M. the Ellipse is the sight of
Twilight Tattoos by the U.S. Army Drill Team, Army Band, and
the 3rd U.S. Infantry with their Fife and Drum Corps.

Shark Day   Late July
National Aquarium   202-377-2826
Washington, DC   Admission fee.

Shark Day is held in cooperation with The Discovery Channel.
Activities center around learning the truth about the various
species of sharks.

Market Fair
Claude Moore
　Colonial Farm
McLean, VA

3rd weekend in July
703-442-7557
Admission fee.

At this 18th-century market fair, children can spin wool, watch a puppet show, make candles, paint faces, attempt woodworking, listen to music, and enjoy refreshments.

Children's Concert
City of Fairfax Band
Fairfax, VA

Late July
703-385-7858

This annual event includes free ice cream and balloons and an evening of music and other surprises.

Civil War Living
　History Day
Fort Ward Museum
Alexandria, VA

Early August
703-838-4848
Admission fee.

Civil War reenactment activities and speeches.

Children's Needlework
　Workshop
Woodlawn Plantation
Mount Vernon, VA

Early August
703-780-4000
Admission fee.

Boys and girls work with 19th-century materials. Activities include making old-fashioned ice cream. Reservations are required. (Nelly's Needlers conduct seminars.)

August Court Days
Leesburg, VA

Third weekend in August
703-478-1856
Admission fee.

Street fair with strolling musicians, a play about the opening of the 18th-century court in Leesburg, and a children's fair with old-fashioned games.

Georgia Avenue Day
Georgia at Eastern
   Avenue NW
Washington, DC

Late August
202-723-5166

Vendors, bands and entertainment, a parade, carnival rides, and live music.

Maryland State Fair
Timonium, MD

Late August
301-252-0200.
Admission fee.

Agricultural demonstrations, livestock shows, midway rides, live entertainment, quilt shows, and thoroughbred racing.

Montgomery County
   Agricultural Fair
Gaithersburg, MD

Late August
301-926-3100
Admission fee, over 12.

Known as the East Coast's largest agricultural county fair, this event features food, exhibits, animals, entertainment, and carnival rides.

National Frisbee Festival
Washington, DC

Late August
Check newspaper for
specific date and times.

This is the largest noncompetitive Frisbee event of its kind. World-class Frisbee champions (both humans and dogs) demonstrate complex throws and catches on the Mall near the Air and Space Museum.

Draft Horse & Mule Day
Oatlands Plantation
Leesburg, VA

Saturday before Labor Day
703-777-3174
Admission fee.

Several kinds of workhorses are on hand to compete in races and demonstrations. Also featured are country music, crafts, tours of the mansion, refreshments, and children's entertainment.

International Children's Festival	Labor Day weekend
Wolf Trap Farm Park	703-642-0862
Vienna, VA	Admission fee.

The rolling acres and many woodland stages of Wolf Trap Farm Park serve as a lovely pastoral setting for this annual three-day smorgasbord of dance, drama, puppetry, mime, hands-on arts and crafts, and music. There's plenty of room to stretch restless legs between enjoying and participating in the worthwhile events.

Fall (September–November)

Children's Chautauqua Day	Fall
Glen Echo Park	301-492-6229
Glen Echo, MD	

Glen Echo is the site of free hands-on arts and crafts activities, as well as performances, for children of all ages.

Prince George's County Fair	Begins Labor Day weekend
County Equestrian Center	301-952-1400, 301-952-0270,
Upper Marlboro, MD	after August 25.

Livestock, arts and crafts, 4-H exhibits, and entertainment are featured at this, the oldest fair in Maryland. 1992 marks their 150th anniversary.

Maryland Renaissance Festival	Late August to mid-October
Annapolis &	301-266-7304
Crownsville, MD	Admission fee.

This reenactment of a 16th-century English fair has entertainment, foods, and numerous activities. Craft items on sale.

Caribbean Festival   September
Fonda del Sol   202-483-2777
   Visual Arts Center
Washington, DC

Outdoor performances of salsa and reggae music.

Car Show   September
Gunston Hall   703-550-9220
Lorton, VA   Admission fee.

Collectors display more than 200 cars, a jazz band provides music, and vendors sell a variety of foods.

Quilt Show   September
Sully Historic Site   703-437-1794
Chantilly, VA   Admission fee.

The house is decorated with antique quilts and outdoor vendors sell quilts and quilt-related items. There also are children's activities.

Adams Morgan Day   Early September
Washington, DC   202-332-3292

This street festival features the cultural diversity of Latin America. It is an opportunity to listen to live music, taste a variety of foods, and purchase crafts.

Steam Show Days   Early September —
Carroll County   301-848-7775
   Farm Museum   Admission fee.
Westminster, MD

Antique farm equipment, steam and gas engines, flea market, food, guided tours of the farm house.

Maryland Seafood Festival
Sandy Point State Park
Annapolis, MD

Mid-September
410-268-7676
Admission fee, 13 and over.

Live performances, Chesapeake Bay seafood, beach activities, and arts and crafts.

Fall Open House
National Capital
    Trolley Museum
Wheaton, MD

Mid-September
301-384-6088
Fee for trolley rides.

Antique European and American trolleys in operation for rides or on display.

Air Fair
College Park Airport
College Park, MD

Mid-September
301-864-5844

This two-day event features stunt pilots, special demonstrations which vary each year, helicopter and airplane rides, a paper airplane contest, and children's entertainment.

Black Family Reunion
Washington, DC

Mid-September
Check newspaper for day
and times.

A weekend celebration of the culture and history of African American families. Held on the Mall, this event includes foods, exhibits, performers, and more.

Rock Creek Park Day
Washington, DC

Mid-September
202-426-6832

Celebrations take place across from Pierce Mill at Beach Drive and Tilden Street in the park. There are activities for children, music performances, environmental exhibits and demonstrations, and lots of fun.

Cheshire Cat Book Store   Mid-September
Butterfly Tree   202-244-3956
Washington, DC

The shop's front window is transformed into a home for caterpillars going through their life stages as they become monarch butterflies. While children and parents patiently stand and watch, butterflies will emerge from their chrysalises.

Open House &   Mid-September
    Arts Festival   202-467-4600
Kennedy Center   Free tickets distributed 30
Washington, DC   minutes before shows on
                                     Plaza in front of Kennedy
                                     Center.

Free music, dance, and other entertainment, indoors and outdoors. There is wheelchair access to all performances and some are signed. Children will enjoy the clowns and mimes as well as the performances.

18th Century Market Fair   2nd Saturday in September
Gadsby's Tavern Museum   703-838-4242
Alexandria, VA

Children and adults will enjoy this re-creation of an 18th-century market fair.

Takoma Park Folk Festival   September
Takoma Park, MD   301-270-4048

Takes place at Takoma Park Intermediate School on Piney Branch Road. There are six stages featuring live music all day, food vendors, dance workshops, mimes, storytellers, crafts, face painting, and more.

Olde Towne Day Festival **Gaithersburg, MD**	Mid-September 301-258-6350 Fee for special events.

Carnival games and rides, music, pony rides, arts and crafts, food, merchant sidewalk sales.

Ethnic Heritage Festival **Around the Armory** **Silver Spring, MD**	June 301-217-6820

Multicultural events and displays. Music and food from around the world.

Bethesda Children's Fair **Bethesda, MD**	Late September 301-652-8798

Petting zoo, clowns, moon bounce, pony rides, crafts, children's entertainment, and refreshments.

Garden Fair **Oatlands Plantation** **Leesburg, VA**	Late September 703-777-3174 Admission fee.

Tours of mansion where competitive floral arrangements are displayed. Garden-oriented vendors, entertainment, and exhibitions.

Kunta Kinte
   Commemoration &
   Heritage Festival
Annapolis, MD
	Late September
	410-841-6504
	Admission fee.

Celebration of African American culture commemorating Kunta Kinte's arrival in Annapolis in 1767. Dance, music, arts, and crafts on the campus of St. John's College.

Fall Farm Festival
National Colonial Farm
Accokeek, MD

Late September
301-283-2113
Admission fee.

Woodcarving, spinning, quilting, and corn husk doll making demonstrations. In addition, apple cider pressing, children's games, blacksmithing, candle dipping, soap making, and refreshments.

Candlelight Tours
Frederick Douglass Home
Washington, DC

Late September–October
202-426-5961

Tours of the home are available in the evening hours.

Open House
Washington Cathedral
Washington, DC

Last Saturday in September
202-537-6200

Demonstrations of stone carving, flower arranging, calligraphy, and needlepoint, and special activities for children. Children ages 9 and up may climb the central bell tower.

Harvest Day
Sully Historic Site
Chantilly, VA

October
703-437-1794
Admission fee.

Includes tours of the house, craft vendors, live music, hay rides, and hay stack. Staff in period costumes demonstrate harvesting techniques such as preserving food and canning.

Fall Garden Tours
White House & Gardens
Washington, DC

October
202-456-2200

Tours of the White House gardens, including the famous Rose Garden, are accompanied by music from military bands.

Autumn Traditions	Early October
Colvin Run Mill	703-759-2771
Great Falls, VA	Admission fee.

Hands-on exhibits, antique tool flea market, woodworking, cider pressing, corn shucking, and apple butter making.

Harvest Festival	Early October
Agricultural History	301-590-9638
Farm Park	Admission fee may be
Derwood, MD	charged in future.

Crafts, demonstrations, antique farm equipment, farming techniques.

Kinderfest	Early October
Watkins Regional Park	301-249-9220
Upper Marlboro, MD	

Children's festival featuring pony and hay rides, carousel, train, carnival games, pumpkin painting, demonstrations of Maryland farming activities, and food.

Virginia Archaeology Week	Early October
Alexandria Archaeology	703-838-4399
Alexandria, VA	Materials fee.

Visitors to the lab and museum of Alexandria Archaeology may tour sites and explore a special hands-on artifact exhibit.

| **Waterford Festival** | Early October |
| **Waterford, VA** | 703-882-3018 |

A Quaker village during the 1800s, this town's fall celebration includes tours of homes, crafts, living history enactments, traditional music, children's activities, food, and entertainment.

Kids on the Bay   Mid-October
Baltimore, MD   301-837-4636

Mermaids, fishing, tales of the sea, singing, and dancing, painting.

Chesapeake   Late October
   Appreciation Days   410-269-6622.
Sandy Point State Park   Admission fee, older
Annapolis, MD   children and adults

Celebration of the contributions of working watermen. Skip-jack races, watermen demonstrations, seafood, scarecrow making, face painting, music, and crafts.

Ghostly Tours   Around Halloween
Woodlawn Plantation   703-780-4000
Mount Vernon, VA   Admission fee.

Costumed guides give ghostly tours of this rambling house.

Halloween Bash   Weekend before Halloween
Capital Children's Museum   202-543-8600
Washington, DC   Admission fee.

Scarecrow stuffing, making masks, magic show, and other entertainment. Come with or without a costume.

How-o-ween Spooktacular   Weekend before Halloween
Baltimore Zoo   410-396-7102
Baltimore, MD   Admission fee.

A special Halloween celebration for children and families.

Annual Open House   Late October
Arena Stage   202-554-9066
Washington, DC

Back stage tours, mimes, storytelling, and face painting make this a special event for families.

Market Fair
Claude Moore
    Colonial Farm
McLean, VA

3rd weekend in October
703-442-7557
Admission fee.

At this 18th-century market fair, children can spin wool, watch a puppet show, make candles, paint faces, attempt woodworking, listen to music, and enjoy refreshments.

Chrysanthemum Show
U.S. Botanic Gardens
Washington, DC

Early November
202-225-8333

Thousands of chrysanthemums are used to present a special theme such as the upcoming "Plants of Magnificent Voyages" and "Circus, Circus, Circus."

Seafaring Celebration
Washington Navy Yard
Washington, DC

1st Saturday in November
202-433-4882

Hands-on activities that celebrate maritime traditions.

Cloister's Birthday
    Celebration
Brooklandville, MD

Early November
301-823-2550
Admission fee.

Entertainment, refreshments, hands-on exhibitions.

Winter (December–February)

Jewish Folk Arts Festival
Addas Israel Congregation
Washington, DC

Late November/
early December
301-230-1369
Admission fee.

Music, art show, Israeli and European dances, arts and crafts, singing, puppets, and kosher food. Sponsored by the Jewish Folk Arts Society.

Hanukah Celebration
Jewish Community Center
Rockville, MD

Late November/
early December
301-881-0100.
Entertainment fee.

This holiday celebration includes food sales, crafts, games, singing, and entertainment.

Hanukah Happening Late November/
Jewish Community Center early December
Fairfax, VA 703-323-0880
Admission fee.

Puppets, book fair, arts and crafts fair, gourmet kosher food booth, and a children's flea market.

Hanukah Extravaganza Late November/
Jewish Community Center early December
Washington, DC 202-775-1765
Admission fee.

Craft fair, children's games and activities, holiday songs.

Candlelight Tours December
Marietta 301-464-5291
Glenn Dale, MD Admission fee.

Music and refreshments are served on some evenings. Reservations required.

Scout Day December
Sully Historic Site 703-437-1794
Chantilly, VA Admission fee.

Scout troups can make reservations to tour the house, enjoy refreshments, and sing carols.

Carlyle House Throughout December
Alexandria, VA 703-549-2997
Admission fee.

House is decorated with Christmas decorations of the 1700s.

Christmas at Harborplace
Baltimore, MD

Thanksgiving–
New Year's Eve
410-332-4191

Daily events include llama petting, choral competitions, celebrity Santas, and a Santa House.

Christmas at Oatlands
Leesburg, VA

Mid-November–Christmas
703-777-3174
Admission fee.

This historic mansion is decorated with handmade decorations gathered and made as they were in the 1880s. There are candlelight tours and living history vignettes.

Festival of Trees, Lights, &
    Music
Washington Temple
Kensington, MD

Throughout December
301-587-0144

Grounds are lit up each evening with 300,000 colored lights. Visitors' Center features community concerts, films, and 14 decorated Christmas trees. There is also an outdoor nativity scene.

Kwanzaa Celebration
Anacostia Museum
Washington, DC

Throughout December
202-287-3369

Each year Kwanzaa is celebrated from December 26–January 1. The celebration of Kwanzaa (which means "first fruits" in Swahili) is derived from a variety of African harvest festivals and stresses the unity of African American culture and family life. Through games, dances, folktales, proverbs, and songs, the meaning of Kwanzaa is communicated to the many children who participate in the festivities.

Santa Express Rides
B & O Railroad Museum
Baltimore, MD

Throughout December
410-237-2381
Admission fee and nominal
charge for train ride.

Children and parents can enjoy a ride on the Santa Express.

Victorian Christmas
    at the Mill
Gingerbread House Display
    & Contest
Savage Mill, MD

Throughout December
301-792-2820
Fee to enter contest.

Victorian decorations by the staff. Winning entries in the adult
and student categories of the annual gingerbread contest are
on display.

Washington Doll's House &
    Toy Museum
Washington, DC

Throughout December
202-244-0024
Admission fee.

Special displays include a revolving musical Christmas tree
that plays Christmas carols and is decorated with original
antique ornaments. There is also an early feather snowman
tree — a tree made from hundreds of dyed feathers. In addition, Christmas toys and games are on display.

Winter Festival of Lights
Watkins Regional Park
Upper Marlboro, MD

December–January
301-699-2407, 277-8456, TDD
Cash or canned food
donations.

From dusk to 9:30 P.M. you can view these holiday decorations
in the park.

Christmas in the Village
Waterford, VA

Early December
703-882-3018
Admission fee.

A Quaker village during the 1800s, this town's holiday celebration includes tours of homes, living history enactments, holiday music, children's activities, and entertainment.

Christmas in the Village
Middleburg, VA

First Saturday in December
703-687-6375

This all-day village fair has arts and crafts, a bake sale, music, and a parade.

National Christmas
    Tree Lighting &
    Pageant of Peace
Ellipse across from
    White House
Washington, DC

Early December
202-619-7222

Each year the President of the United States lights the national Christmas tree and officially opens the holiday season. Trees for each state and territory lead up to the giant national Christmas tree, a spectacle for children of all ages. Each evening Christmas carols are sung on the open-air stage. There is also a Hanukah menorah displayed by a private group.

Scottish Christmas Walk
Old Town Alexandria, VA

1st weekend in December
703-549-0111

Fresh greens sale, flea market, Santa's Breakfast and Lunch, bake sale, craft show, tours of historic homes. The Scottish Walk is a parade of Scottish clans, with each family dressed in its traditional tartan finery.

Christmas Theme Tour
Carroll County
   Farm Museum
Westminster, MD

Early December
301-848-7775
Admission fee, over 6.

An 1850s landowner's house is decorated in preparation for Christmas.

A Woodlawn Christmas
Woodlawn Plantation
Mount Vernon, VA

1st two weekends in
December
703-780-4000
Admission fee.

Living history with actors and storytellers depicting early and mid-1800s in the decorated mansion.

Open House
Beall-Dawson House
Rockville, MD

2nd Sunday in December
301-762-1492

Annual Christmas celebration in this 19th-century historic site.

Memorial Illumination
Antietam Battlefield
Sharpsburg, MD

Early December
301-733-7373

The lost, killed, and wounded from the single day of the Civil War Battle of Antietam are commemorated by more than 23,000 luminaries along a 4½ mile driving tour.

Christmas Activities
Rose Hill Manor Museum
Frederick, MD

Early December
301-694-1648
Admission fee.

Activities include arts and crafts demonstrations, tours of museum by candlelight, and a visit from Santa.

Christmas Carol
  Sing-Along
Wolf Trap Farm Park
Vienna, VA

Early December
703-255-1912
Canned goods donation
requested.

This National Park Service sponsored Christmas carol sing-along features a military band and local choral groups. Song books and candles are provided for all participants.

Holiday Fair
Audubon Naturalist Society
Chevy Chase, MD

1st weekend in December
301-652-9188

The fair includes nature arts and crafts from around the United States, an eatery tent, a raffle for an exciting trip, and a holiday shop where children under 12 can purchase inexpensive gifts and make crafts.

Holiday Sing-Along
Kennedy Center
Washington, DC

Early December
202-452-1321
Admission fee.

Sponsored by the Washington Chamber Symphony, this is an opportunity to sing a wide variety of holiday songs.

Holiday Tours
Montpelier Mansion
Laurel, MD

Early December
301-953-1376
Admission fee.

Guided tours of this 18th-century, decorated mansion.

Holly Trolley Illuminations
National Capital
  Trolley Museum
Wheaton, MD

2nd week–end of December
301-384-6088
Fee for trolley rides.

Displays, holiday sing-along, trolley rides, and a visit from Santa via streetcar.

Christmas Pointsettia Show   Mid-December–early
U.S. Botanic Gardens   January
Washington, DC   202-225-8333

Features displays of white, red, and pink pointsettias and
Christmas greens depicting a special theme — Victorian Holiday and Holidays of Old Washington are upcoming.

Carols by Candlelight   Mid-December
Gunston Hall   703-550-9220
Lorton, VA   Admission fee.

Home is decorated in the 18th century manner and visitors
enjoy refreshments and caroling.

Christmas on the Farm   Mid-December
Oxon Hill Farm, MD   301-839-1177

Pop popcorn over an open fire, drink hot spiced cider, make
ornaments from natural materials, sing carols, and take a
horsedrawn wagon ride.

Christmas Open House   Mid-December
Frederick Douglass Home   202-426-5961
Washington, DC

The home is decorated in 19th-century, Victorian style, staff
are dressed in period costumes, and artifacts are on display.

Victorian Christmas   Mid-December
Fort Ward   703-838-4848.
Alexandria, VA   Admission fee.

A Civil War Christmas features a Victorian Christmas tree,
19th-century music and refreshments, and Santa dressed in
a Civil War costume.

Trees of Christmas
National Museum of
American History
Washington, DC

Mid-December–early
January
202-357-2700

This museum has a beautiful display of ten Christmas trees, each uniquely decorated with crafts from across the nation.

Victorian Christmas
Historic Surratt House
Clinton, MD

Mid-December
301-868-1121
Admission fee.

Candlelight tours, antique toys, Victorian cards and ornaments, fresh greenery, and refreshments.

Christmas Eve Pageant
Washington Cathedral
Washington, DC

December 24
202-537-6200

A Christmas Eve pageant especially designed for the very young begins at 4 P.M. Come early to get seats for this very popular event.

Christmas Open House
Arlington House
Arlington, VA

Mid-December
703-557-0613

This very popular Christmas event features madrigal singers and period food. The house is decorated as it would have been when Robert E. Lee was in residence.

Country Christmas
Colvin Run Mill
Great Falls, VA

3rd weekend in December
703-759-2771
Admission fee.

Visit Santa, roast marshmallows at the bonfire, listen to traditional holiday music, and participate in making crafts.

Holiday Illumination
Sully Historic Site
Chantilly, VA

Weekend after Christmas
703-437-1794
Admission fee.

Tour the fields surrounding this historic site in a horse-drawn hay wagon, watch fireworks, sit by a bonfire and sip hot chocolate, and enjoy singing carols.

White House
Candlelight Tours
Washington, DC

Week after Christmas
202-456-2200

Special candlelight tours are conducted between Christmas and New Year's Day, giving visitors the opportunity to see the President's home with all its Christmas decorations.

Annual Oratorial Contest
Frederick Douglass Home
Washington, DC

Near January 15th
202-426-5961

This one-day contest, in memory of the birthday of Martin Luther King, Jr., is for students at all grade levels in Washington, DC, Maryland, and Virginia.

Valentine's Exhibit
Historic Surratt House
Clinton, MD

February
301-868-1121
Admission fee.

An exhibit of 19th-century valentines and crafts.

Black History Month
  Celebrations
Smithsonian Museums
Washington, DC

Throughout February
202-357-2700

Exhibits and special events focus on the lives of African Americans and their contributions to American history and society.

Chinese New Year Parade
Chinatown
Washington, DC

Early February
202-724-4091

The parade of dragon dancers, floats, and more marches through the streets of Chinatown, on H Street, NW between 5th and 8th Streets in celebration of the Chinese New Year.

George Washington
Birthday Parade
Alexandria, VA

Near February 22
703-838-4200

Old Town Alexandria is host to the country's largest parade in celebration of the birthday of the nation's first president.

Index

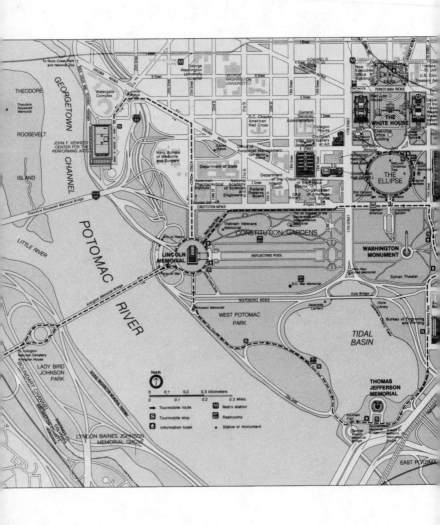